21st Century Meets 1850 Liberty Town

By

Trent Smith

ISBN:0692431799
ISBN-13:9780692431795

DEDICATION

Gina Girl for your countless hours of reading and rereading and reading a few more times the words you've already read before. I love you.

CONTENTS

ACKNOWLEDGMENTS

Kayla Ann Heinze for your wonderful drawings.

Kaley Farwell for your training of an old dog.

Gretchen Zello for your help in editing.

Darlene Williams for your help in editing.

Marjanna Bremer for your help in editing.

"To the sheriff who pulled my teenage boy over for a brake light that magically started working, but gave you time to harass and accuse him of being a pedophile and druggie…" I thank you. "To the IRS that penalized and cheated my father's construction company to the point it went bankrupt…" I thank you. "To the government that decided it needed my grandpa's and mother's land more than they…" I thank you. "And to companies around the globe that have made company policy more precious than human life…" I thank you.

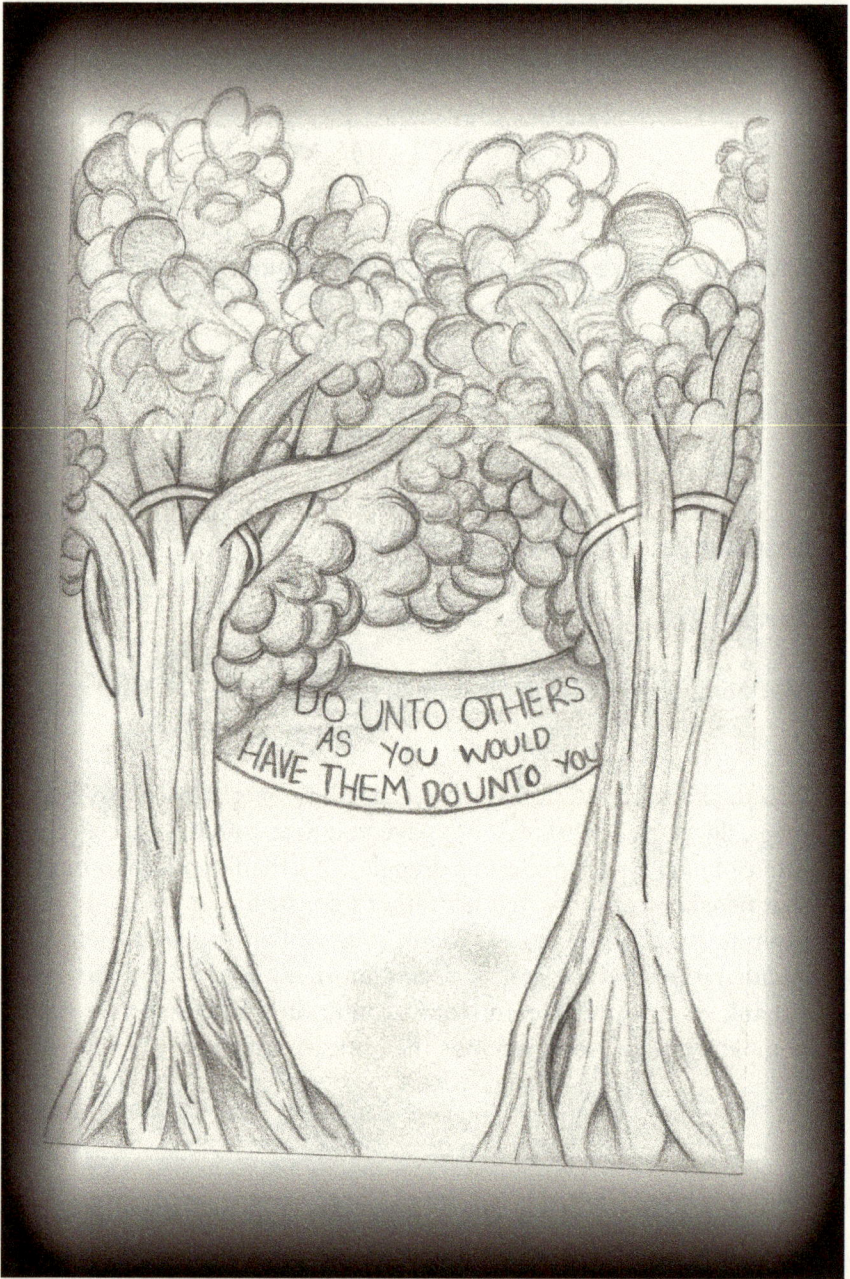

DO UNTO OTHERS
AS YOU WOULD
HAVE THEM DO UNTO YOU

Introduction:

By the mid-1800's, America was fast becoming known as a great land. This in turn brought more and more foreigners to the new nation and each individual that came, they brought in tow their own set of beliefs. Certain settlements grew with people of similar ethics and others grew out of necessity with people of varying belief compositions. As a whole, the genes and DNA of America knew not themselves what America the country would grow to be. What would life be like when an 1850's settlement is introduced to American DNA of the 21st century?

Born in 1832, Johnny was a wild child, and always seemed to be in trouble. It wasn't that he was a bad kid; he just had an adventurous spirit. Heck, growing up in the wild south one had to be adventurous to survive.

Johnny was not the only rowdy youngster living around Liberty Town, because the town was a new town nestled in a new country, it was the new frontier, which gave most that daring spirit. As fathers and their youngsters grew with their land and town, they learned attacking the weak was easier than conquering the strong. Consequently, at a young age, Johnny was tormented and beat up by the older larger kids who found it amusing to torture the children smaller and weaker than themselves. Johnny was unfortunately somewhat smaller than the other children his age.

Johnny's father told his son, "It's not what happens to you, but how you handle it. Hit the largest kid in the nose and chances are they'll leave you alone, finding someone else to torment." The following day when Johnny was being harassed, he followed his father's instructions and punched the leader in the nose making it bleed. Johnny took a beating for doing that, but his father was right, after that day he was left alone. Some of the other smaller children learned from Johnny, you either toughened up or lived a life of torture from others.

When Johnny hit puberty, he grew into a tall, lanky, handsome, young man. At 13, he saw his first love, and was unafraid to announce his love by pulling on Peggy's pony tail, and chasing her around the schoolyard with frogs and crickets. Johnny once found a garter snake on his way to school. He hid that snake in Peggy's desk, and her reaction was no disappointment! She graced him with her response of flailing around and screaming like a banshee. Peggy showed her affection back by slapping Johnny, and shrieking in mock terror at his ridiculous antics. One day, Peggy even screamed at Johnny, "You do that once more Johnny, and I'm gonna kiss you!" Johnny, not willing to accept that consequence, quickly stopped that day's harassment. This affection formed a bond, and the two became inseparable. They could frequently be found fishing at the pond on the outskirts of town, walking to the orchard to pick apples, or just lying on the grass talking about school, family, and life. Their friendship blossomed and developed over the years, turning from schoolyard antics into love.

Johnny's hair was thick and black, his eyes were a deep chocolate brown. Working on his father's ranch made him strong, and his lean arms portrayed strength. His reflexes had become rattlesnake-striking fast. Another youngster took to liking Peggy as well, wanting to prove his dominance in front of Peggy, he picked a fight with Johnny. When he swung at Johnny, Johnny simply dodged the punch and broke the tormentor's nose with a quick solid punch. Never again did that particular fool challenge Johnny.

Johnny was raised to take care of his responsibilities before heading off to the fishing hole, or spending his time with Peggy. Chores and schoolwork came first, and after he'd completed his work in a satisfactory fashion, he was free to play. "Work first, play later," was his motto. He did not care what others thought of him, he felt secure in his town full of his close friends and family surrounding him.

Johnny's dream was to own a ranch with a little four bedroom cabin nestled beside a lake somewhere near the outskirts of his hometown, with horses and cattle of his own. He often visualized seeing Peggy hanging the laundry while he sat drinking his coffee. Peggy would often tease that she was drinking the coffee watching Johnny do the laundry. Having a respectable family of his own was his ultimate goal. The reality was, he was still just a young man attending high school, and Johnny was still miles away from his dream.

When Johnny turned 18 and Peggy was about to celebrate her 16th birthday, their love was in full bloom. The other boys at school were jealous of Johnny because Peggy had become quite attractive, and he himself was tall and handsome. She was slim with wavy blonde hair that ran to her waist. Her eyes were a bright blue when she was happy, but turned a stormy grey as she became angry. Her form was envied by the other girls, and admired by the boys. When Peggy entered school wearing her floor-length Victorian-style dress, all of her peers stopped and fancied her. Peggy was the happiest and sweetest person anyone knew most of the time, but when her eyes turned grey, people avoided her like she was a storming tornado.

Johnny really wanted to show Peggy his love in ways other than pulling her pony tail or chasing her around like an adolescent. Peggy wanted to do more than slap Johnny and run away. One day, Johnny was walking her home from school, as he always did, and he gently reached for her hand swinging lightly at her side. He clasped her small hand in his own callused hand, chills went racing down their spines. Their bonding continued, as did their curiosity of one another. Johnny at one time even thought of kissing Peggy, but the thought of doing such a thing, being unmarried, hindered him from acting on that desire, or any other hormone induced thought that was running through his head.

Liberty Town sat parallel to the Atlantic Ocean. The port built off the peninsula gave the town its roots, it was a perfect location for loading and unloading imports and exports. The fertile land surrounding the town was excellent for tobacco and cotton, commodities the whole world was in need for. The mountain range in Liberty Town's background created a new painting twice a day as the sun rose and set. The rocky region made excellent ground for establishing solid foundations for factories, businesses and homes, Liberty Town was the perfect location for a new town in the new nation.

Shirley, Sue's mom, was born in the the late 1770's. She grew up on a farm-ranch passed down to her parents from her dad's parents. This farm sat on the outskirts of Liberty Town and had a beautiful stream that passed through their land. Shirley loved the farm and her childhood. She would often find herself daydreaming of passing days milking cows and mending fences in her lovely dresses. Shirley also loved her daughter Sue. It was at that farm that Sue met Red when Red was hired on as summer help. The farm/ranch was passed to Red when he married Sue. Red intended to pass it to his first born Johnny when he felt the time was right.

As with Shirley, Liberty Town was founded by adventurous citizens who survived the American Revolution. They held tight to their new freedoms and rights established in the constitution and the Bill of Rights. If necessary, they would pick up their arms and fight again to keep these chartered convictions safe from those with opposing views. As a whole, the founding peoples of Liberty Town were kind and generous, but threaten their freedom and they would become like vicious tigers and lions, destroying those who dare threaten the freedom to roam the land they owned.

The citizens of Liberty Town showed no signs of colored or religious prejudice. The town was built on Godly principles, and it was prospering. The townsfolk were friendly one to the other, smiling, and willing to sacrifice themselves to help others. The town motto was pieced together by the ladies quilting club and hung from two old oak trees that stood in the center of town, reading "Do unto others as you would have them do unto you."

Futureano Americass was a 5'4" potbellied, middle-aged man

born 1817. He had no hair on the top of his head, but the sides of his head had a full growth of grey hair. He let the right side grow very long and each morning he would comb this hair over the top of his bald head in hopes of covering his shiny, smooth scalp. He wore black-rimmed glasses, and did not dress like the other men in town. In fact, he had no concept of cowboy boots or hats until he moved to this southern uneducated town. He usually wore stripped black pants, a colored shirt, and a large colorful tie that ended above his belly.

Futureano moved to this southern town just a few months ago with only 2 things on his mind, money and himself. Because of his character and stature, Futureano wanted to leave his home town where he had earned the nickname 'Punchy Belly.' He had never learned to fight back as others tormented him, he simply let his paunch be hit while inwardly dreaming of creating a society where beatings as he was undertaking were never allowed. "*One should never be physically hurt*," he would say to himself. Futureano figured he could accomplish this simply by creating laws making it illegal to physically or mentally harm another. For that, he calculated, he needed money and Liberty Town had an abundance.

His twin boys, Rudy and Bobby were about the same age as Johnny. Rudy took after his mother, with his wavy chocolate brown hair, piercing green eyes, and tall slim stature, while Bobby took after his father, short, fat and blond. Futureano's wife, Domestica, was reluctant to move from her city up north to this tiny town, but she came with her husband's promise of shaping this town to their dreams.

Rudy and Bobby hated the move. They had spent 4 years secretly fighting their way to the top hierarchy of their class. They had to fight in secret because their father did not believe in violence of any sort. To them this was a hick town with nothing but homely corn fed girls and boys more interested in their horses than anything else. The first day they went to school, they saw Peggy and both immediately became infatuated with her, neither had ever seen a more beautiful young lady in their life. Dressed in designer jeans sagging down to their thighs, exposing their boxer briefs to everyone around, sporting t-shirts with skulls and cross bones and a hat they called a baseball cap, turned backwards on their heads, the boys thought they were the almighty gift to the fairer sex, in fact, where they had come from; Rudy had tremendous success with the girls he flirted with. Bobby always hung back, leaching off his brother's woman leftovers once Rudy was done with them.

1 JOHNNY AT SCHOOL:

Johnny sat outside on Peggy's doorstep waiting. "*Why is she always late?*" Johnny wondered, "*She knows we'll be late for school.*" The front door opened and Johnny stood, then he backed up a step because he was taken aback by her looks, she was so beautiful in that blue dress. Peggy looked at Johnny wearing his worn brown cowboy hat, dark eyes and black stubble because he hadn't shaved that morning. "*Dang, I'm dating the most handsome man in this town*" she thought. She stepped forward to let Johnny kiss her cheek. Johnny looked around ensuring no-one was watching and gladly touched his lips to Peggy's smooth face. They grabbed hands and headed off to school.

When they turned the corner, Johnny paused and picked up a cactus he had found and replanted the other day. He proudly gave it to Peggy. Peggy smiled while wondering, "*Will I ever get flowers*?" She squeezed Johnny's hands tighter and sarcastically said to him, "Thanks Johnny, just what I need, and another thorn by my side." Then she asked, "We going fishing this weekend?" Johnny answered, "Can't, have to help dad with the cows." Peggy sulked and said, "You're always helping your father. All work and no play is making Johnny a dull boy." Johnny replied, "Peggy, you know its winter calving season, dad needs my help." They walked quietly and Peggy started smiling as she was happy that Johnny had taken the time to find, pick and plant her a silly cactus, her eyes were very bright blue.

They entered the classroom and Peggy being the courteous young sweet lady that she was, smiled broadly at Rudy and Bobby in a simple attempt to welcome them to their school. Rudy, thinking Peggy was being flirtatious, decided to take full advantage of the situation. Being the self-assured, cocky, privileged legacy of instant gratification that he was, he winked wolfishly and strutted up to her. Even though he knew Peggy would be outraged, he had found this approach often led to a quick relationship with other women. He quickly pulled her close to him, and before she even knew what was happening, he kissed her rakishly, trying to force his tongue into her mouth. Peggy frantically struggled to push the Americass boy away, but her attempts were futile. She was a delicate young lady and her strength was not enough to do her any good.

Johnny, having never done anything more than hold her hand or pull her pony tail, was outraged! Plowing through the rows of desks, making a bee-line to where Rudy was, grabbed Rudy by his shirt, turned him around and broke his nose with a solid right fist. Rudy's brother, having always stood and fought alongside his brother, ran to the fight. Before he could get close enough to land a fist into Johnny's stomach, Johnny popped him in his chin sending him flailing backwards. Rudy and Bobby, in complete shock at this onslaught, ran to the new principal, their father Futureano. Never before had they been met with such aggressive resistance.

Johnny was called to the principal's office. He sat staring at the bald spots on Futureano's head as Futureano simply asked, "What

were you thinking young man? Violence is never the answer."
Johnny started to answer but Futureano cut him off saying,
"Listen son, we have a zero tolerance policy at this school,
debatable issues should be left in the hands of those in authority.
I have no other choice but to expel you indefinitely." Johnny was
shocked; he stood and asked, "What is a zero tolerance policy?"
Futureano rising from his chair realized that Johnny was much
taller than him, quickly reclaimed a seated position, stated, "Zero
tolerance means no violence of any kind. Now please excuse
yourself off the school property." Johnny never had a chance to
explain why he had hit Rudy and Bobby, as he left the school
grounds he looked up at his classroom window and saw Peggy
standing there. Peggy stared at him confused not knowing where
or why he was leaving.

Johnny's dad Thomas, nicknamed Red because of his full head
of wavy red hair, was a very large man. Standing 6'3" and
weighing 230 pounds, with arms as big as tree trunks, was a hardworking loyal employee at the shipping docks. His free time was
spent on his ranch he inherited when he married Sue. Born in
1814, he believed in loyalty to family and never considered
cheating on his lovely wife. His temper was the only thing in Reds
life that ever got out of control. If he saw wrongdoing, he made
sure it was made right, either by intimidation or force.

When Red got home that night, Johnny was sitting at the
kitchen table with his mom and Red immediately saw something
was wrong. After Johnny succinctly summarized what had
happened and the consequences the new principal had already
doled out, the blood started rising up Red's collar and flushed his
face to an angry shade of red. Red immediately went to pay
Futureano a visit with Johnny in tow. Fifteen minutes later, they

stood at his door.

Futureano's wife, Domestica answered the door, saw Red, and was immediately smitten with desire. She had never seen so much man in one package in all her life. She slowly looked Red over, starting at his worn cowboy hat and ending at his scuffed leather work boots.

Red stood taken aback by the looks Domestica was giving him. She had wavy, raven black hair standing up six inches above her head, and then flowing down around her shoulders. Red had never before seen such black shiny hair, he was not aware of the concept of hair dye. Her eyes were a stark green and she was at least a foot shorter then Red, and a good 6 inches taller than Futureano. What Red couldn't take his eyes off of, was her bosom, which was fully displayed by a scarlet bustier. Red had never seen so much cleavage so shamelessly put on display.

Before asking who they were, or why they were there, Domestica enthusiastically proclaimed, "Come in!" She led them into the foyer, her hips swaying in a provocative manner. Red and Johnny stepped into the house and immediately stopped, amazed at what they saw. Never before had they seen such luxurious possessions adorning a home.

Futureano came down the stairs, smacked Bobby's habitually bobbing head, and went towards his guest. Bobby, looking up and seeing Johnny, told his dad that was the boy who had punched him, and cautiously backed away. Rudy, having heard the commotion downstairs, took a peek and immediately rushed back to his room, having no interest in having Johnny anywhere near him.

Futureano said to Bobby, "I know Dumbo, I expelled him

today!" Turning to Red he asked, "What can I do for you?" Red asked, "Why was my boy expelled?" Futureano responded, "We have a zero tolerance policy. There is absolutely no reason anyone should ever be hit."

Johnny blurted out, "He was manhandling Peggy!" Futureano replied, "My understanding is she was making advances towards Rudy."

Red asked, "Did you even hear Johnny's or Peggy's side of the story?"

Futureano answered, "There is no story to hear. Zero tolerance means no fighting whatsoever. Violence is never the answer. Johnny hit Rudy and Bobby breaking Rudy's nose and splitting Bobby's chin. So I expelled Johnny. I don't understand why your redneck brain can't understand this."

Red, quickly getting annoyed, asked "So it's okay with you if I just start kissing your wife?" Domestica flushed, secretly wishing Red would do that very thing. "Of course not, she's a married woman!" Futureano retorted a little flustered.

"Well, your son was behaving in a manner towards Peggy that only married folks behave. I had to stop him!" Johnny quickly pointed out.

"You could have done that without hitting my boys. Look, I don't make the policy; I only help write and enforce the policy." Futureano answered.

Rolling his eyes heavenward, Red exhaled loudly, "That makes no sense! How do you think Johnny should have handled it?"

Futureano quickly replied, "First, Peggy needs to stop flirting with the boys. Next, she should have simply told him to stop. Johnny should not have gotten involved. These are young adults, and they can certainly handle a minor conflict-resolution situation."

Red, knowing violence was often the only answer and being a logical man, knew Futureano's thinking was flawed. He also knew that there would be no reasoning with him. In a final effort, Red asked Futureano, "So violence is never the answer?" Futureano boldly said, "NO!"

Red looked at Domestica, and despite his moral character, marched up to her, grabbed her and started kissing her, hoping she would display the same reaction Peggy had to Rudy. What he wasn't expecting was for Domestica to kiss him back. Domestica wrapped her arms around Red's broad chest and held him tight.

Futureano was quite the jealous man and his anger flared. This show astounded him, and he quickly discovered his desire to hit Red. However, having just boldly told Red that violence was never the answer and having expelled Johnny for hitting his sons for this very reason, he knew he would be playing right into Reds plan and proving Red's point. Johnny saw Futureano's shock, and then stared in disbelief at his dad and Domestica. He immediately understood what his dad was doing and he couldn't help but chuckle.

Finding his feet, Futureano rushed over to Red, and attempted to utilize his previously suggested method for solving a conflict such as this. He gingerly tapped him on the shoulder, suddenly more aware of Reds strapping figure. Red knew he was close to getting the response he wanted from Futureano, so he grabbed Domestica tighter and simply picked her up, Domestica gave an excited shriek. Futureano, getting desperate to put an end to this ridiculous man's antics, tapped harder. Red got more passionately aggressive with Domestica and turned her back into her husband. Futureano finally screamed, "EXCUSE ME, SIR!" He tried splitting the two apart, but his strength was nothing in comparison to Red's. Domestica clinging to Red didn't help him either, Red continued to ignore Futureano.

Futureano was beginning to lose control. None of his diplomacy was working, and his wife was not even attempting to rebuff Reds attention. He had been taught that violence was never the answer, yet it seemed that he had no other answer at this time.

Futureano watched his wife willingly kiss this stranger and he felt helpless, having not the strength, nor the character to stop Red. He choked back a sob, and punched Red in the kidney. Red barely felt the punch and he smiled as he pushed Domestica off of him. She would not let him go and continued trying to get Red to continue with his passion. Red finally pushed her away and she landed on the floor, still aflame from being kissed by a real man, clung to Red's leg.

Red turned to Futureano and grabbed him by his shirt, raising the short man up to his level. He looked at Futureano and said, "I thought violence was never the answer." Futureano started sweating and tried to answer, but he had no answer to give.

Red and Johnny walked to the door and Johnny laughed as his father drug Domestica with them. At the door, Red lightly kicked his leg and she fell off, then immediately started pouting.

The following day Johnny went to walk Peggy to school. They usually met at her house and walked to school together from there. Johnny was sure that Futureano would allow him back into school, having learned that, at times, violence is the only language some understand. When Johnny reached Peggy's house, she was again nowhere to be seen. Johnny again thought,

"Why is she always late? She knows we'll be late for school."

Johnny heard Peggy's voice loudly asking, "What do you want?" Johnny turned the corner into the alley and saw Rudy and Bobby talking to Peggy. He walked closer and heard Rudy say, "Where I come from, we call girls like you Cock Teases!" Johnny took two steps forward, and without thinking, punched Rudy in the nose, re-breaking it, Bobby's groin was met with a swift kick from Johnny's pointed boot, and both boys fell to the ground. Johnny chuckled and thought, *"Genes like these have no place in my town. Imagine, thinking that Peggy has ANY similarities to the family rooster!"*

He grabbed Peggy's hand and walked her to school. Knowing that after today's episode he would most likely just be leaving again, he stopped at the door and looked at Peggy. Peggy smiled at him and asked, "See you after school?" Johnny blushed, poking her in the ribs, "Sure," he answered, smiling as he turned to walk away, "at my dad's ranch. You can help castrate the cows."

2 JOHNNY'S FIRST WAGON

Johnny's ethics and morals were being overridden by
Futureano who had different standards for his personal morals
and values. "No longer could you defend your family or those you

love without facing consequences?" In just a short time, Johnny
could see that there were many new ideas coming to his town
that did not coincide with his own. It seemed that more people,
that shared Futureano's character, were arriving daily from coach
or ocean liner. Each time another "Futureano" came into town
Johnny and Peggy's families would laugh and joke saying, "Here
comes another Americass!" Johnny knew that people like
Futureano were going to overrun his beloved hometown one day,
and that made his dream of a home and land of his own even

more important to him.

Since Johnny had been kicked out of school, and had so much free time on his hands, he decided it was time to build himself a wagon. He had no problem landing employment at the factory to earn the money for his project. He saved his money until he had enough to purchase parts and pieces to piece together his first set of wheels and buy his first horse. Johnny bought his front springs for his wagon at a salvage yard, the back springs he salvaged from a wrecked carriage that had lain abandoned for many years outside of town. The frame Johnny made himself from freshly fallen pine trees. His father Red had brought home scavenged packing crates that Johnny used for the floor and sides. As the pine wood frame dried, Johnny's wagon took on a different form as only two wheels would rest on the ground simultaneously. Johnny thought great wheels would make the wretched wagon look awesome, so he spent half his saved money on flashy wagon wheels. The other half of his saved money Johnny purchased an unsightly horse, that some would have called a mule. Johnny had acquired this dreadful creature from an old friend living his last few moons. The building of the wagon had taken a considerable amount of creativity, time, and patience.

With a basket full of freshly baked bread, sliced roast beef, and a homemade cherry pie his mother had baked, Johnny was ready to take Peggy for a picnic. He was taking her to their special place by the river a few miles out of town, he was pleased to be showing off his first wagon to is love. Peggy was a little concerned about the looks of the wagon because it did not compare to any other wagons she had ever seen, in fact, at first sight she was wondering what exactly it was. Peggy saw that Johnny was very proud of his creation; she also did not want to discourage him in any manner, and so she held up her head and let Johnny help her into this pile of debris with wheels, worrying that she was going to fall through the floor.

Peggy asked, "Is it safe?" Johnny proudly smiled and answered, "Built her myself." Peggy again questioned, "Is it safe?" Johnny said, "We'll see." and with a commanding voice, Johnny said "Giddy up!" The four legged creature groaned and the wagon followed suit, Peggy and Johnny were being carried down the street to the sound of loud squeaks and groans.

Trying to hold a conversation between the minor bounces and noise of the wagon, Peggy pointed at the thing pulling the wagon and asked, "Is it a mule or a horse?" Johnny simply said, "Don't know, couldn't get a straight answer when I bought him." Peggy, having a name for each of her animals, asked "What's its name?" Johnny looked at Peggy and chuckled, "I think I'll name it after you, Creature." Peggy hit Johnny and Johnny was happy that their relationship was advancing to the next level.

Both Peggy and Johnny were extremely excited to be making this journey. They felt that they were chasing liberty, and pursuing happiness, just as they had a right and a privilege to do. As they rode side by side they shared a silent dream of a future together, one far away from Futureano, Bobby, Rudy, and all the other Americasses moving to their town. Peggy and Johnny were so happy and excited that they did not notice all the people laughing at them and their noisy contraption, as they made their way through town.

Midway through town, they passed the local businesses and deputy Jaerk, who was riding down the street. Jaerk, the ever-loyal, law-abiding, enforcer of the law, quickly rode his gelding to

Johnny's wagon side saying "Pull over!" Johnny pulled over in front of the newly erected local saloon. "What did I do now?" Johnny quietly asked. Peggy whispered, "Just be polite, everything will be fine."

Jaerk had moved to town 6 months ago, it was rumored he received the deputy sheriff position because he was some relative of Futureano's. Jaerk approached Johnny and Peggy wearing his brown, 10 gallon hat and dark sunglasses, in which no one had ever seen him without, even at the local diner. He neither smiled nor frowned, his stark brown uniform gave him an aura of authority. He was not very tall, maybe 5'5". Because he wasn't very strong, he enjoyed the feeling of the vest he wore under his uniform, for it made his chest seem very broad.

"License, registration, and proof of insurance." Jaerk stated. Johnny, dumbfounded, asked "Excuse me?"

In a louder voice, Jaerk sarcastically hollered "You have a hearing problem? I need your license, registration and proof of insurance!"

Johnny, having never heard of these items before, asked. "Could you please tell me what these items are? I honestly don't have any idea?"

Jaerk, thinking Johnny was being insolent, said in a patronizing voice, as if explaining something to a small child, "License: it tells us: who you are, that you are of a legal age to drive, and that you are competent enough to drive this beast and wagon. Registration proves this wagon is yours, and insurance guarantees anyone you injure on the road will be compensated for their property damage or personal harm."

Johnny chuckled, "You can't be serious?"

Jaerk drawled, "Certainly am. I must ask you both to step down, out of the wagon." As Johnny and Peggy complied, Jaerk started writing several tickets. When he was done, he gave them to Johnny, saying, "You have 30 days to mail in your fines or you can appear in court to appeal these citations."

Johnny was flabbergasted. He started to mount his wagon when Jaerk said, "You can't move that wagon until you have the items we discussed." Johnny and Peggy furiously marched down the street to the local courthouse to get their registration and insurance. They both continued to ponder why they needed a license, registration and proof of insurance when they had been riding horses and driving wagons since childhood. Upon entering the courthouse and spending an hour in line, the clerk informed them that nothing could be done until they had a license, she instructed them where to go for that.

Johnny and Peggy marched to the other side of town to the DWV, Department of Wagon Vehicles. Once there, they waited another hour to be given their written test. After they passed their written tests, they were informed that they needed to pass a driving test. Because they had to leave the Creature and wagon along the street, they marched back to get them so they could prove that they could drive the wagon and get their license. They both wondered ironically how they were expected to move the contraption without a license, registration and proof of insurance. What a mess this all was.

Rounding the corner from where they had left the Creature and the wagon, Johnny was the first to notice that the beast and wagon were no longer there. Running to where he had left them,

Johnny found nothing but Jaerk loitering about, talking to a dancing girl who was taking her break.

"Deputy Jaerk!" Johnny shouted. "Where is my horse and belongings?" "How should I know?" Jaerk responded mildly as he continued eyeing the dancer. "I left them here, per your instructions, and now they're gone!" Johnny panicky said.

"Well," Jaerk said, "If you think they have been stolen, you can file a report at the sheriff's office. Once the paperwork is in order and we believe you indeed have items that have been stolen, we'll start an investigation." Johnny and Peggy angrily walked to the sheriff's office and made a report of their stolen items. "I can't believe this" Peggy stated. "Me either," Johnny angrily replied. Peggy asked, "How can he not believe they were stolen?" Johnny answered, "I believe where he comes from, protection of one's self is as important as the protection of others. If he does anything not governed by the paper trail, he might get himself in trouble." Peggy said, "All this paper and the paper trail, it can't lead anywhere good." Johnny agreed and the two spent the afternoon holding each other. Both were very depressed because they realized how quickly trying to follow the laws of man had led to them losing their possessions. One months' worth of hard work, sweat, savings, and sacrificing extravagances, was all gone. Playing by the laws of man was indeed very expensive, confusing, and heart-wrenching, not to mention down right irritating.

Johnny and his little brother borrowed their parent's horses to look for Johnny's wagon and the ugly beast, with no luck. A few weeks passed, and Jaerk came to Johnny's house to get a statement from Johnny about what goods were supposedly stolen. Johnny gave the deputy a very detailed description of the Creature and wagon. Jaerk left saying, "A lot of things get stolen;

doubt we can do you any good. The more time that passes after a theft, the better chance the thief has of getting away." Johnny closed the door angrily, muttering under his breath. Hours of sweat and labor went into that wagon and horse, and all he gets from the authorities is, "Doubt we can do you any good!" He wondered if Jaerk would have handled the situation differently if the stolen goods were his own.

3 JOHNNY'S DAD RED

Red's father was a very controlling man, nothing Red did ever seemed to satisfy him. Even if Red would outperform his father, as he sometimes did, his father was never quite content with Red, pushing him to unreasonable standards of perfection. Even though Red knew his life was full, he still felt as though there was something missing. Now as Red sat at his kitchen table with his lovely wife, Johnny, Peggy, and his youngest son Jordan, Red thought, "*I am so blessed, so why do I feel dissatisfied?*"

Red was truly blessed; he had a lovely, devoted wife and two wonderful sons. There was no shortage of complements from the town folk about his beautiful home. Even his job was one coveted by many. Silently he wondered if he could blame his dissatisfaction on his controlling dad. Not necessarily, he concluded, as he continued his introspection. Even though growing up with a choleric dad brought misery to his childhood, his dad had long been out of his life, and he could not blame the present on his past.

"*Maybe it's the lack of money for all the things I still want,*" Red contemplated. Then he thought of all the wealthy acquaintances he knew that went home to the bottle every day, drowning their troubles in alcohol. *"No,"* he thought, *"they are, in some cases, more miserable than I am. Money truly does not buy happiness,"* all of Reds needs were met. Red looked at Johnny and could not help but be impressed. Johnny was every dads dream son. *"Well,"* he thought, *"it's certainly not Johnny that's causing my dissatisfaction."* Red looked at Jordan and thought the same. He had two wonderful boys, both very different but equally great.

Red eventually tired of moving the food around on his plate and decided to call it a night. He clapped his sons on their backs, kissed his wife, and went outside to think. *"Why was this bothering him so?"* Staring up at the sky, Red prayed internally, "God, thank you for my life, my wife, and my sons. I give them into your hands to do as You deem necessary. Please give me the wisdom to do, and to feel, what is right." Red went inside to turn in for the night.

The following morning, Red rolled out of bed, got dressed, packed his lunch and headed to work. Monday through Friday, the same thing every day, Red's routine was set. Nothing changed from day-to-day but the circumstances. *"What a rut I live in,"* Red thought. *"The sun rises and sets, day after day, week after week, and my life does the same."* He felt a sense of purposelessness, and restlessness.

Red was eating lunch alone at the ship docks where he worked when another transport arrived from up north. Red figured this was not any ordinary ship, it was far too spectacular to be carrying normal hard working citizens in search of a new start. Red was amazed at the craftsmanship of the clipper ship. Its main mast was sanded to a glass finish, as was every other piece of wood on the ship. The rigging was shiny brass and hard exotic wood. "*No*," Red thought, "*whoever was on this ocean liner were very important. Ones savvy in ways of business.*" Red was proud that his town was now attracting more prosperous people.

The first pair that exited the platform were two giddy girls, one had long straight blonde hair, and the other had long straight black hair. Their perfectly parted hair flowed around their beautifully slim faces. They were holding hands, skipping down the dock, one dressed in a vibrant bright green dress, the other in blindingly bright orange. Red could not take his eyes off the girls, they were stunningly beautiful and their colorful clothes clung to their slender bodies, they were hard not to look at. The clothes barely covered anything at all, their plummeting necklines revealed most of their chests, and the hems danced around the mid-thigh, there was young skin everywhere. These were the only fully unclothed lady legs Red had ever seen, other than his wife Sue's, now he was staring at more leg than Sue would dare show in public.

As they skipped and danced towards Red, they looked at each other, raised their prefect eyebrows and smiled devilishly at Red. The girls then seductively touched their bright red lips to each other's, after a brief second they looked at Red then took off running down the dock laughing. Red had not noticed he had dropped his afternoon coffee or that his mouth was wide open. His first thought was, "*Holy mongrels, what just danced into my town?*" Then his mind swept to thinking how Jordan would behave around those two walking porcelain dolls. Red placed his hand on his six shooter thinking it might be best to never give Jordan that chance.

Red heard more clattering on the plank. He turned and saw a

stunning blonde dressed in a knee length, skin-tight, white dress. The dress was a brighter white then Red had ever seen, and was so tight that Red would later swear the sun reflected off of it. Her white blonde hair was so tightly bound that Red wondered how she could even smile let alone blink, then he noticed that she didn't smile or blink. Marching down the platform she portrayed an air of arrogance that seemed to suggest that she owned, not only the ships and the docks, but the people that accompanied them as well. Again Red was astounded at the amount of leg this blonde was not covering.

She stared straight ahead, not glancing to the left or to the right. The only thing Red thought she might be concerned about was the glossy black briefcase she clutched in her hand. Red did not notice the two large black men walking a half-step behind, on either side of the blonde. His eyes were too distracted by the form fitting dress and the way she walked. Red didn't have time to form a conclusion about "Tight White Dress" before he heard more people exiting the ship. Red turned to see yet another passenger sauntering down the ramp, Red's eyes widened, Red thought in confusion, "*what the hell is that*!?" The individual had long raven colored hair, dressed in black shoes, black slacks and a black t-shirt covered over with an open black trench coat. His skin was deathly pale, his eyes looked as though they were painted with blacks and grays, his lips were an unnatural deep purple, and his expression stark and cold. As the individual passed Red, he thought it curious the shuffling motion this person used to traverse. Reds jaw was hanging further down then it had before, he stepped away from the black dressed young man hoping he hadn't already caught the disease the kid was carrying.

A couple of young boys, probably 15 or 16 in age, were the

next passengers to disembark. They seemed to be dressed casually enough: some sort of leather-looking, discolored shoes, blue jeans, and t-shirts with drawings on them. One was carrying something on his back inside some sort of pack. It was not until they passed Red that he saw a baby staring back at him with his tiny body bouncing up and down with the step of the young boy. The baby smiled at Red, Red smiled back and raised his humongous arm and waved back at the baby. Red dropped his waving arm as he watched the two young boys grab each other's hands. Red closed his mouth and immediately wondered, "*Where was that baby's mom?*" He went to take a sip of coffee but saw it was lying spilled on the ground. His mind was running rampant, "*The two girls, had they no modesty? That straight faced blonde, where was her husband and children? Had she no modesty either?*" Then he remembered the white face of the young kid, and Red wondered if he should move before his family caught that disease.

Red heard spurs clanking on the wooden plank. He turned and saw gold spurs attached to alligator cowboy boots with gold toes. He looked up at slacks made of sparkling blue and silver and a huge gold plated belt buckle. The man walking down the plank smiled at Red and tipped his outrageous pink and blue cowboy hat in greeting. Red noticed a line of golden teeth, and underneath them hung 2 gaudy gold chains that plunged down into a very hairy chest. Red immediately thought this man was some sort of trader, trading what he didn't know. Then Red saw a ton of filming equipment following the gold toothed man. Red was happy that their town's progress was going to make national news.

Several other characters exited the ship and it was not until the very last one that Red paid careful attention. A tall, slender man with graying hair, dressed in a navy blue pinstriped 3-piece suit with a stunning red tie, was being followed by ten other men, who were also finely dressed in suits. The ten men were nervously looking around, but the slender graying man walked calmly forward in his shiny black shoes.

Red noticed out of the corner of his eye that Futureano was running toward the fancy-suited man and his companions. When Futureano reached Mr. Blue Suit Red Tie, he could not stop his jabbering and bouncing. It was ridiculous watching Futureano's stomach, tie, and loose grey hair bounce up and down, he seemed so excited to be greeting this individual. The following ten did nothing but gaze around blankly.

Futureano couldn't stop blabbering. He was jumping up and down saying, "Uncle Charlie, Uncle Charlie, it's so great you are finally here! This town is a gold mine and the people follow like lost sheep in a pasture. They do exactly what I ask of them with no questions asked! Now that you're here, they'll follow your leadership more reverently than they do mine. I'm so excited about the upcoming years. We'll be dining in the best restaurants, living on the best real estate, and governing these people like tyrants." When Futureano finally finished, Mr. Blue-Suit-Red-Tie Charles Marcus, reached into his jacket pocket, pulled out a 3 x 5 card, studied it, and finally stuck out his right hand to shake Futureano's right hand and said, "Hello." Mr. Marcus then took the card he had just read and stuck it back into his coat pocket. He looked at the next 3 x5 card, read it, and asked, "Shall we proceed?"

Red had never been so confused in all his life. *Who were these people and where did they come from*? Most of the people he had seen come to town wore rags, looked under fed, and were willing to work hard to survive. Red could usually tell the occupation of any new immigrant, whether they were farmers, factory workers, or dock workers like himself. Red could not guess the occupation of any on this transport ship, other than the man who came to capture their prosperous little town on film.

Red picked his emptied coffee cup up off the ground, and noticed that the others were heading home, he decided that that was a good idea. That night Red explained to his family all of the strange people he had seen exiting the ship. Johnny sarcastically said, "Great, more Americasses." Sue immediately became nervous about the girls with perfect bodies, perfect hair, and risqué clothing. Something in Sue instinctively told her they were bad news and should not be trusted. Sue had heard of business women up north and decided the blonde in white was some important business woman looking at business avenues in their southern town. Sue also deducted the boys with the baby we're probably brothers and raising their younger sibling on their own. The black dressed boy with a white face was to be avoided. Sue told Johnny and Jordan to avoid him at all cost, he was probably carrying some new sort of disease, Red agreed. The man with the golden chains and boot tips horrified Sue; she immediately visualized a fat warty man. The last character intrigued her, she couldn't say until she saw him, but the ultimate conclusion was that a boatload of Futureano Americasses just came to town. Red suddenly felt his life might have more purpose then he had thought last night.

4 JOHNNY GOES TO WORK

Thomas' Factory Produced Wagons was a large manufacturing company, owned by a self-made businessman named Thomas. TFPW assembled unique wagons, using the first steel bearings and springs, TFPW's wagons were known for their smooth agile ride. People from all over the area wanted TFPW wagons. Soon word of these magnificent masterpieces of manufacturing spread across the ocean. Thomas became a very influential man, and his factory grew, which in turn helped the town grow. New saw mills were commissioned by TFPW to provide wood for Thomas' wagons, and new housing for all the new workers. People came from all around to fill the new jobs created by the economic boom of the once tiny town. The town was having a hard time keeping up with all the new demands this sudden growth was bringing.

Johnny couldn't sleep any longer, he was too excited about his new job at TFPW. He loved this new job, not only did it pay better than any job he'd had before, but he was also able to take pride in the work he was performing. Johnny was getting closer to his goal, of replacing his stolen wretched wagon and the Creature with an upgraded rig. He jumped out of bed, dressed, and headed off to work with a smile.

Johnny always stopped at the local café to get a morning cup of coffee before his 6:00 am shift; it seemed that caffeine was a morning necessity. He ordered his coffee "black to go" as he always did and this morning, his cup of liquid sunshine tasted better than ever. As he walked down the street to work, Johnny saw his old friend Sherriff Wright. "Morning Johnny," Sheriff said as he tipped his hat and spit a mouthful of brown, tobacco induced, spit on the dry dusty street. "Morning Sheriff," Johnny replied. "See you at the Friday Dance?" Sheriff asked pleasantly. "Wouldn't miss it," Johnny said, returning the sheriff's smile.

Johnny continued his walk to work, smiling broadly as he thought of twirling Peggy around on the dance floor. Watching her golden hair dance as they spun was something Johnny truly enjoyed about Peggy's beauty. Johnny thought himself blessed to be courting such a fine young lady, and he started laughing as he pictured giving her a jar of crickets as a prank date gift. Johnny couldn't be any happier; he had the perfect job, great cup of coffee, and beautiful girl to share his dreams with.

A few blocks from work he saw deputy Jaerk. "Morning Deputy," Johnny greeted happily, his thoughts being on Peggy and not on his stolen goods. Ever on the lookout for suspicious activity, Jaerk suspected Johnny of walking the streets while inebriated because he was happy and had a spring to his step. Jaerk ignoring Johnny's greeting asked, "A little happy today?" Johnny smiled easily, turned to Jaerk and said, "It's a great day," his vision being shifted to Jaerk and not to where he was walking, tripped on a loose nail that had worked its way up through the wooden boardwalk. He stumbled, but continued walking. "NOT SO FAST!" Jaerk shouted, a little giddy at the prospect of putting someone in jail, or issuing a pricey ticket, especially to this insolent dummy. "I noticed you're not walking straight. Something in that coffee helping you get your day going?" Jaerk interrogated. "Just coffee" Johnny replied quizzically. "Mind if I take a whiff?" Jaerk sneered. Johnny immediately thought *"Are you serious?*" But replied asking, "Why Jaerk? Someone get up on the wrong side of the bed?"

Jaerk, not liking Johnny's seemingly disrespectful attitude of his authority, took further dislike to Johnny's happy attitude, demanded "Please set the cup down, and step over to the wall." Johnny thought this was ludicrous, and was irritated that he was now going to be late for work because of some ridiculous accusation from this stuck up Americass.

Jaerk proceeded without checking the contents of Johnny's coffee cup. "Looks like you've had a little too much alcohol added to your morning coffee Johnny. Ya wouldn't mind doing a few simple tests for me?" Jaerk questioned. Not giving Johnny time to reply, he immediately started giving Johnny a series of tests to prove his intoxication.

One of Johnny's co-workers snickered as he passed Johnny touching his middle finger to his nose while jumping up and down on his right foot. Jaerk had Johnny repeat this process while on his left foot and Johnny's face flushed red as the young children passed on their way to school.

Jaerk, getting frustrated that Johnny was passing these tests, had him clap and count backwards from 327. Several of Johnny's co-workers clapped along with Johnny as they passed him on their way to work. Johnny smiled and now Jaerk turned red. Furious, Jaerk told Johnny to stand on his left foot and count by thousands for five minutes. Johnny started wavering a tiny bit at four and a half minutes, his left leg did not let him down though. In a last attempt to prove Johnny was walking the streets inebriated, Jaerk asked Johnny to calculate the product of 4,568.36 and 89.52 divided by 73.25. Charlotte, the school teacher, yelled to Johnny as she was passing by, "63.59." Johnny said to Jaerk, "63.59." Jaerk angrily looked at Charlotte and scowled, then turned and stomped away. Johnny and Charlotte smiled at each other and then went about their morning travels.

Johnny was fuming inside, his coffee was cold, he was late for work, and he had been asked to do the most unbelievably illogical tests. Many of his companions had passed him, while he performed Jaerk's sobriety tests. Although most knew Johnny was not a drinking man, all of them had chuckled as they passed Johnny, including his boss Thomas. Johnny had to admit to himself that it was probably rather comical watching him jumping around in his old clunky cowboy boots giving Jaerk the "bird" as he was instructed to.

Some wondered how they had let Johnny misguide them into believing he did not have a drinking problem. Others were thankful they weren't the ones being given the test, knowing they wouldn't pass. A few felt sorry for Johnny at having been delayed on his way to work, knowing it had to of put a damper on his day. When Johnny finally reached TFPW, his floor supervisor told him the boss wanted to see him. "*Could this day get any worse*?" Johnny wondered. Embarrassed at having to pass his co-workers who recently passed him while being questioned by Jaerk, Johnny headed up to Thomas's office.

Jaerk raced back to the sheriff department and darted back to the file room to pull Johnny's record, searching for anything that he could use to put Johnny in his place, behind steel bars. Jaerk did not like Johnny or his goody-two-shoes behavior, but Johnny had passed all the inebriation tests. Pulling Johnny's file, he immediately saw that Johnny had a record for violence and had been expelled from school. As Jaerk skimmed over the file all he read was "violent behavior... adolescent female... Expelled for unacceptable actions." Jaerk hopefully assumed that meant "lewd violence on a minor." He smiled, jumped on his horse, and galloped to the factory where Johnny worked.

Johnny's boss, Thomas, was a solid built man born in 1810. He had grown up with Johnny's dad, and knew that Johnny's family blood ran thick with good morals and values. However, this morning, he had seen Johnny being given the inebriation tests and wondered if Johnny was alright. "Why'd Jaerk give you the alcohol test this morning?" Thomas asked.

"Cause I was whistling, and smiling, and seemingly enjoying life!" Johnny responded with a hint of sarcasm in his voice.

Thomas asked, "What all was in your coffee?"

Johnny, a little concerned at the question coming from Thomas, grinned and said, "Nothing but water and old coffee grounds."

Thomas chuckled, "That'll get you in trouble every time."

Johnny wanted to vent his frustration. "I just don't understand..." Johnny began to say, when Thomas' office door swung open, and in stepped deputy Jaerk. Wearing his brown ten gallon hat, sunglasses, and wrinkle free suit, Jaerk solidly planted his dark boots and stated, "We have a problem."

Thomas, not liking the attitude of the young deputy, agreed. "Yes, we do. You're standing in MY office, unannounced and uninvited." Jaerk, unmoved, blurted, "Your worker here happens to have a problem with under-aged women. I would like to question him further about why he was so happy this morning."

Thomas and Red had sat at the bar many nights talking about Johnny's incident at school. Thomas himself had great concerns about the same thing happening to his own son William. If a young man could not protect himself or his loved ones, how long would it be before an adult was not allowed to protect his own life and his loved ones? Thomas had been very displeased with the whole situation.

"And what, pray tell, is Johnny's problem?" Thomas roared, "That he protects the woman he loves? That he is happy and in love? That he has dreams of moving away from the likes of you? Or does the problem lie with you and your wrongful accusations? Last I read, constitution says a man is innocent until proven guilty, and, you're standing on privately owned property, onto which you were not invited! Seems you're breaking more laws than anyone else right now!"

Jaerk knew he was breaking the law. However, he had also been taught that it was "OK" for an officer of the law to break the law in order to ensure the safety of others. Which, of course, includes issuing tickets to discipline the wrongdoer. Jaerk's philosophy was simple: If a law is broken, a citation is given, even if no one is or was in any sort of danger. Jaerk was unmoved. "I need to question Johnny a little further," and, wanting to prove to others that Johnny was a threat, Jaerk loudly blurted, "He has a problem with young women!"

Although this was untrue, the words had been spoken and subconscious seeds of doubt had been planted into the minds of the hear-Sayers loitering outside Thomas' door. They would go home to their families and discuss Johnny and his "young girl problem." Those with daughters would warn their daughters to stay away from Johnny. Jaerk's simple statement had marred the view of Johnny's character for life.

Thomas was furious, he knew Johnny. Johnny was an outstanding young man, a youngster any father would be proud to call son. Johnny was one of his best employees, he was punctual every day and worked harder than most grown men. All 6-3, 230 pounds of Thomas rose from behind his cherry wood desk and hovered over Jaerk. "You can leave now." Thomas billowed darkly.

Jaerk took in the full head of Thomas' silver hair and his grey eyes which seemed to be screaming "You are 2 seconds away from dying!" Jaerk wondered *"What the hell is wrong with these people? Have they no respect for authority?"* Jaerk also knew that Thomas and Sheriff Wright were on good terms with each other, he did not want to start a feud with Thomas, and his quarrel was with Johnny. Jaerk looked at Johnny and said, "We are not done young man." He turned and stormed away.

Johnny was fuming. First Futureano Americass got him expelled from school; now this Jaerk Americass was jeopardizing his new job and ruining his reputation. Being embarrassed in front of his boss and coworkers, Johnny was unsure what to do. Thomas took the initiative, "I will talk to Mr. Wright. Get this straightened out. Go on and get to work." Thomas gave Johnny a pat on his back and sent him out the door. Johnny ignored the questioning stares of his workmates as he went to his station.

Thomas was raging mad, he wanted to speak with Sheriff Wright about Jaerk immediately. He tried to hurry through his morning meeting with his factory staff, but they had a long list of questions and concerns. It was mid-morning by the time Thomas was rushing to the sheriff's office. There the secretary told

Thomas the sheriff was busy and could not be interrupted. Thomas went to the diner for lunch, then headed back to the sheriff's office. The Secretary told Thomas that the sheriff had to go out of town for a few days, he could leave a message with them, if he wanted. Thomas could not put into writing his current thoughts concerning Jaerk and Johnny. He would wait until the sheriff got back.

A week later when the sheriff did get back, he seemed to avoid Thomas at all costs. Finally when Thomas caught Wright in the street, his temper had subsided. What Thomas did not know was that Sheriff Wright had heard about the incident at TFPW from Jaerk. Wright and Jaerk had looked at Johnny's file and had seen Jaerk's misunderstanding.

Sheriff Wright was a man in his late fifties. He was lean and strong, with even stronger character. He wore his grey hair long and he never seemed to shave, his long handlebar mustache and thick grey beard left people with a gruff impression of him, though he was an honest, decent man. Sheriff Wright stood a good 6 inches taller than Jaerk, who was intimidated by Sheriff Wright's size.

Wright was furious with Jaerk. Jaerk being a relative of a city official, was protected against Wright's discipline. Wright asked Jaerk, "Why are you falsely accusing Johnny?" Jaerk simply stated, "The law clearly states public inebriation is wrong. Johnny looked inebriated and I had to act on that!" Wright continued his questioning, "And the pedophile accusation?" Jaerk was at a loss for an answer to this question. He simply shrugged his shoulders, knowing the powers high up would give him protection against the laws he had broken. Wright sat at his desk, unhappily trying to find a reason to give Thomas for the accusations. He knew

Thomas desperately wanted to see him concerning Johnny and dreaded the upcoming confrontation.

By the time Wright met with Thomas, Wright had prepared a response. Thomas asked Sheriff Wright, "Your deputy accused Johnny of being intoxicated while on his way to work then accused him of being a pedophile. These accusations were unmerited by your young deputy." The sheriff simply said, "Sorry about the misunderstanding. My deputy had referred to a file of a person who shares Johnny's name." Thomas, not believing that another boy with the same name as Johnny existed in this town, questioned the sheriff further. "You mean there is another Johnny running around town with the same birth date?" The sheriff turned a little red and stammered "Afraid so."

Thomas knew Sheriff Wright was lying, but could not understand why. They had been friends for years and had never lied to one another. Thomas pondered what sort of misconstrued politics could make an honest man lie to a friend. Thomas, knowing he would not receive any further information from Sherriff Wright, turned and left. Thomas would never know the reason for Wright's statement other than Jaerk and Wright. However, the damage to Johnny's reputation was already done. Fortunately for Johnny, the incident did not go into his file.

5 CHARLES MARCUS and SUSIE POWERS

Futureano's' uncle, Charles Marcus, sat at the center seat of the old oak table, situated on a slightly raised platform on the far side of the largest room in city hall. Dressed in his fancy pinstriped suit, crisp white shirt and vibrant red tie, he looked very commanding in the large arm chair. As Futureano had surmised, Charles was easily elected town mayor. He spoke like a man who could govern the needs of the prospering town, and looked like a man in charge. Charles sat in the old wooden armchair wanting just a little more time to study his 3x5 cards which were being held by Susie, to prepare for this evening's speech. There was still a little time before the meeting commenced, he smiled as he remembered his nephew's enthusiastic greeting as he stepped off the ship 3 months ago. Futureano was right, exploiting the towns concerns and convincing them that Marcus was the only person capable of running their town had been easier than expected.

Sitting on Charles' right was Futureano, and to his left, his sister Susie Powers, Futureano's aunt. Susie's golden hair was tied back in its' customary tightly woven bun, not even a trace of a smile on her face, her navy blue power suit clung securely to her thin frame. The only thing really noticeably different about Susie since she exited the ocean liner was she no longer clutched her black briefcase, the case and its contents were now safely locked away.

Susie had grown up a headstrong, power-hungry, entrepreneur. Her first successful business venture was establishing a black market food distribution ring in junior high. Supplying more appetizing food options instead of the green pea mush soup the school cafeteria offered. In college Susie excelled far above her classmates, but her being a woman outdoing her male counterparts caused friction. The boys in her class would often chastise her and try to make her life difficult, but Susie didn't care. The adversity made Susie even more determined to outdo them all. Graduating college at age 21, she was ready to face the world thinking she was the wisest individual around. Because of her shrewd business savvy and ability to control others, Susie excelled at every business venture she undertook. But being an authoritative woman in the male dominated society of the late 1800s was not easy; she knew she could advance no further than she already had.

Immediately after receiving a letter from her nephew Futureano explaining a gold mine down South, Susie started formulating her personal business plan. She lost hours of sleep as she masterminded her way to the ultimate powerful position in life, controlling the New World. Sitting at the round table of this prospering town was her first step. Susie knew that being a female would limit her capabilities; she deviously enlisted Charles as her unsuspecting marionette for her scheme. Charles reluctantly thought "*he was not as smart as other homominions.*" Fortunately his sister Susie had taught him how to compensate. As long as he could remember, Susie was always dressing him spectacularly and teaching him - not the 3 Rs, but the DWTR, how to dress, walk, talk and relate to others.

The strange bond between Susie and Charles happened when Sister Susie was selling food in middle school. Charles was promoting the health benefits of his sister's candy over the schools' green vegetables. From that first success, he knew there was nothing they could not accomplish together. Charles became the public figure and Susie stayed in the shadows watching and directing Charles with carefully composed 3x5 cards as he performed each of her painstakingly magnificent masquerades.

They separated for a brief period of time while Susie attended business school and Charles went to acting school. Susie went to an agnostic liberal college specializing in cunning business practices, Charles went to an acting school in the far west. When Susie graduated, Charles dropped out of college and the two reunited. After receiving ridiculous Futureano's letter telling of the booming little town down south, Susie had locked herself in her room for months. She began devising her plan outline for her end goal in life, controlling the entire world. It took every ounce of Susie's mental energy to engineer and compose her scheme. After a thought was conceived, it was written on paper, the piles grew and were separated and placed in folders. When a folder was finished it went into a shiny black leather briefcase. When Susie had finished her scheming, she emerged from her room looking like a vogue model, ready to conquer the world. Her silky blonde hair was tightly secured to her head; her dress was not the traditional Victorian but a formfitting pencil skirt and matching blazer that she had specially made for herself by a tailor friend. The bold power suit made her look powerful, elegant, desirable and completely untouchable. They boarded the next luxury ocean liner leaving their city.

After arriving in Liberty Town Susie and Charles purchased a large three story house near the center of town. They filled it with all the comforts of "home." Every room was filled with the most magnificent of everything. Susie's office was no exception, her beautiful cherry wood desk sat in front of a large bay window overlooking the town from the second floor, her mastermind plan locked up in the safe wall that was camouflaged behind a pirate ship oil painting in her new home office. She removed her first folder for review; page 1, paragraph A. REMOVE GOD. Susie smiled as she considered God, the Creator of heaven and earth, having no place in the schools of Liberty town. Since God was not in the constitution, Susie determined the forefathers had wanted the government to guide people's morals and ethics. If people could not keep their behavior in check, then they should fear the government and not God to keep them obeying civil and moral law.

Susie had learned from her favorite professor at college that a child's basic beliefs were set in stone by the age of 12. When she was building her master plan, she decided she would instill in the small children an agnostic view. This one simple step would be the foundation for her master plan. It would eliminate her competition with God. Destroying the moral fiber of "do unto others" and plant the seed of self-worship. She would no longer have to waste time with stupid fights between government and religion because the people would really have no religious doctrine on which to base their behavior.

So, now they sat at the same table as their nephew, little Futureano Americass, bringing their agenda to this new world, starting in this booming town. This agenda was simple enough in theory to them, but logically insane to those who held tight to their constitutional rights. Charles sat tapping his fingers, drumming faster and faster, all he wanted was just a second or two to study those 3x5's Susie was holding, before the town meeting commenced. He hated when his sister did this to him, deny him time to study his speech. Charles lightly kicked his sister's ankle. Susie ignored her brother's interruption; *it was not time for the marionette to perform.*

Susie scanned the crowded meeting room, more and more people were pushing into the already full hall. She looked at her brother and saw him seething. She had prepared him for tonight, but Charles couldn't grasp the importance of this meeting. He kept asking stupid questions and was continuously trying to joke with her. Finally she had told him, "I'll write your speech, just make sure you execute it with precision." She hoped he had learned his lesson. Susie took a deep breath as she handed the stack of 3x5's to her brother and sighed to herself, *"it's now or never."* Charles shot his sister an evil glare as he grabbed the cards and stood in front of the podium. As the townsfolk began to settle Charles reluctantly thought that "*he was not as smart as other "homominions.*" Fortunately his sister Susie had taught him how to feign components for as long as he could remember, Susie was always dressing him spectacularly and teaching him – DWTR, how to dress, walk, talk and relate to others.

Charles knew they were an unbeatable pair, his charisma and her intelligence, he just felt like his sister was the one pulling all the strings. Charles read the first card, Susie watched the reaction of the people, being ready to terminate the gathering at the slightest hint of hostility.

"Ladies and gentlemen, citizens of our great town, I am grateful to each and every one of you who took time out of your busy lives to discuss these fundamental matters..." Charles paused as he flipped to his next cards, "of our town's prosperous future. That is, the education of our young children. Without proper education, this town will not survive." Charles again paused shortly to flip to another card, Susie continued to watch the people. She thought she saw a hint of doubt in Red's eyes. Charles continued, "Our children need, no, not need, deserve to be educated to the highest of standards." Charles thought he would enhance his sister's ruse by adding "And you should all feel ashamed for not giving your children the best education available." Susie saw Charlotte's eyes darken, Susie immediately pushed her glass of water off the table, making its contents drench Charlotte's leg, and the glass roll to the floor. Charles and Susie both bent to pick up the fallen glass. When their faces nearly touched, Susie whispere to her brother, "You deviate from the script once more and I will make you beg for death." Charles' face beamed red as he stood straight; most thought he was embarrassed at having looked as though he had pissed his posh slacks.

Charles, being angry with his sister, read his speech word for word with a heated expression. "Our current teaching methods are far below acceptable standards. It is menial teaching at best. Not to say our children are not taught to the utmost of small town standards, they are, but our children deserve the best education available anywhere, to standards that are a prerequisite for success."

Charles continued reading from his 3x5 cards and as usual, he persuaded the masses that he was right. Even though many did not really understand what he was talking about, his eloquent speech made them want to agree with every word he said. When Susie saw that not all were on board with her plan, she handed Charles another stack of 3x5's. Charles read the second speech, "It is impossible for a working parent to teach the children to a minimal acceptable level of education (pause and flip card) that will ensure his acceptance into the adult world having reassured himself that he knowingly was educated by the best possible curriculum. (Pause and flip card) Knowing that you willfully and voluntarily submit your children into the hands of the delegated representatives that will ensure an elucidation to the education dilemma (pause and flip card) that you appreciate being offered for your betterment of the exceptional education your children will receive." Charles continued reading a rewording of the first 3x5's that seemed to say something almost entirely different, and again took the crowd around his oratory merry-go-round. By the time he had finished, the audience was alight with excitement, although none really knew what they were excited about other then they saw their children being better educated. Susie sat at the end of the table and for the first time in months, she cracked a smile because the people had just placed the education of their children completely into her hands.

After the town meeting Susie beamed at Charles, "I can't believe the people just gave us control of their schools." Charles, wanting to sound educated, replied "Most homominions aren't that bright sis." Susie started to correct her brother's misinterpretation of a non-existent word but realized she liked that term for the people, clueless people who just seem to follow blindly the path placed before them, kind of like sheep. Susie hooked her arm through Charles's and the two set off towards home, tomorrow was going to be a busy day.

That night at the dinner table Red asked Johnny, "What exactly did we vote on this evening?" Sue answered for her son, "I think we no longer have much of a say in what or how the children are taught." Red grimaced at the thought.

6 **RUDY AND BOBBY**

Charles had convinced Futureano and others that Susie's idea of education was so spectacular that he immediately adopted them and hoped to persuade all schools, throughout the nation, to implement the same reforms. Futureano chuckled to himself. Charles is so right. *"Children can't learn from their parents."* Futureano thought further. *"They really do need schooling. Since children need governmental guidance, it should be a priority in every town. Since we, the government, are a priority, we should be given whatever we need. Since I'm the head master of this school, I should be given whatever I desire as well. I do need a new horse..."* Futureano screamed, "IM GETTING A NEW HORSE!" Just then, Charlotte walked by on her way to teach her Math class. She looked oddly at Futureano, smiled, and continued to her class. Futureano saw Charlotte smile and inwardly his heart beat faster. He knew that deep down Charlotte liked him, after all, she did just smile at him.

Charlotte was an attractive teacher that Futureano not-so-secretly had a crush on. Charlotte had curly auburn red hair that turned a little bit orange in the sun. She was not skinny, nor was

she overweight, Charlotte's weight was distributed just right, with curves in all the right places. Her dark green eyes would change color with her emotions. When she was happy they were a light glinting green, as the tint or her mood darkened so would the shade of her deep green eyes. Some days Futureano would interrupt her class just to look at her; Charlotte's eyes would darken to a smoky clouded green. Charlotte, on the other hand, despised Futureano and his sons, Rudy and Bobby. She knew Futureano was married, which she called Strike one. Futureano's' boys did nothing but behave obnoxiously in class and tried to sneak peeks up the girls' skirts, including hers. Strikes 2 and 3, she thought.

Charlotte glanced out the window and saw Jaerk writing a ticket, Johnny had been riding to work when a youngster darted in front of him, trying to make it to school on time, and Johnny swerved to miss the child, and was now being issued a reckless driving ticket by deputy Jaerk. Charlotte chuckled, thinking, *"One of these days Jaerk might not be protected by his uniform."* If and when that day comes, she could picture Johnny beating the tar out of Jaerk. She visualized Johnny's right fist connecting with Jaerk's left eye. She knew Johnny was tough, she knew Jaerk harassed Johnny under the protection of his uniform for nonsense accusations. She herself would like to see some sense beaten into Jaerk. She visualized herself smacking his right eye and kicking his ribs. She silently cursed as she had to rush off to class rather than finish her thoughts of Jaerk ending up lying in the street bloody and bruised. She lifted the hem of her long white dress just above her feet to prevent ripping as she hurried off to her class.

Inside Charlotte's classroom was chaos. The thin blonde wearing a short neon green dress was sitting on her desk telling two younger boys to kiss. These were the same two boys who held hands while one carried a baby off the ocean liner. The boys turned red and told the green neon dressed blonde, "NO!" The raven haired girl who was scantily clad in a blindingly bright orange dress giggled, "We know you do it at home, we want to watch." The local town's children were stunned into silence, never had they seen anything like they were now witnessing. It was hard enough accepting Rudy and Bobby into their school, now they were watching the newly arrived neon dressed girls encourage other new students to do unimaginable things right there in public school. The boys couldn't quit staring at the girls in the florescent short dresses; the girls were intrigued to see if two boys would actually succumb to their taunting and kiss. One of the taunted boys asked the long haired blonde, "Are you two related?" The dark haired girl answered for her sister, saying, ""We're twins." The other pressured boy said, "If you kiss your twin sister, I'll kiss him." Without hesitation, the neon dressed twins kissed. There was gasping throughout the once deafening classroom. The twins looked and smiled at the boys and simultaneously said, "Your turn!" The boys grabbed each other's faces and joined their lips in a shockingly passionate kiss just as Charlotte walked into her classroom. Charlotte's jaw about hit the hard wood floor as she tried to comprehend the astonishingly confusing sight before her.

Charlotte dropped her books and stammered, "WH...AT THE H...ELL?" The twins turned to Charlotte and the blonde said, "Miss C, you shouldn't cuss like that in front of small children." Charlotte ignored the reprimand and ordered her class to take their designated seats. She cautiously walked to her desk and lowered herself into her chair, she dizzily wondered what these new Americasses had brought into her classroom. She was too shocked at what she had witnessed to speak and silently cursed the "Neon Twins," the name her subconscious just tagged the girls with, for entering her classroom. She had them pull out the bible and start copying Romans chapter 1.

Futureano was excited about the new horse he had decided he was going to get. Seeing Charlotte's long wavy auburn hair resting on top that bright white dress had him excited in unspeakable ways. He decided he should drop into Charlotte's class and ????, hmmm, why did he need to see her? Futureano smiled as he remembered the new school policy. He grabbed the policy papers and headed to Charlotte's room whistling as he attempted to hide his balding head with his ill-conceived comb over.

Futureano didn't knock, he barged into Charlotte's room hoping to surprise her. He loved seeing her startled face and darkened green eyes, which is what he expected to see. What he didn't expect to see was all the students copying the bible. Futureano dropped his papers and forcefully declared to Charlotte and her class, "There will be no more bibles allowed in any public school!" Charlotte stood in shocked outrage, "Why not!?!?" Futureano simply said, "New school policy," as he casually began gathering the bibles from the dumbfounded students and placing them into a large bag he had collected from the rack next to the door. Peggy came rushing breathless into the room apologizing to Charlotte for being late, Peggy was about to give her excuse when Charlotte grabbed her hand and walked her out of the classroom muttering, "Class dismissed, go home and get your chores done." The local children rushed out, happy to be able to get their chores done early. The 'Americass' children stayed back, not knowing what to do. Charlotte told Peggy, "I'm so thankful you were late." Charlotte didn't expound and she walked with Peggy holding her hand for comfort, her mind was too busy trying to sort out today's events.

The next day Charlotte sat in class looking at her students. She was so proud of her students, well the ones who she had known before the "boom" happened, the ones before all the Americasses invaded her quaint little town. Now as she looked around she saw Rudy and Bobby, the Neon Twins, Gothard and the others, and how disappointing they all were in her eyes. Not only in dress and nature, but also for their lack of motivation, none had made better than a D on any of the work she had assigned. As the class settled, she passed out todays test. She immediately heard Rudy say, "Another test Miss C? I would think if you had a man in your life you wouldn't have time to make all these tests." The class erupted in laughter. Futureano entered the classroom smiling at Charlotte as if to say, "I'm your man." Charlotte's eyes darkened a shade. She finished passing out the days test and sat at her desk. As the test progressed, she heard the Neon Twins giggle, but paid them no mind. Later, as she graded the papers that evening at home, she was shocked as she made her way through the stack, the new children's test scores were perfect.

Rudy and Bobby borrowed their father's keys to the school that they might spend extra time at school "preparing" for future tests. Futureano was so proud of his boys; they seemed to know that education was the key to Liberty Towns' success. Rudy and Bobby entered the school and headed straight for Charlotte's classroom. Once there they opened her top desk drawer and removed next week's test. Not wanting to spend any more effort than absolutely necessary, they would copy the answers onto their desk lids. The boys loved the popularity they were receiving for sharing the answers on testing day.

Charlotte immediately knew foul play was at work after scoring the mid-term tests. Overnight the newer students had gone from almost failing to perfect scores. It took her all of two more weeks to figure out the testing conspiracy. Having a good sense of humor, she allowed the conduct to continue for a couple more weeks, inwardly laughing as she saw the squinting eyes and odd movements during test days. The more success the children had each week with their tests, the more blatant they became about their cheating, thinking Miss C really was not all that bright, and couldn't possibly have a clue.

Finally Charlotte decided to end the charade. As the children calmed the next morning for the days lesson, Charlotte said, "I would like all of you to change your seating arrangements before we start today." The children mumbled and started switching desks one with another. Bobby stood and declared, "All right, but I'm taking my desk with me." Rudy and Bobby both grabbed their desks, Rudy moved his beside Peggy and Bobby moved his between the Neon Twins. Peggy was repulsed at having to sit near Rudy, but she held her tongue and thoughts. Charlotte laughed and dropped on the floor with gut-wrenching laugh cramps as she watched the two boys awkwardly rearrange their desks and themselves into a new classroom position. Charlotte asked Rudy and Bobby to please sit up front. They grabbed their desks and positioned themselves at the front of the class. Charlotte laughed louder. Rudy asked, "What's so funny Miss C?" Charlotte replied, "I've never seen two boys so in love with their desks before." The classroom erupted into louder laughter.

The following day Charlotte found herself in Futureano's office. "I will not have you laughing at my boys" Futureano said grudgingly. Charlotte watched half of Futureano's hair fall off the top of his head and land on his shoulder. She giggled, which made Futureano more angry, thinking Charlotte was not taking this seriously.

Charlotte stated the reasons behind her laughter, how his boys were behind a cheating conspiracy, and that their actions in trying to continue their cheating behavior was just too hysterical. Futureano defended, "Education is the key to Liberty Towns' future success, and a child's self-esteem is important. To laugh at these children is to damage their self-worth. I will not allow this destructive behavior to be around the children." Charlotte angrily replied, "They were cheating and helping others to cheat!" Futureano retorted, "They should be commended on their ingenuity! You're dismissed! Two weeks suspension without pay." Futureano made sure he lightly pushed on Charlotte's back as he ushered her out of his office, taking any opportunity he could to touch this beautiful woman. Futureano would have terminated any other teacher for laughing at his boys, but he liked having Charlotte around, she was very attractive and fun to touch.

When Charlotte returned to work she was given the new school curriculum. Having read what she was expected to teach, she was utterly infuriated. In spite of her rage, Charlotte knew it was better to just follow the new regulations instead of voicing her fury. She had just come back from disciplinary vacation, and was in no hurry to leave her class full of impressionable children to someone else again. She sighed and made a determined promise to herself, *"One day we will get our school system back."*

7 **Susie's Plan.**

Susie was thrilled, the Town Hall meeting had gone splendidly and her education proposal had passed virtually uninhibited. The Bible was out of the classroom and the town government had complete say over what was to be taught to the school children. Susie smiled to herself as she sat behind her desk in her City Hall office; she slid her high heeled shoes off her tired feet as she pondered her "re-education" program. Re-writing a curriculum was going to be a long and tedious process, Susie knew this, but she was excited all the same. She entertained the idea of having her secretary take notes, then she rethought the idea, her thoughts were better kept to herself for the time being, locked in her sturdy black briefcase. Susie cleared her desk to make room for her "re-education" revisions. She set out the education file from her case and beside it her yellow legal pad, "The right of ownership and handling of firearms shall be reserved for military use only," Susie nodded decisively at her first line of slander. She swore at the constitution, the idea giving everyone the right to carry a gun was appalling. She knew the writers of the constitution wanted the government kept in check. *"Well"* Susie thought, *"It will be a cold day in hell before I will allow guns to be used against me."* Susie wrote on a clean sheet of paper, "Our founding fathers were inhibited by the effects of smoking marijuana when they wrote the phrase 'all men have the right to bear arms.' What they must have meant was that 'the militia should always carry firearms for the sole purpose of protecting the government and its people.'" Susie sealed the paper to be sent via messenger to Futureano, included were instructions to start teaching this thought in history class immediately.

Susie skimmed her notes and read a quote from Thomas Jefferson, "No government can continue good, but under the control of the people." --Thomas Jefferson to J. Adams, 1819. Susie thought, *"That's bullshit TJ. It's pretty ridiculous to think that those governing the people should be led by the people. Those ignorant homominions."* Susie scoffed, she flipped to a clean sheet of paper in her legal pad and began writing. "Elected officials are chosen by the mass majority for a reason. People are too lazy..." Susie crossed out the last four words and re-wrote, "People realize that there are different levels of comprehension and therefore they elect the ones they know will be capable of the wisest governing. When a political position is filled, the elected official decides and acts upon what he feels is in the best interest of the people. The people should trust in the elected official, and abstain from questioning their authority." Susie thought sourly, *"to have the people tell the elect how to govern is nothing more than a showing of ignorance. Surely the governed should unquestioningly follow the elected and their decisions."* Susie re-read her work and sent it off to Futureano to have taught to the children in political science. Susie smiled as she watched the messenger leave her office, thinking, *"It's pretty ridiculous to be asked to serve the people and then the people not follow the elected directions or decisions."* Susie read her educational notes once more and decided to agree with TJ this time when he said, "If once [the people] become inattentive to the public affairs, you and I, and Congress and Assemblies, Judges and Governors, shall all become wolves. It seems to be the law of our general nature, in spite of individual exceptions." --Thomas Jefferson to E. Carrington, 1787.

Susie would have liked the day's work to be done but knew there was one more piece of business for her to attend to. On the outskirts of town there was a beautiful ranch that she wanted, *"Of course, to help govern the people better,"* she thought. Sighing heavily at the thought of even more work, she went to the record room to gather the papers on her future property; she cussed under her breath as she made her way back to her office to review them. *"This is bullshit,"* she muttered to herself, *"this would be so much easier if there was a way for me to just decide I want something and just make it mine."* She paused, *"is there a way for me to make that happen?"* She thought of herself as a "superior being," She wanted a place all her own, she giggled to herself as she thought of the ideal name for her own little corner of the world, *"Superior Area."* "Yes" she said aloud, with a girlish giggle "I should call my home Superior Area, eminent domain. Now all I have to do is figure out how to get it." She wondered if it could be so simple as to just want it and take it. Susie scribbled on a clean sheet of paper, "The government reserves the right to claim as their own any land or assets they deem necessary for the betterment of the people." Susie smiled triumphantly at this thought; she considered sending the transcript to Futureano but decided he probably had his hands full with the new school regulations and curriculum. She would implement this new law at a later date. Susie went home and slept like a rock, she felt that since she had worked at least 3 whole hours today she deserved extra sleep.

The following day Susie locked up her educational file and pulled out the next file on her agenda marked, **POWER**. Having successfully started her plan on the educational system, she was now ready to proceed to her next phase. She giggled to herself as she thought *"how ignorant people really are. Tell them there's free food and they'll come running to pay the one dollar fee to enter the park where the free food is."* She smiled as she visualized the masses dressed as sheep following whoever held the staff. *"Hit them with fear, or promise them power, people would always be willing to follow."* Even her brother Charles was happy doing as she said as long as his power continued to grow. Susie's ultimate goal was to be the most powerful human alive. She didn't just want to control the people, the businesses, and the corporations; she wanted to control the world. She did not mind not holding elegant titles, but knowing she was in control of everything, that did send goose bumps down her arms. If she could control four men in great power, then she was 4 times more powerful than any one of those men. Susie considered, *"If I could increase the title holders' power over individuals, my power grows as well."* Then another thought flashed through her mind, *Religion*. People would die defending their god. Her mind was jumping from thought to thought until she couldn't think straight. Finally she decided to act on man's first basic motivator, fear. She called for another town meeting for tomorrow evening.

The next evening, Futureano, Charles and Susie sat at their respected chairs in the town hall's large meeting room. Susie sat in her white dress at the end of the table, she did not want to be noticed, but she did not want to miss the reaction of her sheep either, or *homominions* as Charles would call them.

Charles took out his 3 x 5s and started reading. "Ladies and gentlemen, I am so happy that many of you could make it. You, your families, and your livelihoods are very important to me. I care about each and every one of you. I often sit up at night thinking of ways I can make your lives better. After all, we are all in the pursuit of happiness together." Charles stood and started walking the crowd. He stopped at the front row and tapped a young man on his shoulder and asked him his name. The young man answered, my name is..., Charles wasn't really listening all he heard was "Baaa Baaaa." Charles flipped his cards and read, "Baaa Baaaa, you're very important to me. I want to see you healthy, I want to see your family well fed, I want you to be safe, to be able to return home from work each day unharmed." Baaa Baaaa turned red at having been singled out. Charles moved to the next row and shook hands with a young lady. Charles warmly asked her name. She answered, my name is "Baabaaa Too." Baabaaa Too blushed at having been touched by such a distinguishing handsome man. Charles smiled at her and continued reading. "Baabaaa Too, I know you love your husband." Baabaaa Too thought, "*I don't have a husband*." But she kept quiet wanting to take in every word that was being spoken to her. Charles continued, "And I know he is a hardworking man and that you want him to come home safe each night after work to you and your children. It's for people like you we are immediately forming a special committee to ensure you and your family's safety each and every day."

For 30 minutes Charles spoke concerning the importance of safety. For those same 30 minutes Susie was inwardly hula-hooping with excitement over seeing the people relinquishing more of their individual power as they melted away, right into her hands. They were all nodding their heads up and down in agreement with every word Charles spoke. None liked the idea of injury or unsafe environments, and now Charles was promising to make their lives safer. They had no idea that in the name of safety many of their rights to freedom of choice were being ripped away. They were nothing but sheep, following her brother Charles, the charismatic man dressed in a fancy blue suit, white shirt and brilliant red tie.

Susie stood and left, she was bored listening to the words she had written for Charles to speak. She had seen that her sheep were willing to let rules be put into place to ensure their safety. She knew with each rule she imposed; more power was given to her and taken away from the people. She walked outside and stepped in a pile of manure. Her expensive white stilettos were now a stinking brown mess. She was furious, Susie muttered, "What the hell! I could have slipped and fallen in that shit. First thing tomorrow, in the name of safety, there will be no more horse crap in my town."

8 BANK SHOOTING

Susie's new health and safety laws were being enforced on the pleasant people of beautiful little Liberty Town. Horses were no longer permitted to relieve themselves on the street, horses and horse drawn wagons had to be dismounted and walked through school zones. Owners of horses exceeding a certain speed, determined by local officials, were to be immediately issued citations. There were other laws as well. Laws dealing with guns, families, businesses practices and employees. When Susie tired of making laws, she hired lawmakers to make more laws. These laws were based on the assumption that they helped keep her citizens more safe, and the environment cleaner.

It was a hot day in May when the Espinoza gang rode into town. Their first stop was the local saloon. There they drank, ate, and partied until they were well beyond their senses. By midafternoon their coin was low and their common solution to this problem was simply to go and take some more. Gathering their guns, they exited the saloon mounted their horses and headed towards the local bank. There were eight members to this nasty little gang, the towns folk had made themselves scarce after seeing the ominous group of men riding silently down Main Street. Their long black trench coats only partially hid the arsenal that each man seemed to be toting. Dust rose from the dry ground as the horses' hooves stirred the earth below. Johnny had hitched his father's horse and wagon to the post outside the general store across the street from the bank. Inside Johnny was paying for the supplies, his six shooter hung securely on his hip. Peggy was across the street depositing her daddy's money at the bank, as she faithfully did every payday.

The gang dismounted and marched single file into the bank, spreading themselves out into a line inside the door. A large man stepped forward drawing his silver revolver from its leather holster and discharged two blazing bullets into the ceiling. Peggy screamed, dropping to the floor, the other bank customer followed suite and fell to the floor. Another shot was fired into the ceiling, the three tellers behind the banks counter all raised their hands as they stared into the Espinoza gang leaders face and gun. The large man who had fired the first shots smiled and walked to the first bank teller behind the counter, it was safe to assume he was running the whole show. He politely said, "I'd like to make a large withdrawal, all the money in the tills will be a good start." The teller, thinking no-one would kill another for money and being very frightened, didn't move. The large and in charge man pointed his glistening revolver at the tellers forehead and fired, his face never changing expressions. Gasps and whimpers filled the bank as the customers and other tellers stared in horror as the dead teller toppled to the floor in a puddle of blood. The large man walked to the next teller and asked in a pleasant voice, "Maybe you'll be more helpful?" She quickly glanced at her dead friend on the floor and started gathering up the banks money. Anytime a customer moved, a shot was fired in their direction by one or more of the seven supporting gang members.

Johnny, who was gathering ranch supplies at the general store, heard the shots coming from the bank dropped his bags of flour and started running towards the bank entrance. Pulling out his six shooter, Johnny spun the cylinder ensuring that all the chambers were loaded. He knew Peggy was in the bank and he would do anything possible to ensure she and the bank's other customers were safe. Johnny loved Peggy and his heart was rapidly beating as he imagined her lying on the floor bleeding out with a gunshot wound.

"Whoa there Mister" Deputy Jaerk said while grabbing Johnny's arm as he exited the general store on his mad dash to the bank. Johnny was swung sideways from his momentum as he was halted by Jaerk's grasp. "May I see your gun permit?" Jaerk asked. Johnny, bewildered, asked "What!? What the hell is a gun permit?!" Jaerk started telling Johnny what a gun permit was. "A gun permit is a piece of paper that states you are permitted to carry a gun."

Inside the bank, a young man's foot started cramping, he straightened his leg to relieve the strain on his muscle. A gang member with long black hair, matching beard that covered his chin, whirled around, setting his sights on the moving leg and shot. The man who had stretched his leg let out a deafening howl.

Johnny interrupted Jaerk's speech, "Did you hear that!?" Johnny hollered, "That was another gunshot from within the bank and a man screaming bloody murder. The bank is being robbed, you should be gathering your men and help protect the people in the bank, not lecturing me about gun laws!?" Jaerk said, "I can only handle one law infraction at a time son." He continued telling Johnny what a gun permit was. "You get these gun permits, which lawfully allow you to carry your gun, at the city hall. It'll take a couple of weeks, it usually does by the time they finish your background check, your immediate families background check, your uncle's background check and your unborn sons or daughters background check. Then you can lawfully carry this gun. Until then, I'll have to confiscate it." Jaerk took Johnny's gun. Johnny wanted nothing more at that moment then to punch Jaerk square in the jaw, but instead shook his arm loose from Jaerk's grasp and took off running across the street towards the bank. Jaerk took off after Johnny, rather annoyed that Johnny hadn't waited for the completed lecture and citation.

Inside the bank, the presumed leader of the Espinoza gang was finishing gathering up the money from the remaining 2 bank tellers. Peggy hadn't moved, the man with the shot leg was squirming and whining next to her, he was holding his hands on his bleeding wound muttering to himself, *"Jeff, why are you the only one who has to deal with this shit? I mean come on it's not my fault I didn't listen and keep still."* The leader yelled, "Ladies and gentlemen, it's been fun doing business with you. But times a tickin and we have some whiskey that needs drinkin!" He laughed at his witty rhyme. He took a drink of whiskey that he had pulled out from under his large trench coat, drew his gun and shot the man with the wounded leg in the head saying, "I hate partyin with whiners. Anyone else a whiner?" No one moved or made a sound.

Johnny heard the gunshot, turned and yelled at Jaerk. "There's shooting in there, you ignorant ass. Quit harassing me and let's go protect those people in the bank!" Jaerk finely caught up to Johnny just below the steps to the bank entrance, Jaerk turned to face Johnny gasping for air and replied with a long drawl, "Son, you just don't ever seem to learn. Cursing at an officer of the law? That carries quite a fine." He whistled as he started writing Johnny another citation to add to his carrying a gun without a permit ticket.

The gang emerged from the bank. Johnny turned white and froze as he saw the hairy grey beard of the leader brushing against Peggy's pretty white cheek, one of his guns was positioned under her chin. Peggy was whiter than normal, but her countenance showed she was alright. The gray bearded man noticed Jaerk talking to Johnny. He said, "Mighty ridiculous hat your wearing there mister." Jaerk, still looking at Johnny, ignored the procession emerging from the bank and continued whistling as he continued writing Johnny's double citation. The outlaw restraining Peggy, irritated that he was not being paid attention to, drew his other gun and shot at Jaerk's feet. Jaerk dropped his papers and turned to face the leader of the Espinoza gang. He thought about drawing his gun, but he counted through his dark glasses eight guns pointing at him. He swallowed and said "Morning to you sir." The outlaw stepped forward removing his gun from Peggy's neck and shot Jaerk's left foot with a villainous grin. He laughed as Jaerk bounced around holding his huge hat on his head and screamed out obscene sentences. When Jaerk calmed and sat whimpering on the street, the ringleader ominously said, "Evening to you too." The leader of the gang, having quickly realized that this law official was no threat to him or his gang, threw Peggy on the ground and calmly walked to his horse, the rest of the gang followed suit. Jaerk didn't move, he was frozen by fear and pain. Johnny's eyes took in the whole scene, watching as the seven men began mounting their horses, and Peggy sitting stunned on the ground.

The last to mount his horse was the gang member that shot the leg of poor Jeff. He looked at Jaerk, smiled and drew his gun. Jaerk froze, thinking his life was about to end. Johnny, without thinking, reached and grabbed Jaerk's gun out of his right holster. He rolled, took a one kneed stance and shot the gang member in his heart before he could take aim at Johnny. The Espinoza gang, having heard a gunshot, took off galloping away on their horses, except the one with a thick black beard. As he fell to the ground he managed to discharge one last bullet from his revolver, before his body slammed into the dirt motionless. That shot missed Jaerk and Johnny but did put a rather nice round hole in Jaerk's brown ten gallon hat.

Peggy sprang from the ground, launching herself at Johnny, he stood to catch her as she embraced him in an almost suffocating hug. Jaerk gathered his composure, picked up his dropped papers and handed them to Johnny. Johnny gave Jaerk an evil glare, he was too stunned to speak. He turned, still holding Peggy tightly with one arm, and began slowly walking Peggy away from the scene. Jaerk yelled, "Not so fast Johnny." Johnny turned and angrily asked "What?!" Jaerk answered, "You drew the weapon of an officer of the law. Can't do that son." He started writing Johnny a third citation. He did not whistle but rather moaned as the pain in his foot continued to throb and bleed. Johnny was thinking, *"I just saved your life you ignorant bastard!"* Jaerk finished filling out the third citation, "All these laws are for your own protection son." He turned and slowly hopped away, making sure he didn't put much weight on his wounded shot foot.

Johnny turned back to Peggy and asked, "You ok?" Peggy kissed Johnny on his cheek and said, "I think I'll live." She smiled and returned the question, "You ok?" Johnny thought a second and answered in a subdued voice, "No, It seems my town is turning upside down. Where else do you get punished for doing good?" Peggy couldn't answer and the two walked huddled together across the street as the townsfolk came running to the recently robbed bank.

9 **The Damn Dam**

Work on the damn dam had been a pain in Jimmy's butt since the project began. Jimmy silently swore once again as he approached his work. *"Damn, Murphy's already here."* "What's up Murphy?" Jimmy asked. Murphy chuckled, "If things can go wrong, they will."

Jimmy was Red's younger brother, and just like Red, he was a stoutly built man with arms and legs like tree trunks, huge. Jimmy had large ears, but not many people noticed since he was every bit a huge man, but his family jokingly called him Mule behind his back. He was raising 3 daughters, of 14, 15, and 16. After Jimmy learned his last born was another daughter, his hair turned grey. Now that they were all teenagers, he had no hair. His eyes were smoldering blue that contrasted drastically with his fair white skin. Jimmy was every bit as polite and kind as his nephew Johnny, but his size and stature intimidated most.

Jimmy was one of many mangers of WBIC, We Build It Construction. He was good at his job, and did not tolerate laziness on his worksite, nor was he lazy himself. He managed with patience, good humor, and by example. Every morning of Jimmy's shift, he would greet each worker by name and often tease them, if the occasion arose. He was a good leader and fun to be around, his coworkers respected and enjoyed working with him far more than any other WBIC Foremen.

No-one knows where Murphy came from, he just seemed to have appeared one day. He was tall and lanky with small features; his dark olive skin proved his Middle Eastern heritage. His eyes were a bright silvery gray, his black eyebrows met in the middle above his pointed nose. Neither Jimmy nor Murphy were very pleasing to look at, in fact, they often got laughed at for their looks. Seeing the two stand side by side was comparable to looking at a huge old oak tree growing beside a spindly aspen.

Because of Murphy's bad luck, WBIC had to continuously promote him. If the company had not paid Murphy in career advancements, Murphy would now own the company through payouts of losses of court lawsuits. When a mishap happened where Murphy was involved, he would simply say to the board, "It wasn't my fault that such and such happened. I can either be promoted or I'll take you to court." The controlling members of WBIC knew the local circuit judges always favored the individual in frivolous lawsuits; WBIC would always give Murphy his career advancement.

The workers at WBIC despised Murphy; every project that they worked on under Murphy's supervision took at least four times longer than the estimate and someone was always undoubtedly going to be hurt. On sunny days or cloudy days it would always rain on the Murphy project site. The materials used on his projects would often arrive damaged, his workers' seemed to find every wood splinter or improperly driven nail to snag themselves on. The traveling laborers that would work during the busy seasons, always seemed to find bed bugs in their hotel rooms, or food in their lunch pails that seemed to make them sick, if they were unfortunate enough to find themselves on Murphy's crew. None of these things seemed too happened at other WBIC worksites or in other crews, just Murphy's.

WBIC despised Murphy as well, they continuously checked to make sure all of his instruments were calibrated after a job where all the buildings he constructed were far out of spec. After an investigation, WBIC learned that the tape measures Murphy used on that job were miss made and far from regulation quality. WBIC was forced to pay enormous sums of money to injured employees from Murphy's construction sites, far more than any other supervisor of their projects. Everyone dreaded the possibility of being assigned to Murphy's team, mostly out of fear of the perpetual bad luck that seemed to hover over and around him. When WBIC won the contract for the water conservation dam, they placed Murphy and Jimmy together to oversee the construction of the gigantic containment wall. Jimmy was still furious over this arrangement and when he had asked the higher powers at WBIC why he had to work with Murphy, Jimmy was simply told, "You're the best, he's the worse. Someone has to babysit him and even out his luck."

One month into the project, it seemed to Jimmy that Murphy had more control of the project then he did. Today scaffolding was being built so construction of an inlet tower could commence. Under Jimmy's command in other scaffolding building projects, this was a simple process. His workers would build a chain and pass the scaffolding material piece by piece, one to the other, erecting the scaffolding like an efficient machine. Today however, the workers looked like a swarm of ants that had been poked with a stick. Workers were scrambling around everywhere carrying parts and pieces to places they belonged. As some climbed the stairs of the built scaffold carrying their loads, Jimmy could sense something bad was about to happen. Just as Jimmy was about to yell "EVERYONE STOP!" Bob's morning coffee was knocked off a rail by the scaffold brace that Joe was carrying. The large thermos of hot coffee fell onto a group of workers that were climbing the scaffolding, each hauling arm loads of material and each of the workers, having been slightly burned, dropped what they were carrying. Gravity sent 12 semi heavy pieces of construction material falling 40 feet onto a local laborer named Steve. A rather large wooden scaffolding plank hit Steve on the thigh, bruising the muscle and snapping the bone. Jimmy watched the whole scene and turned to Murphy saying, "Look what you've done." Murphy nonchalantly responded, "What? I was here all the time." Jimmy took off running to help Steve, thinking, *"Murphy you're the damn supervisor on this watch, it's your fault."*

News of the accident spread through Liberty Town like a brush fire. Upon learning of the accident, Susie was one of the first to arrive at the tragedy's location. She silently cussed as her white shoes turned brown when she stepped out of her horse drawn carriage into a sloppy mud puddle. When she felt the slime on her ankle, her smooth forehead furrowed. Susie quickly looked over the scene and ran through her head what had transpired and thought, *"How great it would be to ensure no one would ever be injured on a job again!"* Then it struck her like lightning, what if she could ensure that safety? What if she could somehow ensure that all workers would be safe on every job sight, by creating and managing agencies that monitored and created safety regulations? And oh the influence she would have over the working class. She smirked inwardly at this poor man's misfortune and thought, *"Could life get any better?"* She stepped around the mud puddle and crawled over the driver's seat to hers. The driver looked at the trail of mud Susie had left, but said nothing as he tried cleaning his seat with his handkerchief as best he could.

Susie sent a messenger boy to announce to the other town council members that there was a special meeting taking place that afternoon. The boy ran to the first house, lightly tapped on the door, waited a brief second, and then took off for the next. After knocking on each of the other council member's doors and receiving no responses, he headed back to town hall where he found Charles, Futureano, and Susie waiting at a fancy table for the council members. The young boy said to Susie, "Can't get no-one to answer my knocks." Susie smiled at the child and dismissed him. Then she said, "I guess where the only ones concerned about this town." Charles stood and called the meeting to order, Futureano read the treasury report and prior business notes. Charles then asked if there were any new orders of business that needed discussing. Susie raised her hand and said, "I would like to create positions to ensure no-one ever gets harmed on a jobsite again." Charles called for a vote and all three found themselves in favor of Susie's idea.

Susie had already determined who she would place in charge of the new safety agency, Marshna, her 2nd best friend. Marshna, seeing how large the demands Susie was making were, asked for help with the safety project. She asked that Oshna, her best friend, be able to help her. Together the two spent weeks contemplating any possible work hazard and made rather large documents addressing each issue. Susie set into motion the necessities to ensure Marshna and Oshna's documents were enforced. After all, safety was Susie's primary concern to her homominion sheep. Susie started wondering, *"Why do I refer to the citizens as mine?"* Then she laughed as she thought, *"they are slowly becoming mine, to do with as I please."*

Murphy had taken a mandatory 52 week vacation after Steve's accident and under Jimmy's watch the Power plant was progressing at a rapid rate, without incident or accidents. Oshna and Marshna arrived at the job site early morning and started observing the construction site. Jimmy came up to the two and said, "Good morning, ladies. How may I help you?" The ladies did not respond but started walking and looking at every minute detail of the construct/mine site. Jimmy asked, "Something I can do for you ladies?" Oshna replied, "We are here to ensure the safety of your workers" and the two continued walking. Going down the steps to a platform, the ladies stopped and wrote Jimmy a citation. It read, "Platform steps .25 inches out of compliance 36.495.368 subparagraph 2B section D. Fine 50.00 dollars." Jimmy stood still, reading the paper in shock, thinking, *"What the heck?"* He coughed as he read the fine amount.

The ladies continued walking. A few paces later they stopped again and wrote another citation reading "Edge of board sticking 1.33 inches into walkway. Tripping hazard. Per 295.467.824 subparagraph 4x section A. Fine 32.00 dollars." They gave a copy to Jimmy. Jimmy said, "Wait a minute, I don't understand." Marshna said, "Since you can't create an accident free work environment, we've taken it upon ourselves to do that for you. It is for you and your employee's safety." Jimmy replied, "We do have a very safe work site." Oshna said sarcastically, "Yes, you proved that last month when Steve lost his leg." The 2 continued walking. They came to a man hammering a nail. He wasn't wearing safety glasses nor was he using pliers to hold the nail freeing his fingers from the possibility of being hit by the hammer. Two more citations were written and given to Jimmy. When they came to a corral for the horses, they again stopped and started writing another citation. "Horse tie ropes are frayed and might fail. Horses can possibly run free. Hazard 732.688.925 subparagraph 8D, Section O. Fine 62.00 dollars."

Jimmy followed Oshna and Marshna around the work site watching the citations in his hand grow. Then Oshna, a very slim athletic girl, took off running up a slope. Jimmy remained behind and watched with interest as Oshna stopped on top of the hill and surveyed the surroundings of the work sight looking as far away from where any work was actually being done. She came down the hill and tripped on a rock. She slid on her bottom to the bottom of the hill and was stopped by Jimmy's tree trunk of a leg. Jimmy smiled and helped her up. She did not smile back; she calmly got her paper and pencil from Marshna and started writing more citations. Jimmy lost his cool when he read the citation for a dead tree a half mile from the current worksite. A branch could blow off in a strong wind and strike a worker. Another was for not cutting the slope of the hill she had just climbed to a safe pitch that could be traversed with ease. Jimmy, about to erupt, yelled at Oshna, "That tree is not on this jobs property and this hill will never be climbed." Oshna calmly wrote Jimmy a personal citation for arguing with a government official that was there for his safety.

By the time Oshna and Marshna were finished inspecting Jimmy's WBIC construction site, Jimmy held over 132 citations for WBIC totaling $18,734, enough to bankrupt WBIC. In the months that followed, WBIC did go bankrupt because of these citations and 1084 workers sat unemployed. Oshna and Marshna were proud of themselves for they had their first accident free construction site. Susie, having a new source of revenue and controlling two more governing department services, propped her feet on her desk and thought, *"job well done."*

Oshna was having fun. Being a skinny girl that could barely see with stringy greasy black hair of waist length, she was ridiculed and teased her whole life. Now she had power given to her by Susie Powers herself. Oshna was confident as she roamed the other businesses and factories in town. She visited Thomas's wagon factory, there she wrote Thomas citation after citation. No guardrails on walkways, walkways not painted, machines moving parts have no guards, the worker's break room have no covered trash can, reflective clothing not worn, stairs not labeled as being stairs. The list was endless. Thomas agreed that some of these ideas would benefit the employees, but the fine that went with these citations nearly cost him his company.

Thomas sat with his employees and they agreed to take a cut in pay to help him pay the citations to Susie and help get the factory up to Oshna's specifications. Thomas had to increase the cost of his wagons and the rise in cost sent customers to other wagon makers in neighboring towns. Although the quality was not as good, the other wagons were affordable. Exports became less and less frequent. Thomas suddenly didn't have as much money to invest in his company and employees. The booming Liberty Town began to feel the effects of one of its major cogs helping turn the city to prosperity begin to break.

Oshna and Marshna both visited the saw mills. The human danger factor was unimaginable, sharp blades turning at fast speeds were everywhere and the belts turning these blades ran beside walkways. Some of the trees were bigger than the machines designed to lift them. By the time Oshna and Marshna had finished, the saw mills had to shut down as well, there was no way they could pay the fines and make hazardous equipment danger free. In time, other business capitalist would try reopening the saw mills, but they all quickly learned there was no way for the saw mills to meet the standards of Oshna and Marshna with the current technology, it was just impossible. Lumber had to be imported at a grossly inflated price.

The imported lumber cost Thomas twice as much which raised the cost of Thomas's wagons even more which made his sales drop even more. He had to lay off a few more of his employees. The town was seeing an influx of unemployed workers. Grocery store sales dropped, revenue to Susie dropped as goods were no longer purchased. The more businesses and factories Oshna and Marshna put out of business, the more sprockets in Liberty Town's prosperity machine cracked and broke.

Susie and her hired money counters sat in her office contemplating the drop in revenue. The cash produced by Oshna and Marshna did not compare with the cash she made from business taxes. To compensate, she raised the taxes of the few safely operating companies even higher. Thomas had to raise the cost of his wagons even more and more of his sales dropped. Thomas was saddened as he had to lay off half of his remaining factory workers because he could no longer afford to pay their wages.

With the closing of the saw mills, Thomas's factory running at a quarter production, exports nearly nonexistent and imports at a record high, the prosperity gears of Liberty Town came to a complete stop. Liberty Town was no longer a booming little town and many of the residents left their beloved town in search of work in other towns.

Charlotte was on her way to school dressed in a new purple and pink dress. She passed the remaining workers of Thomas's factory and froze as she watched them slowly walk past. They looked more like brown ghosts then factory workers. Charlotte recognized the dark eyes and lanky stature of Johnny and she stopped him. Charlotte said, "Johnny, you and your coworkers look ridiculous. Is there some town play I missed hearing about?" Johnny laughed and removed his thick leather hood so he could speak. He replied, "No ma'am, these are our new work uniforms we have to wear. They keep us safe." Charlotte said, "You can't be serious, you can barely move." Johnny said, "I know, but we are safe. The heavy leather shoes make our feet sweat, the thick leather pants and shirt restrict our movement, the protective leather hood is nothing but an annoyance causing extreme heat and fatigue." Charlotte asked, "Why the glasses?" Johnny joked saying, "To restrict our vision. No, seriously, they protect our eyes." Charlotte was stunned at this ridiculousness, "I can't imagine working like that." Johnny replied, "We don't accomplish a quarter as much as we used to, but Thomas can't afford any more citations from Oshna." Charlotte was dumbfounded. She asked, "How is not being able to barely move safer than regular work attire?" Johnny shrugged, "It's not, but if it keeps Oshna from breathing down Thomas's neck, we'll help him however we can." Johnny put his leather hood back over his head and tried catching up with his co-workers. Charlotte contemplated if it were possible to be too safe as she watched Thomas' workers lumbering along in their ridiculous attire.

It took a year for the dam construction to once again commence. In that time Susie had built a nice house overlooking the river where the water conservatory dam was being built. The morning the construction resumed, Susie was drinking tea on her lovely white porch that overlooked the valley below, with the small river that flowed gracefully through it. Her smooth bare legs and feet were propped up on a white table, her white cotton t-shirt felt refreshing as opposed to her normal formfitting constricting work attire. She ran her fingers through her long golden hair and relaxed as she surveyed the surrounding maple trees. She watched deer drink from the river and she even saw a cute little cotton tail rabbit bounding through the clover. Then she saw the tiny specks of the construction workers in the distance starting work on the dam. Susie envisioned her back yard becoming a huge mud hole, she was instantly furious. She stood, bound her hair into a tight bun, dressed in a stark navy blue power suit, and stormed out her front door.

The dam was needed for city water, irrigation, and testing a prototype hydro electric generator. With the towns businesses grinding to a halt from the repercussions of becoming "more safe," Liberty town's growth depended, almost entirely, on the dam. Susie was unconcerned with the need for the dam; her beautiful view was being threatened by the completion of the dam. She called an emergency City Council meeting and again only three members happened to show up. After the meeting, it took Susie a couple of weeks to find the leader she wanted for her new agency she had yet to name. Her choice of leaders was to come from overseas, a biologist and scientist, with doctorates in both fields, his name was Henvirones Mentals. People simply called him Mr. Environmental.

Susie took Mr. Mental to her home and showed him her predicament. Dressed in bleached white shoes, socks, slacks and shirt and shrouded in a stark white lab coat and black rimmed glasses, Mr. Mental shook his head thoughtfully as he listened to Susie. He pulled a pencil from his white coat pocket and made notes. The following day Mr. Mental knelt beside one of the catch ponds beside the river filling tiny glass flasks with the precious water. It took another day for Mr. Mental to discover what he sought, he had found a never before discovered mosquito larva that would later spread malaria all around. To dam the river would destroy this larva; the dam project had to be stopped.

Charles stood at the podium addressing the town people, reading his 3 x 5's written by Susie. Dressed in his brilliant custom blue suit, white shirt and silk maroon tie, he read, "We have a beautiful City, and building this dam will make us undistinguishable from any other town. Beyond that, we will be destroying our beautiful land, making it uninhabitable for our children and our children's children. Building this damn dam will destroy the ecological system of that which has been created. If the Creator had wanted a surplus of water in this region, he would have built his own damn dam. I will not allow the construction of this dam to proceed, we must stop its construction." Charles talked for another hour explaining the importance of protecting the environment. By the time he was finished, all the towns newly appointed leaders agreed, the dam project should be terminated for the protection of the environment for our children to enjoy. Since most of the old towns folks were busy with their farms and work, very few had showed for the meeting. Charles read his speech with a booming powerful voice. By the end of the speech, the new Americans were horrified at the thought of killing the mosquito larva. The dam construction should and would be terminated. The few native townspeople attending the meeting were appalled and outraged.

Mr. Jones, a farmer with ten acres outside of town, stood and tried voicing his concerns to Charles, "You mean we're not going to build the dam because of some stinking mosquito? Why? I don't fully understand." Charles answered saying, "Thank you for your wonderful question." He found the 3x5 he wanted and read, "The mosquito is born from eggs and grows into a larva. They live...." Susie grabbed her brother's arm, cutting him off. She stood, directing her piercing blue eyes at Mr. Jones. She didn't know this annoying man's name, nor did she care to, all she could think about was what a burden this man was to her plan. Susie squared her shoulders and addressed Mr. Jones, "The mosquito, Mr. Burden, is the base of the world's eco system. It feeds the birds; the birds eat the mice and rats." Susie walked to Mr. Jones and stared at him face to face. Mr. Jones began to sweat and Susie continued, "Do you want an infestation of rats Mr. Burden?" Mr. Jones couldn't quite figure what was wrong with Susie's logic; he was too stunned and confused to answer. Susie continued, "Mr. Burden, Rats carry diseases and the plague. Is your measly ten acres of beans worth the whole town dying? If it is, I'm sure all of us would gladly build the dam." The crowd chuckled, Mr. Jones, embarrassed, sat down. No-one else dared to open their mouths. Susie stormed out the door, the crowd parted in front of her, clearing a path. Outside Susie cracked a smile and thought *"Man, men are so easily swayed."*

Inside, the native townsfolk did not agree with Charles or
Susie's views, they agreed with Mr. Jones but were too afraid to
speak their mind. They were not educated and could not respond
to her firm confabulation or his fancy dialog or their insane logic.
They knew to stop growth of their homesteads and town to save a
mosquito larva was just plain ridiculous. Futureano called for a
vote and the new Liberty Town citizens won by majority. The dam
project would cease. Those employees who were unemployed
from the recently closed factories, who had found work at the
dam, were once again out of work .

10 HISTORY

The late 1700s were a gruesome time. The American Revolution would come and go and the foundation of a new nation was beginning to take shape. The legacies of great men and women who lived through this trying time would be passed down for generations. Some of these great stories are still taught today in history classes in schools. Unfortunately, along with the great tails of triumph and conquest, the selfish pride and lust for power seems to have also been passed down through the generations.

Charles, Susie and their brother Billy's grandfather was a legendary pirate. The stories were that he would sail the seas taking only from the wealthiest travelers and killing only when absolutely necessary. Susie, Charles, and Billy's mother and father were wonderful parents and good honest people. Their mother and father met a few years after the revolutionary war, both had lost their own parents to the revolution. It was the death of the grandparents that drew the three together, each parent believing their loss was unjust and the new nation was to blame, and therefore owing them for their loss. This belief was inadvertently passed down to Susie, Charlie and their brother Billy, the father of Futureano.

Jaerk, Futureano's cousin, was indeed the son of Susie and

Charles. In their teen years, Susie and Charles' parents spoke very little of matters pertaining to sex and sexuality which peaked the young teens curiosity, which wasn't helped by the talk of their peers. The consequence of this curiosity was Jaerk. To avoid destroying the family name, Jaerk was taken from Susie and given to Billy to raise. Futureano and Jaerk grew up as rivals under Billy's supervision. Billy was always partial to his biological son, Futureano. Susie always loved her son Jaerk, but she kept their relation hidden from others. The end result was Susie and Billy were slightly estranged but tolerant of each other, Charles remained neutral.

Red and Jimmy's mom was a Quaker, their dad was a Puritan. How the two had ever came to be married was hushed by the family because of its scandalous nature, and left the frowned upon nuptials out of the family tree storytelling. Red and Jimmy's parents were adolescents during the revolutionary war. They were both too young to fully comprehend the significance of the revolution, all they were taught was that they were born during a new beginning. This belief was always spoken to Jimmy and Red by their mom and dad, "You're the beginning of something great" they would say.

Shirley, Sue's mom, was born in the late seventeen seventies. Shirley grew up on a ranch passed down to her parents from her father's parents. Shirley loved the farm and her childhood years that she spent there. She would often find herself daydreaming of passed days spent milking cows and mending fences in her lovely dresses. Shirley dearly loved her daughter Sue. It was at that farm that Sue met Red when Red was hired on as a summer hand. The ranch was passed to Red when he married Sue.

The day of the town dance was fast approaching. Jimmy,

having learned that the dam project was permanently terminated, was not in a happy mood. The dam was the largest project he would have ever supervised and that would have led to many future financial advancements. Moreover, he had heard the stories of how the Americass family had controlled the town meeting, where the vote for the dam project had taken place. Consequently, when Jimmy passed Susie, who was flamboyantly flaunting her John Richmond dress, he purposefully stomped his size 13 shoe into a muddy pot hole, spraying muddy water all over Susie's expensive dress. "Sorry ma'am," Jimmy apologized sarcastically, "Just thought the malaria mosquito larva might need their water spread about, just doing my job helping protect the environment." Susie chided back, "You stupid, slimy, scurvy ridden jack ass. My dress is ruined." Susie started to say more, but Jimmy interrupted, "My job is ruined and this town's growth is ruined." Susie replied, "This town is perfect other than the likes of you." Jimmy retorted, "We were doing just fine until the likes of you sailed in from God only knows where." Susie pompously said, "We sailed in from up North, you all need cultural enlightening." The two continued to quarrel, Johnny rode past on his new mare. The well-built horse stopped, raised her beautiful silky black tail, and proceeded to drop her waste on the street. Deputy Jaerk was only seconds away and proceeded to start writing a citation to Johnny. "What in the name of God did I do this time?" Johnny blazed. "Watch your language son, we now have a 'no waste' law in this town. Your animal lays waste, you pick it up and dispose of it properly." As Jaerk was finishing the citation, his horse did the same as Johnny's had. Jaerk gave Johnny the ticket and started riding away. Johnny yelled at him, "And the waste of your horse?" Jaerk smugly replied, "Just because I enforce the law does not mean I must adhere to the law. I'm here to protect and serve, you should remember that son." Johnny thought, "I'd rather eat dung beetles then be called your son, you're no relation to me, thank God." Susie chuckled as she watched Jaerk ride away. "Good blood runs through that boy." Jimmy was stunned to silence at hearing this, what had just transpired with Johnny outraged him further. He walked over to Johnny, put his arm around him, and the two walked off together, Johnny's newly purchased mare in tow.

Susie turned on her heels and stormed away to retrieve a clean new dress. Johnny and Jimmy started talking, "What has happened to our town uncle Jimmy?" Jimmy pondered and said, "It seems as though the ones up North want to bring their lifestyle to us." Johnny responded, "I don't like their lifestyle. Why should we have to live like they want?" Jimmy thought more, "It seems that the more politically powerful they become, the more we have to follow their thinking." "I don't want to Uncle Jimmy" Johnny said. Jimmy sighed "I know, me either."

The two continued meandering down the dusty street towards the park, where the final preparations for the town dance were being made. Near the center of the park the dance floor was being constructed out of plywood, and next to the dance floor a small stage for the band. Jimmy and Johnny both watched in horror as an eight man team chopped the four giant oak trees in the center of town down to stumps. As the last tree fell to the dirt, the banner representing Liberty Town's spirit floated behind it in tatters. They watched the banner settle into the ground and felt as though the last piece of their town had fallen with it. A tear ran down from Jimmy's eye, Johnny felt hollow inside, Futureano was walking past and Jimmy asked him, "Why'd you cut down those trees?" Futureano happily replied, "We have a special treat for the town dance, needed the extra room." Jimmy and Johnny were shocked and silent as they mournfully walked away from the awful sight; both felt that some part of their body had just been removed. Jimmy silently wondered "*how is protecting mosquitoes healthy for the environment but living trees aren't'?*"

When Susie arrived at her office, she found many of the dam workers were waiting to speak with her. Having voiced their complaints to Susie for no longer having jobs and needing money for food, Susie told them she would see what she could do. She then closed the door in their faces, sat down at her desk, and thought. Susie's heart was sometimes in the right place, she truly wanted to help these townsfolk, but she was always looking at new ideas to increase her power. She talked out loud to herself as she tried bringing these two thoughts together. "I am learning to deceive and control people in authority, how can I control the lay people? They have needs, if I can continuously fulfill the needs, I will control the people." She smiled at herself. "All they need is money. I shall give them money. Where shall the money come from? I shall make money off what people use, like sugar and flour." Susie continued working this out in her head for the remainder of the day. When she was finished, Susie had determined she could raise thousands of dollars just by adding a simple tax to sugar, flour, wheat, corn, tobacco, alcohol, all things bought and sold. Susie shouted, "I SHALL TAX EVERYTHING!" She grinned at herself as she locked up her office and headed home to prepare for the dance next evening.

11 - THE TOWN DANCE

The town was charged with excitement the morning of the annual Liberty Town dance. It wasn't often that the towns' people could leave their work and chores and enjoy the company of their neighbors and friends. But the day of the dance was a day set aside by all for fun, food and dancing. This was the day that young boys found the courage to approach that special someone and ask them to the dance. Young adults anticipated "playing" in the nearby woods with their dance partner. Married couples looked forward to renewing their lost puppy love, and the old timers sat around reminiscing about the "good ol' days". Johnny could hardly contain himself, tonight he was going to propose to Peggy. Yes, the dance gave most the courage to do what they were sometimes afraid to do.

The community organizers were spending the morning adding the finishing touches to the decorations. They scurried about, trying to finish their tasks quickly so they would have time to go home and prepare themselves for the dance, the whole town tried to look their very best. Johnny and Red were finishing placing the last table when Johnny spoke, "Dad, when was it that you first saw moms knee?" Red chuckled, thinking back to that day when he had first seen his wife's knee. "WOO HOO," he had thought. Red cautiously answered, "Johnny, I did not do anything with your mom until it was made right through marriage."

Johnny, with hormones raging, replied, "Dad, I'm going to marry Peggy. Why can't we behave with each other as married couples do?" Red remembered he himself had thought the same and replied with what his father had said, "Son, it comes down to respect and attitude. You must respect her because too much can happen between now and your wedding day, and, because you govern your life by Gods standards. When you do this, your attitude will remain in check."

Johnny, not wanting to express any more of his thoughts to his father, agreed while inwardly thinking "maybe I will get a glance at Peggy's knee tonight, if she agrees." Johnny and Red started walking home and passed Futureano, he absently smiled at the two. Futureano was busily thinking, "This town will never be the same after tonight. The money I've spent for the special guests will be well worth it."

Jaerk spent his day preparing for the dance by scouting the surrounding area, looking for the best place to view the festivities. He knew there would be heavy drinking tonight and many would get inebriated past the newly allotted tolerance level. He decided to get a jump on things and would later pre-write a booklet of tickets; writing in everything from the date and time to the location, the town square. The only thing not complete on the citation would be the name. Jaerk figured he could issue more than three times the tickets this way. He limped away on his bum foot to investigate the rest of the square.

Peggy spent her morning making a cherry pie and afternoon ironing and trimming her powder blue dancing dress with beautiful ivory lace. Although it was plenty hot outside, she still had a small fire burning to heat her iron. She smiled as she thought of holding hands and dancing close to Johnny, these thoughts made butterflies flutter in her stomach. "What would a kiss do?" She stated to no one in particular. "Probably make my heart explode." She laughed, "OH NO, tonight I'm going to die!" She threw her arms up in the air, then, placed them over her heart as she slumped to the floor in a mock death scene. "Well," she said vindictively aloud, "If Johnny is going to kill me with a kiss; I'm going to kill him with a glimpse of my knee." She hoisted her skirt and admired her smooth thigh and knee. She finished her ironing and spent the rest of the day twirling and dancing wherever she went as she beautified herself for the dance.

After the initial stage, dance floor, and tables had been placed and the town organizers had gone home to ready themselves for the dance, 8 large freight wagons came into town and pulled into the square. Futureano directed the wagons and drivers to the appropriate location. They were instructed to park their wagons in a semi-circle surrounding the back of the stage. They then erected a curtain to keep any curious eyes from peering inside. What they were constructing was Futureano's secret surprise - and a surprise is what the workers set out to build.

The Neon Twins had but one thought for tonight: "To seduce the Americass boys." They knew a boy could be easily distracted and controlled by the mere sight of their "barely there" dresses that left very little to the imagination. The two had successfully worked their seduction magic on many boys before, tonight they challenged each other to see which of them could entice her date to take them into the woods first. With this in mind, they dressed accordingly. Neon One would wear her snug blindingly bright pink dress that had a slit in the side clear up to her left hip, underneath the impressive dress was a matching set of black imported French lingerie made only of sheer lace. Neon Two would wear a fluorescent green knee length dress with a practically see through middle and back. Under this, Neon Two wore a stunning set of deep purple net imported lingerie trimmed with silk ribbon. They knew the mismatched colors and immodest dresses would draw most men's eyes to places they didn't belong. Neon One said to her brunette sister as she wiggled into her tight dress, "Bobby probably won't even last to the woods." Neon Two giggled, "You're too naughty for anyone's good." It was all part of their game: get their date's attention focused on where they shouldn't be looking. They then laced up their mismatching 6 inch green and orange thigh high lace inlayed boots with the intent of showing their dates no mercy. They spent another hour on their final step, carefully applying lip stick, eye shadow and other cosmetic tricks in an effort to seductively enhance their feminine features. By the time they were done, both knew no man was safe from their malicious game of seduction. The two left hand in hand with the knowledge they were displaying a whorish sexuality.

Futureano's boys left for the dance dressed in their normal fashion, loose fitting jeans and worn t-shirts with sporadic designs all over them. Tonight would be special for them because each carried a white pill that their drug suppliers up North had called ecstasy. Neither knew the mind altering effects of the drug, nor did they care about any harmful side-effects. Their greatest desire was to find and experience a new and stronger euphoria.

Red and his family all walked to the dance together. Red, Jimmy, and Johnny proudly carrying his lady's pie in one hand; with their free hand they tenderly led their partners to the town square. They all were happy and looking their best, talking excitedly about the upcoming evening.

As the group walked through town, they passed Susie Powers' town house, her door opened and down the stairs she came. Red's family immediately stopped and watched Susie descend the stairs, none had ever seen anything so beautiful. She wore an evening gown of shimmering midnight black, it clung tightly to her slender frame to her knees where it loosened into an elegant flowing flare. Around her neck was a sparkling diamond necklace that glistened in the evening light, as did the diamonds on her striking black high heels. Her usually tightly restrained hair was loosely pinned up; golden curls flowed around her face and back of her neck. Susie's six inch stiletto heels and impeccable posture made her seem much taller than any of the town's people. As she approached her carriage, which was parked in front of her home, she acknowledged Red's family with a curt nod, then turned and entered her carriage. Jimmy stared at Susie's back. To him it looked like she wore no dress at all until the fabric started just below the small of her back and flowed to the ground. Jimmy turned red and his wife Tammy turned white as she watched her husband admiring Susie's flashy attire.

Red and his family stood unmoving as Susie was carried away in her elaborate carriage. Each somehow felt a little less significant than they had just a few short seconds ago. The ladies were thinking how ugly and plain their Victorian dresses were in comparison to Susie's impressive northern dress. Their dresses seemed to pale in comparison, the only slightly fitted bodices and large fluffy skirts just seemed so unextraordinary. Susie's evening gown looked like something a princess would wear, the women lost a bit of their confidence as they compared themselves to Susie and all her glamor. She was taller and far more slender then any of them. Her skin was flawless, her dress was so spectacular that the color black actually glowed, and that diamond necklace, it looked like it was a gift from God the Father Himself. They had instantly forgotten that the most important thing about a person was what they carried inside and the strength of their character. After a few moments, the group continued on their way, Talk was sparse - the ladies were lost in thought about what they had seen, while the men were feeling inadequate, knowing that they could never afford a dress or necklace like that for their loved one.

When Red and his family arrived at town square, the commotion and excitement around the stage was growing deafening. The women, in their finest long dresses, were gathered around the freshly baked goods, happily exchanging recipes and complements. The cowboy gents were readily handing their six shooters to a collection booth attendant, since guns were not permitted at this function. Jaerk was on top of the courthouse surveying the scene. The old men and their wives were seated near the stage, smiling at the bustle of activity around them. Domestica was gazing at Red, seductively licking her bright red lips, she had dressed thinking only of Red. Her heavy bosom was clearly exposed to one and all, if one looked closed enough. Red and his relatives quickly found two tables and settled in for the festivities, each having swiftly forgotten the loss of self-respect at the mere sight of Susie Powers.

When the town band was trying to set up their instruments, Futureano kept turning them aside, saying, "Your presence is unnecessary. I've arranged the entertainment for tonight." Charlotte appeared in a satin emerald green dress, extending from her shoulders to the floor. She was a truly lovely sight, her stunning red hair cascading down her back in perfect curls. Charlotte's eyes were glowing her happy shade of green. She sat beside Thomas and Red's bunch. Futureano saw Charlotte and immediately lost himself as he dreamt of dancing with her. He knew Charlotte's wavy red hair would feel delightful against his balding head.

The air was alive with the sound of excited chatter from the town's people as more joined in this yearly reunion in Liberty Town's square. From behind the curtained stage a base driven rhythm began pulsing from the speakers. Futureano appeared from behind the bold red stage curtain, dressed more extravagant than usual, he flipped his loose hairs back over his bald head and started to speak. He spoke through a fancy, new-fangled gadget called a microphone; it projected his voice through a series of speakers making it loud enough that even the neighboring towns could possibly hear. "Ladies and gentlemen, welcome to the festivities! Please welcome our special guests, the White-Eyed Chickpeas." With that said, smoke rose from the stage as the impressively large curtain parted. The bass seemed to double in volume, deafening the town's ears, and Futureano's imported entertainment was only slightly visible through the cloud of manufactured smoke. Eight singers stood in the haze, they began rhythmically chanting, their voices harmoniously echoing through the enormous speakers, "This is the night" (base boom) "This town comes alive" (base boom, base boom) "you're going to see, but you won't believe" (base boom base boom) "You're going to hear, but it'll be unclear" (base boom base boom) "And what you feel, is not really real" (base boom, base boom). Then in harmony the eight sang backup to a lead female vocalist singing and swaying her hips with her arms raised above her head, "What I make your body do. The way I make it swaa-ay. It's telling your mind simply this, that everything's Okaaaaay." As she sang, her whole body moved suggestively with the rhythm of the music, her tight leather clothes left little to the imagination, and put even more un-needed focus on her overflowing corset. "Go ahead and grab yourself, it's what you want to do. Don't care what other people think, to your own body be true." She moaned on as her provocative dance continued.

The deep boom, boom of the bass was deafening, the town's folk covered their ears in an attempt to mute the painful sensation, with little success. The vibrations from the speakers pulsated through their bodies, making them move involuntarily with the music. The native Liberty Town citizens started backing away from the speakers, but the Neon Twins immediately ran to center stage and started gyrating their bodies in time with the music. They swayed and bent and wiggled into each other. The men's jaws dropped as they watched this dangerously provocative display, their eyes were drawn to every place they knew better than to look. Most of the native town women turned away in disgust, the others were too shocked to move. The women saw where their men's eyes were focused and slapped their dates in disgust.

Rudy and bobbing Bob felt like they were in heaven. The pills they had taken 20 minutes earlier were starting to work their magic. They staggered through the crowd in a joyous daze, the vibration of the music working harmoniously with the chemicals of the drug. The Neon Twins, spotting Bobby and Rudy, jumped off stage and ran giggling to the brothers. The girls pressed their bodies against the boys and started dancing with them. The boy's bodies, being more chemically influenced then hormonally influenced, danced with the Neon Twins but did not respond to their sexual advances. This rejection from the boys started an inward challenge to the girls, making them even more determined to succeed in their seduction scheme. They both grabbed the boys and started dancing as though they were having sex at that very moment.

Johnny was expecting to dance with Peggy tonight. He wanted to see her hair flowing in the breeze as they twirled around the dance floor. He wanted to calmly sit with her and watch the other couples dance. He wanted to make her feel special and loved. When the timing was right, he was going to kneel on the dance floor and ask her to be his wife. What he heard had his heart beating, but not because of his love for Peggy. The loud "BOOM BOOM" of the bass made everything in one's body beat. There was a slim chance, if any chance at all, his plans for tonight could take place with this so called "music." He glanced around and his eyes automatically stopped on the Neon Twins grinding their bodies into the Americass boys. A quick thought flashed through his mind. "Maybe I should act like them, I sure would like Peggy dancing with me that way." Then he looked at Peggy, her beautifully innocent face, her loving temperament, and her pure heart. Johnny cussed at himself for having thoughts like he just had about Peggy.

Peggy was watching the Neon Twins kiss each other in public view. She wondered what that would be like, "kissing another girl." She gagged and moved her eyes to Rudy and Bobby. Bobby was bouncing his circular head up and down. He turned and acted as though he had not a single care in the world. She wondered what that would be like, "not caring about anything." The Neon Twin in the bright pink dress grabbed bobbing Bobby's butt. Peggy thought about grabbing Johnny's butt and blushed. She quickly turned her eyes to the stage and watched the dancing of the performers. She had never before seen such actions and wondered what many of them meant. She was trying to focus on the music when Johnny grabbed her hand and started walking her away. Peggy was a little hesitant, wanting to watch the behavior of the Americasses and her body being drawn to this strangely alluring music.

Red was trying to figure out how the voices were so damn loud, they hurt his ears. He looked at his lovely wife Sue covering her ears, with a look of shock on her face. He knew Sue was hating this moment in time. Red glanced around and noted the people from up north were having a glorious time while the rest looked as though they stepped into hell. Red grabbed Sue's hand and left with Johnny and Peggy.

Charlotte found herself caught up in the music; something about its beat struck her to the core. She was standing on a table swinging around. Her red hair was swaying with the rhythm of the music; her green dress was following around her like a wave. It was a marvelous sight. When Charlotte started swaying her hips, Jimmy stood and grabbed her with one arm. He picked her up and placed her on his giant shoulder, carrying her away from the music like a giant would carry a rag doll. Charlotte's body continued to move to the music and she giggled and laughed as she was carried away.

The Neon Twins were still kissing Rudy, Bobby and each other. Rudy stood taller than most, and was slightly bent over kissing the twins back, his butt wiggling in the wind. This scene disgusted the women and the men who had their roots embedded in Liberty Town. Because of the noise and the sexual behavior, they all began leaving in a hasty fashion. Jaerk, seeing that he was not going to be able to place names in his book of written tickets, got depressed and made his way to the pies. Peggy went to gather her pie to take back home as her and Jonny made their way out of the town square. When she came to the pie table, she sighed as she saw it had already been eaten. Johnny, seeing the disappointment in Peggy's eyes, and seeing that Jaerk had cherry pie covering all sides of his mouth, walked to Jaerk and yelled, "YOU SELFISH SON OF A BITCH!" Jaerk, unable to hear Johnny over the volume of the band, shrugged his shoulders, put his left hand over his left ear, and indicated to Johnny, "I can't hear a word you are saying son." He did however think "anyone in their right mind would not willingly approach an officer of the law." Jaerk wrote Johnny's name on a prewritten citation, gave it to Johnny, and then stuffed a whole slice of blueberry pie into his mouth. Johnny threw the ticket on the ground and left with Peggy, both depressed that her knee was not the center of their attention.

Futureano and Domestica danced and danced. A few times Domestica's boob would topple out and she would unconsciously cover herself back up. Futureano couldn't have cared less about his hair; it was sweaty and sticking to everything but his bald head.

The only remaining native townsfolk were the ones who had lost the majority of their hearing and most of their sight. The vibrations of the music made their bodies move. The aged elders were all sitting and bouncing their creaky knee joints up and down with the beat of the music. Futureano, seeing that most of the town elders were enjoying themselves, considered the dance a success.

The band, unable to see the audience because of lighting, continued playing, being ignorant that half their audience had left. Rudy and Bobby ended up sitting a few feet from the speakers gazing up into the stars. In their minds, it was a perfect night. Johnny and Red, home at the ranch, were thinking the exact opposite.

Susie Powers stood down the street, her eyes not missing a single response or behavior. At last she sighed and thought, "I shall avoid entering into entertainment."

The Neon Twins, having been denied sexual pleasure from the Americass boys, left together and sat behind the courthouse pleasuring each other. Gothard, the pale faced boy, stood in the shadow of a nearby tree watching the evening unfold in front of him. He scowled at the smiles and laughter of the people, he himself found little reason for such things. He walked to where the guns had been checked by the town's folk and grabbed the last remaining six-shooter from the unattended booth. He glanced around and thought this action was unnoticed. He thought, *"People should not be happy."* Charles sat in his office listening to the heavy beat of the drums. He was angry at his sister Susie for not allowing him to attend the dance. She had said to him, "You're too important to chance doing something stupid tonight. Best you stay out of sight." He thought that maybe he did not need his sister's help to keep advancing his growing position in the public's eye. Oshna and Marshna sat at a table taking notes of possible injuries public entertainment could cause. Mr. Mental sat staring at Oshna wondering if she would dance with him, but decided it was safer not to ask. The festivities came to a close and the remaining participants made their way back to their homes for the night.

The following Monday Charlotte started class by asking how each enjoyed the dance. Rudy and Bobby asked, "What dance?" The Neon Twins, having gained everlasting popularity with the boys, simultaneously said, "We had a damn good time!!" Peggy said, "I had better times cleaning up the horses manure." From then on the class was divided into those who enjoyed the dance and those who had not. Gothard sat stroking the six shooter he had stolen at the dance, which was well hidden in his long black cloak.

At the café, sitting around various tables eating breakfast, the same conversations were taking place. The town was divided by those who enjoyed the dance and those who were appalled by it.

Futureano pulled funds from the town depository and paid off the White-eyed Chickpeas. They, in response, asked to come perform again. Futureano, speaking for the whole town, said, "That would be most enjoyable." Futureano knew some of the town natives were unhappy about the provocative and vulgar show, and if those unhappy few knew he was paying the band via the town's holdings, they would probably have him shot. He decided to keep private how the entertainment was being paid.

Susie sat in her office, drumming her manicured nails on her desk. She was thinking about the small minded towns' people, "If the music at the festival was too much for them, they will all have heart attaches when they see all that I have planned for this town," She muttered to herself. She was going to make this town the most powerful town in the world. With the prosperity gears at a halt, she contemplated other alternative ways to keep her masterminded plan alive.

12 - **More Money**

The desire to fulfill the needs of the less fortunate would not leave Susie's mind. Susie would not admit to herself that she was the cause of the lost work; instead she blamed the leaders of the divisions she had created. She thought about calling them into her office but decided she really had nothing to say to them, they were following her business model but a little too aggressively. *"How could I yell at them for that?"* She wondered. Susie knew that she needed to find a way to fix the damage she had done to the town's economy. All she needed was money, then she could freely give it to any and all individuals she deemed worthy. She sat thinking for hours as to why she couldn't simply make her own money. The pros were immense; she could give the pauper people food, clothing, and shelter, anything she thought they needed. She could help businesses reopen, build bigger structures for her and the new agencies she was creating. She could build an army to protect her and her growing infrastructure of people and agencies. She could build a navy to protect their coast. She could pay her employees handsomely and they would spend that money on things the pauper people created. She could make Liberty Town the prettiest town in the world. Susie could not think of any cons to making her own money. She yelled for Charles, "Get me a money making machine!!" Charles was at a loss, *"A money making machine?"* he thought *"What the heck is that?"* Susie saw the lost look on Charle's face and yelled, "A money machine, Idiot!! You know a PRINTING PRESS TO PRINT OUT MONEY!!!" Charles quickly backed out of Susie's office. He hated dealing with his sister when she was in these moods, wanting something that no-one's ever heard of. He hurried off to find a printing press that printed money, knowing it was an impossible task.

As Susie contemplated ways to spend the money her money making machine would make, Johnny was out hunting rabbits on Peggy's fathers land. Johnny was proud of his Colt Dragoon black powder revolver, and of the fact that he was a fairly good shot. Johnny could not believe his luck when he saw two rabbits and a rafter of turkeys. Johnny contemplated the situation, and figured he could probably hit four of the animals; he took aim and fired four shots. He hit two rabbits and a turkey, not the four he was hoping for but still an admirable feat. Johnny imagined patting himself on the back, complimenting his hunting skill. As he headed home, he decided to walk through town so he could proudly parade his kills for all to see. Just when he was imagining their shock and awe at such perfect hunting specimens, Deputy Jaerk walked up demanding to see Johnny's licenses. "Let me see your small game license." Johnny was completely dumbfounded at Jaerk's request. "What in tar nation is a small game license?" Johnny questioned. Jaerk, once again annoyed at Johnny's ignorance, asked "Were you born in a barn?" To which Johnny said, "Yes." Jaerk, unmoved by Johnny's reply, started telling Johnny what a game license was, "Well son, a game license allows you to shoot wild game. It sets limits on the amount of game you can shoot, and you can only get one after you've completed your hunter's safety course." Jaerk asked Johnny, "You do have your hunter's safety certificate don't you?" Johnny, who had been hunting since he was four, again had no idea what Jaerk was talking about. When Jaerk saw Johnny's confusion, he whistled and started writing another citation. When he was finished he handed Johnny three tickets saying, "These here are citations for shooting small game without a license or permit and for hunting without a certificate of hunter's safety. Pay your money within thirty days of today at the town hall." Jaerk then took Johnny's kills and his gun walking away saying to Johnny, "Nice shooting." Johnny looked at the fine total and thought he could easily buy a cow for what he was being fined. Having Jaerk take his new gun almost sent Johnny into a rage, he had to talk to lawyer Abe sometime soon.

The following morning the town was a virtual swamp due to the downpour the previous night. Charles and Susie were walking to town hall when a coach happened to rush by. Naturally, Charles and Susie were both splattered with the mud that was flung by the quickly spinning wheel. Susie looked at Charles and said, "We need brick roads." Charles, wiping the slimy mud from his fancy suit with his handkerchief, readily agreed. "You know, Charles," said Susie "This town has quite a few needs. I really think we ought to call a meeting with the rest of the town leadership." Susie whistled and her messenger boy appeared at her side like an obedient little puppy. She said to him, "See if you can't round up the other council members." The boy smiled and took off running down the muddy street, anxious to knock and run on the preselected doors.

The selected council members gathered in the meeting room, Charles, Susie and Futureano were holding this conference to discuss the needs of the town. Susie sighed, as she often did, and said, "I sure wish other members of the council would take an interest in our town." After the morning mud escapade, they all agreed the town needed a storm drainage system and brick or cobblestone roads. The only problem was securing the funds for such an expensive endeavor. The people were already being heavily taxed and Jaerk was issuing citations faster than new ticket booklets could be printed. So many factories and businesses had gone bankrupt with the citations from Oshna and Marshna that the supply of revenue from the town operations was quickly ending. Susie asked Charles "How is your hunt for a money making machine progressing?" Charles cautiously answered, "The only resemblance of one I'm able to find is the town's printing press." Futureano had been promoted to town community organizer after the dance and seeing an opportunity to slam his uncle, tauntingly asked, "So what are you waiting for? Go get it!" Charles looked at the younger bald man with his belly sticking out like he was expecting to give birth at any moment, comparing it to his own toned stomach and smiled at the pitiful comparison. It further irritated him that his nephew was trying to assume leadership over him. *"How could Futureano even act as though he was in charge of me?"* Charles wondered. Then he looked at Futureano and snarled, "You never ever tell me what to do again or you will find yourself serving food to the pauper people at the bread line. You might be a big shot in the eyes of the town, but to me you're nothing. Understand?" Susie supported her brother saying, "Just because you hold a fancy title doesn't mean you're capable of handling my problem." Futureano quieted. Charles smiled at his sister in silent appreciation of his triumph. He was now even more determined to fulfill his sister's request.

Charles voiced his concerns about the owner of the newspaper being quite upset about losing his printing press. Susie simply said, "If he gives you any grief, tell them that the town is taking ownership for the better good of the community. If they still complain, just tell them that times are tough for everyone and we all must do our part to ensure your continued freedom." With that, the meeting adjourned, the three shook hands and congratulated one another for solving the financial crisis.

Charles had never been personally involved in Susie's dirty work. He hated confrontation and knew taking the town's printing press would surely cause an argument. Rather than face all the difficulties of diplomacy, Charles grabbed 10 large burly men to help him and headed to the town newspaper. He sat outside as the 10 impressively large men simply walked in, grabbed the press and loaded it onto his wagon. The owner of the newspaper came running out raging mad. Charles met him, shook his hand and said, "Thank you for your support. You're doing your town and country a fine service. I'm glad you'll continue giving me your support in the upcoming elections." The owner of the press was flabbergasted. The print masters' stunned silence seemed like agreement and support to Charles and he left smiling broadly as he rode away with the printing press sitting in his wagon. The owner of the press sat on the front steps of his business and wept, unsure what he could, or be allowed, to do.

Gussio Contriour was a French builder with impressive innovative intellect. There was nothing Gussio could not build with great speed; consequently his speedy constructing skills earned him the nickname of Gusto Contructo.

Gusto could crush his own lime for mortar, cut and mill his own timber for fine furniture, and mold metal into any shape. Gusto was good at everything he did and he made a lot of money teaching factory owners up North how to be efficient in manufacturing and producing an array of goods in one factory instead of several. However, he soon tired of the suffocating smog, high crime, and noise of the larger cities, and wanted a more peaceful lifestyle, so he and his wife moved south, settling near Liberty Town.

People would talk about Gusto and his wife as though they were one. The couple were complete opposites, but their differences seemed to make the love they shared even stronger. Gusto was a few inches taller than his lovely wife Regina, and quite round and bulky in comparison to her small thin frame. Regina's thick glossy black hair and olive complexion were quite a contrast to Gusto's balding blond hair and very much white skin. Regina mainly spoke Spanish but spoke reasonably understandable English, and Gusto, her polar opposite, knew very little Spanish and desperately tried to teach her more English to help clear up some of their very confusing conversations. The devoted loving bond the two shared was so very inspiring to those around them that many tried imitating their relationship.

Regina had many ideas of her own, which she was always more than happy to share with Gusto while he was hard at work. Gusto would be focused on a project and his ever loving wife would always find ways to improve on her beloved husband's plan of action. She would spend hours informing him of all improvements he could make while Gusto tried to work. When she would finally leave her husband to his task, he would take what she had said and do the exact opposite, and the end result was immediately perfect construction, at least to his momentarily triumphant mind.

Gusto was loading the last of his three wagons with rough wood and other construction materials when Charles and Susie happened by. Charles, who did not know the difference between a hammer and a saw and thought a nail was just something on a finger, asked Susie, "You think he knows what he is doing?" Susie humphed and replied, "I doubt it." As she spoke, a precious thought struck home, and she started to see dollar signs. Susie spoke aloud. "We should ensure everyone who builds, builds properly." Charles asked, "What do you mean?" Susie explained, "What if you were to build a house?" Charles laughed, "Right, like I could do that." Susie said, "Imagine, you build a house and someone buys that house. What would happen?" Charles responded. "In a short time it would fall down and possibly hurt someone." "Exactly!" Susie exclaimed, "We need to ensure everyone's safety." The two hurriedly walked back to their town hall offices with this new found idea, she could not contain her excitement.

Gusto had constructed his dream homes' foundation on top of solid rock with granite. He already had placed the rough wood frame for his house and was in the process of laying pipe for water that flowed from a river above the house's elevation a mile away into his catch basin. Gusto was also constructing a leach field for a septic system. Jaerk rode up to Gusto's new house and watched him work for ten minutes trying to figure out what in tarnation Gusto was doing. Gusto, getting annoyed at someone, other than his wife, inspecting his work, finally asked, "What can I do you for Jaerk?" Jaerk asked, "What's ya building?" Gusto, not wanting to waste time explaining himself, simply said, "A septic system." Jaerk, never hearing of such a thing, whistled and started writing Gusto a citation. Gusto chuckled and asked, "What's that ya writing Jaerk?" Jaerk said, "This here's a citation for not having a building permit for a, what did you call it your building?" Gusto harshly said, "A septic system." Jaerk finished explaining his citation. "A septic system. You can get your permit at town hall. Please pay your fine within 30 days." Before Gusto could speak,

Jaerk threw the paper at him and galloped unsteadily away on his horse. Gusto picked up the paper and read in bold print, **"Failure to comply with Building Department of Revenue,** no septic system building permit." Gusto saddled his horse and went to town hall where he was directed to the basement in his search for the building department. There he stood in line for an hour before he could speak to an old skinny man with long stringy grey hair and wire rim glasses. He kindly informed Gusto that all buildings were now required to be built to a specific code. When Gusto asked to see the building code for septic systems, the old man retired in the back room for 30 minutes. He returned and informed Gusto there was no code but doing work without a building permit still carried a fine. Gusto reluctantly paid the fine and rode home. He gave the receipt to his homestead accountant, Regina. She looked at the yellow building permit and its cost. She looked at her husband and said, "Are you funning me, you gave them money for this? Just wait till I wrap my hands on their neck..." Then she took off saying 8 letter words in Spanish that Gusto did not understand but presumed they weren't very nice no matter what language they were said in.

The following week Charles sent Jaerk to Gusto's building site. Gusto was just finishing framing one of the walls when Jaerk approached and told Gusto he needed another building permit. Gusto growled, "I have a building permit!" Jaerk answered, "Doesn't anyone know anything around here? You need a permit to frame your walls, pick one up at town hall." A frustrated Gusto asked, "Why should I?" Jaerk smiled and said, "If you don't, you continue to be fined. If the sum of the fines becomes large enough, we empty your bank account and confiscate your house. It's for the good of the community and for safety of the people. It's in your best interest to simply comply with the law." Jaerk left whistling.

Gusto went to the town hall, yet again, to purchase a building permit for framing. As he left, he noticed that the piece of paper he was holding cost as much as all the lumber he had recently purchased. *"This is crazy!"* he thought in horror, *"Almost as crazy as some of my lovely wife's ideas."* However, he knew he could not ignore buying a building permit the way he ignored taking his wife's good-intentioned advice.

The next week Gusto was setting a door when Jaerk, once again, appeared on his property. Jaerk handed Gusto yet another citation for not having a building permit. Gusto, flabbergasted, showed Jaerk the building permit he had recently purchased. Jaerk said, "That was for basic framing, you're setting a door. Please pay the fine and purchase your permit at town hall."

The following day, as Gusto was placing a window in the front of his new house, Jaerk again approached. "What now!?" Gusto asked in anxious annoyance. "Just want to see your building permit," Jaerk said nonchalantly. Gusto produced the permits and Jaerk, of course, proceeded to write a citation. Gusto cussed. Jaerk said, "You're setting a window, you need a permit. Might want to purchase all your permits in advance and avoid these fines."

Gusto went to town hall with his fourth fine. He then proceeded to purchase permits allowing him to build his home to completion. As he had left, he tallied all his permits and fines and was appalled; the cost of the fines and pointless permits equaled the cost of his new home. A few months later Gusto had finally completed his house, and decided it would be nice to plant a few trees since it was still spring. After planting his first ponderosa pine, he turned, startled by Jaerk's whistling. Gusto, wanting to punch Jaerk's smug face, snapped, "What!?" Jaerk continued whistling as he counted trees and said, "I thought you would have learned gramps, you need a building permit for any improvement on your land. Please pay your fines down at town hall." Gusto suddenly found himself wishing he had moved somewhere where government didn't exist.

Susie sat in her plush town hall office calculating the increased permit revenue and deducted the lost revenue from non-issued citations. She concluded it had been well worth creating a building permit division because now the sheep were willingly paying to ensure their homes were safe.

In a couple weeks' time, Susie had raised enough money to start her storm drainage and brick road project. Construction was underway when Gusto and his beloved were walking through town. As usual, Gusto would stop and watch the new construction. Gusto's wife immediately took notice of poor workmanship, especially compared to that of her husband, and shared her observations with Gusto. Gusto, still furious over the loss of so much money for nothing more than mere pieces of paper, walked over to the man who was just standing at the construction site. "You the supervisor?" Gusto asked a large man holding a copy of the plans in his hand. "No, just taking a break. The supers' over there drinking coffee." Gusto casually wandered over to the supervisor and asked, "You the supervisor?" to which the man cautiously answered "Yes." "My name is Gussio Contriour, people call me Gusto Constructo," Gusto said as he held out his right hand in introduction. "Pete Noitall" Pete replied as they shook hands.

Gusto then explained to Pete how he had seen roads fail after just one rain when built in the same fashion as Pete was implementing. "Without a base, the water seeps through the brick and the road turns to paved mud," explained Gusto. Mr. Noitall simply replied, "You don't need to teach me, I was hired for my expertise as a cer-tee-fied engineer, graduated 23rd in my class. I know how to build a road." Gusto, frustrated at knowing the work would not last, and remembering ol' Pete had to purchase a permit for his brick laying, then asked, "Can I see your building permit for this job?" Pete simply replied, "We're Government financed, we don't need any stinkin permit!"

Thomas sat watching his workers. They could barely move, sweat pouring off of them. They were a loyal bunch, but they were miserable. Thomas gave them breaks every 30 minutes to hydrate. He watched a wagon come off the assembly line. The fine craftsmanship was no longer apparent due to the worker's clunky protective attire. It was impossible to do fine work with your hands covered in thick rubbery leather. The wagon had taken ten times longer to build and Thomas knew he could no longer keep his factory open without losing everything.

He called his loyal employees together and discussed their options. They all agreed that the fine wagon factory had to close. Most were relieved that they no longer would be sweating all day, but all had concerns about finances. Thomas hugged them all as they left out the huge factory doors. Then he closed and locked the factory that had so greatly contributed to Liberty Town's booming birth.

Susie sat across the street and watched Thomas close his factory doors. She was unmoved. In a few short days her money making machine would make everything better. She smiled as she thought about people becoming more dependent on her.

13 - **The Wild One**

Charlotte sat in her classroom teaching history. She was appalled that she was now being asked to teach that the revolutionary war really didn't take place, heck; some of the fighters in that war had barely been laid to rest. She was even more appalled that she could no longer reference God or any of His teachings. Her eyes were a very dark angry green, she was furious. Finally she threw down her book and said "We're going on a field trip." The class cheered as they all thought, *"Anything was better than sitting in class."*

The class walked through town, the little youngsters holding hands one with another and skipping on the cracks between the smooth new brick road. The young teenagers were happily chattering with each other and making remarks about the old men playing checkers on the plank sidewalk and snickering to themselves. The Neon twins were holding hands and chattering away at Rudy and Bobby. Bobby, who was infatuated with the twins, was attentively taking in their every word. The twins, still slightly hurt over being rejected at the dance, had vowed to never give Bobby another chance at their wares. After all they had said one to another, "He isn't handsome or cute or funny, and he basically has no character." However, Rudy was another story; both twins wanted a night alone with him.

Rudy, Bobby and the Neon Twins, all but ignored all of their classmates, they were never polite and rarely smiled at anyone but each other. Gothard walked a few yards behind the four, secretly wishing he would be acknowledged by them. Ironically, in the past when he was acknowledge by other students, Gothard would stare straight ahead completely ignoring the politeness being offered to him. Gothard walked with his hand cradling the six shooter he had stolen, thinking, *"Today someone dies."*

William, Thomas's son, was an average young man with average looks. He had brown hair and observant hazel eyes and was not much of a talker. He spent most of his time watching other people and became very skilled at recognizing character traits and subtle actions of others. Today he watched Gothard and recognized the handling of a gun under Gothard's long black trench coat. He was not the leader of any sect in the school, nor was he a follower, but today he decided action was necessary. William slowly made his way up the line of children to Charlotte. He whispered in Charlotte's ear, "I think Gothard is going to do something bad."

Charlotte, astounded at these words, asked William to explain. William simply said, "I'm fairly sure Gothard is handling a gun under his coat." Charlotte answered, "William, kids don't shoot other kids." Charlotte looked anyway and continued walking.

A thousand thoughts raced through Gothard's mind as he followed his classmates down the street. He hated being a loner but despised the idea of having or wanting friends. He knew he was smarter than others but still seemed to struggle immensely to achieve even minimum passing grades. Gothard was not an athlete like most of the other boys, and didn't put much effort into trying either, he just felt like he didn't belong. Inside he was fuming at Rudy and Bobby for being friends with the Neon Twins. He had tried to date girls, but they treated him like an outcast. He enjoyed watching the twins, hell, every boy enjoyed looking at the twins. Today Gothard was just too tired to deal with life anymore and its complexities, he just didn't see much point in it all.

The Neon Twins knew Gothard was watching their butts as they walked in their customary hip swaying way. They grabbed Rudy, bringing him to a halt, looking directly at Gothard, they grabbed Rudy's butt and tried touching tongues with him, but there was one tongue too many. Gothard was outraged at this deliberate mockery. He pulled out the stolen handgun and aimed in the general direction of the four. The twins quickly recognized the danger and instantly pushed Bobby between them and Gothard. Bobby, with his head bobbing at a rapid pace, stared dumbfounded at Gothard's' gun.

Charlotte's mouth dropped open as she watched Gothard pull out a gun and aim at Bobby. Charlotte screamed **"GUN!!!"** just as she heard the noise of a single shot. The children all screamed and ran in different directions. Gothard dropped the gun in a panic when he noticed the river of blood coming from his wrist. *"What the fuck, I didn't even pull trigger and that damn gun injured me."* The Neon Twins wondered why Bobby was still standing. Bobby was a little shocked himself, *"Crap, I've been shot and I don't feel a thing."* He steadied his twitching head with his hands preparing to breathe his last breath.

Thomas had been drinking coffee with Johnny, discussing different options for the closed factory. Thomas watched as the school children made their way down the street, he noticed Gothard pointing a gun at some of his fellow students. Without thinking, Thomas drew his own gun and shot for the gun in Gothard's hand. The bullet went through Gothard's wrist, through the window of the sheriff's office and came to rest in Jaerk's morning blueberry muffin.

113

Jaerk, having heard a gunshot, grabbed his muffin and dove to the floor. When he heard no more shots, he stood and casually took a huge bite of his muffin as though nothing had happened and he hadn't hidden under his desk like a scared little school girl. As he chewed his ginormous bite of muffin, his lower left molar crunched down on a very solid lead ball. He was outraged. He marched outside the office with his gun drawn, somebody was going to die or go to jail for breaking his tooth. Thomas saw the red angry face of deputy Jaerk and immediately holstered his gun as nonchalantly as he could. Jaerk surveyed the scene and marched up to Charlotte, who was still mildly in shock. "Mind explaining what just happened here ma'am?" Jaerk asked. Charlotte answered, "That boy drew a gun and fired at Bobby and the Neon Twins." Jaerk went to the twins and said, "Tell me what just happened?" Blonde Neon One broke out in tears. The brunette simply said, "That asshole just shot at me." She was pointing in the direction Gothard had run off, which was directly towards Johnny. Jaerk looked at Johnny, spit out some blood, and marched towards him.

Johnny saw Jaerk approaching him and immediately wondered *"why?"* Thomas sat back in his creaky wooden chair. Jaerk looked at Johnny and simply said, "I knew you would screw up someday. It'll be fun watching you hang." Jaerk pushed Johnny to the wall and placed him in handcuffs. Thomas smiled and told Jaerk, "I'm the one who shot Gothard." Jaerk, a little confused, replied, "You can't protect him anymore. Your power in this town is nearly dead. Best you quit trying to obstruct justice." Jaerk started walking Johnny to his office.

The twins, still infatuated with Johnny, ran to Jaerk and said, "He didn't shoot at us, Gothard did." Jaerk, unmoved, continued walking towards the sheriff's office and tripped on Gothard's gun with his still sore foot. Charlotte walked up and said, "I told you, Gothard shot at the twins." Jaerk picked up the gun, smelled its barrel and said, "Nice try ladies, but this gun hasn't been fired." The twins, more confused than normal, took to helping Charlotte gather up the younger kids, all being embarrassed at their words being found to be false. Thomas chuckled and tried to explain what had transpired to Jaerk. Jaerk, again, rebuffed Thomas's words and continued walking Johnny to the jail house. Thomas finally yelled and said, "LOOK deputy dog, just follow the blood".

Jaerk looked at the trail of blood and decided that that might be a good idea in solving this riddle, although he really wanted Johnny behind bars. Charlotte sent the twins to take the children home and she trailed after Jaerk and the others who were following the blood trail towards the corral. There, behind the corral, they found Gothard lying dead because his severed artery had bled him out. Gothard had the first smile on his face that any of them had ever seen. Jaerk placed both Johnny and Thomas in jail for cold blooded murder. Thomas and Johnny now had a new topic to discuss other than the closed factory, "the justice system."

The following morning Charlotte dressed for her day, then strapped a gun to her side. Never again would she be caught unable to defend her children. She looked sexy as all hell wearing that gun. Nobody at school even seemed to notice that Gothard was gone, which wasn't surprising since he never socialized and always sat in the back corner of the room, out of site and mind. Charlotte decided to try another field trip, thinking anything was better than teaching what she was being asked to teach and hoped it would take her mind off Gothard. Charlotte led the children down the red brick road and wondered if she would ever feel excited and inspired about teaching in this town again. The children were again excited at having another day free from the confines of the school room walls. They walked for two hours to a meadow; there Charlotte taught them the difference between edible and poisonous plants. She taught about safe berries and green leaves, most importantly she taught about mushrooms that could instantly kill and those the Indians used to take as a hallucinogen.

An apache, who had been too proud to head west with his family, silently sat watching the white children as they trampled all over his gathering grounds. He cursed in apache as he watched a round kid with a strangely bobbing head eat his spiritual mushrooms. He camouflaged himself crouching next to a tree, as he quietly pulled an arrow from his quiver and set his arrow for a shot. He sighted in on a brown haired child standing beside a tree alone, watching the other children. He released the string and sent the arrow soaring towards its target.

William was watching Bobby eat the mushrooms that Charlotte had told them to avoid. He heard a very soft whistling and turned just in time to see an arrow lodge into the tree just inches from his nose. William drew his gun and fired in the direction that the arrow had come from. Charlotte, aghast at having heard another gunshot so near her children, turned to see William pointing his gun at a tree. Seeing the arrow in the tree next to William, Charlotte drew her gun. She followed Williams gaze to a tree up the hill and aimed her gun, she saw nothing.

The apache prepared another arrow and once again took aim at William. William saw the movement and fired, the Indian ducked to the other side of the tree where Charlotte saw and shot him in his chest. He died saying in apache, "Damn, I thought this was a gun free community!?!?" It sounded something like this *"Wewoo woo woowoo!"*

The stunned children stared at the scene in front of them. Having determined there were no more Indians, they quickly took to poking and prodding the dead indian. None of them had ever seen a red man before. Bobby, hallucinating on mushrooms, saw at least a hundred savage Indians circling him and screaming a war cry. Charlotte and William stood silently watching the children, both saddened that someone had died.

On the way back the children were all chattering about the exciting Indian war. The twins were rapidly discussing the scene in great exaggerated detail. Neon One was saying to her sister; "I can't believe all the Indians we fought, there must have been at least 50. And the way Charlotte shot them all. She's like the most awesome teacher ever." The brunette Neon Two dressed in a red dress responded, "50!? You so underestimate everything sister. There was at least a hundred."

Jaerk sat with his arms crossed listening to his mother. He was happy that she couldn't see his petulant eye rolls from under his dark sunglasses. Susie was pacing and ranting her disapproval that under no circumstances would violence be allowed in her town, anyone who shot a gun was to be jailed immediately, regardless of the circumstances. Yesterday's gun fiasco had her in a tizzy. Susie's usually impeccable hair was flying this way and that as she waved her finger in her son's face and continued lecturing about the importance of zero violence. Jaerk left with Susie's last words ringing in his ear, "Get a new hat, I'm tired of constantly being reminded how close I came to losing you". When Jaerk had left, Susie loudly said to herself, "I hate guns!!!"

As Jaerk walked down the street he heard the chatter coming from the Neon Twins and his ears perked up. He thought, *"A hundred Indians shot. Dang, wish I could have gotten me some of that hunting action."* Then a view of his mother's finger poking his nose flashed across his mind and the word "SHOT" froze him. He grabbed Bobby whose head was bouncing five times faster than normal, and asked, "What happened?" Bobby said, "Dude, a 100 Indians!! Arrows were flying everywhere!! Teach and that kid killed em all!!!"

Jaerk grabbed Charlotte and William and sternly asked, "You two fire your weapons today?" Both, still saddened at killing an individual, mournfully replied, "Yeah." Jaerk had them follow him to jail where he ushered them inside the cell with Thomas and Johnny. Charlotte asked why and Jaerk said, "For murdering a hundred Indians." Jaerk ignored the protests as he tried figuring out how to explain to his mom that there was more gunfire on his watch. William explained the situation to his father. Thomas was thankful that his son wasn't hurt and hugged him like he had never hugged him before.

Sheriff Wright had just returned from a conference in Texas about "constitutional law" and was headed to his office to check in on things, he was met with the sight of his friends filling the jail, and Jaerk paying attention to no-one while hiding under his ridiculously oversized hat. Mr. Wright listened to Thomas, then Johnny, then Charlotte, then William. He looked at the hole in the window. He went to the coroner's office to examine Gothard and after that he interviewed many of the other children who had witnessed the incident. Then he began investigating the Indian debacle. Wright rode to the meadow where the dead Indian was still lying and inspected the entire scene, arrows, tracks and all.

The irritated Sheriff galloped back to his office and asked Jaerk how many Indians had died. Jaerk said with great confidence, "At least a hundred." Mr. Wright shook his head and marched to Susie's office. There he spent an hour waiting before Susie finally saw him. She rudely asked, "Enjoy your vacation while the rest of us slaved away making this a better community?" Sheriff Wright's trip had been terrible and he had not enjoyed it at all. It was long, hot and dusty. It was not a vacation; it was a conference concerning the citizens and the constitution, but he ignored the rude comment and said, "Citizens of America have a right to bear arms and protect themselves. You're wrongly holding innocent people behind bars."

Susie missed nothing in her town. She had people watching people and others watching the people watchers. She was more interested in watching her son squirm while trying to explain why another gunshot was fired in her town then listen to this old timer explain the constitution to her. She knew the constitution and she knew it was flawed. However, she had yet to write enough laws to change the constitution to her liking. She could care less about a ghostly looking kid and even less about a savage Indian. She would let Mr. Wright win this battle because she knew she would win the war. She simply said, "Fine, do what you want but put a leash on your people." The sheriff knew not to fight her, not when he was getting what he wanted. He left being greatly concerned, but about what he didn't really know.

He returned to his office only to find the Neon Twins jumping up and down, holding huge signs written in fluorescent green and yellow over their heads. One read, FREE THE TEACH. The other read, SHE KILLS THE BEASTS. The twins were dressed in corresponding mismatched outfits. One was wearing a right neon green thigh high boot and a pink left boot; the other wore the matches to her sister's boots. One wore a scarlet red skirt and yellow belly shirt; the other wore a red top and sunshine yellow skirt. The twins took turns jumping and yelling what was written on their large card, making the shortness of their shirts even more noticeable. The result was that a bunch of men had gathered to watch them and cheer them on as the girls protested. Half the men's heads were watching the blonde, the other half were watching the brunette. Mr. Wright watched the men's heads move opposite one another in up and down motion, it was somewhat comical and if one could see underneath his large grey handlebar mustache, they would see a thin smile. He took this opportunity to gain public popularity. He went inside and freed the captives, he smiled and had the three men stay back while he gave the public Charlotte.

Charlotte laughed as she took in the situation from the window. When she stepped out onto the front steps, the crowd roared. The Neon Twins yelled in delight as they ran to hug Charlotte, they resumed jumping as they squeezed her tightly. Many of the men smiled at Sheriff Wright as if to say, "Well done sheriff." Charlotte hugged the twins and part of her thought she might really like these two if she would just give them half a chance.

14 - **The Money Making Machine**

Susie, Charles, Futureano and Jaerk all met the incoming wagon train 10 miles outside of town in the dark of the night. In the wagons was Susie's answer to the problems pile, piling up on her desk, and the ever growing line of pauper people standing in the bread line each day. Oshna and Marshna were demanding higher wages, yet their work load had been cut by three fourths as business after business continued to close their doors at their hands. Susie ignored the fact that many businesses closed at her own hands because of her outrageous taxes. The cost of constructing her official buildings was skyrocketing as more building materials had to be imported rather than manufactured locally. In short, most of her citizens were unemployed and those still working at the few still opened businesses were quickly joining their peers in the unemployment line due to the growing cost of tax and safety regulation requirements. Times were tough in Liberty Town, but it was nothing that more money couldn't solve.

Susie had told Charles that he was in charge of building a special structure for this much anticipated money machine. Charles hired Gusto Constructo as the engineer, foreman and designer of the "ahead of its time" custom vault. The impenetrable building was embedded into bedrock of a mountainside west of town, with a two foot thick concrete slab as its front. Gusto had blasted a trench for sewer and water that led under the self-sufficient building. There was only one way in, a 6 inch thick solid steel door. This door was an impressive feat of engineering and Gusto's crowning achievement. This steel door hinged on a railroad car axle and wheels that Gusto modified and partially embedded into the concrete wall to stabilize the giant door. To operate the door a pair of strong mules and a multiple pulley system was used to make opening and closing this monster of a door possible. When the building was completed, Susie hired twenty men to break in and rob the building. To her joy, all of them failed.

Susie, Charles, Futureano and Jaerk quietly rode the wagon through town towards the newly erected building, Susie started grumbling about the lumpy brick road they were now passing over, it did the machine no good to be bounced this way. She thought to herself, *"It was so pretty and smooth a couple months ago before the rains."*

It took the trio two weeks assembling and fine tuning the immaculate money machine. When completed, Charles turned a crank on one end while Susie joyously played in the money falling onto the floor at the other end. Futureano stuffed money down his britches and thought about buying Charlotte's love with a sexy red dress like the Neon Twins wore.

The following day Susie had Charles contact the owner of Liberty Town's newspaper printing press, Mr. Bias. Mr. Bias's printing press just wouldn't print money, no matter how hard Susie and Charles had tried. Charles struck a deal with Mr. Bias, if he would print what was asked of him by Susie and himself, he could have his printing press back. Mr. Bias was at first reluctant, but when Charles offered him free monthly tickets to the all you can eat seafood buffet, Mr. Bias, an ample bellied man, readily agreed. The headline of the first paper printed after this arrangement was made read, "GUNS ARE INHUMANE!" in huge bold letters. Below that was a photograph of the recently deceased Indian who had been munched on by a bear and a wolf since his demise. Then a story followed telling how this unrecognizable individual was shot, a ridiculously exaggerated, hundred times with a gun.

Susie had Charles hire a courier to deliver the newly printed pieces of money to all the people she liked to call "pauper people" who were unemployed. The only requirements to accepting this money was a signature and a check mark in two boxes next to the words, "I am not currently working" and "I have looked for work". The paupers were then told that if they came by every other week to the town hall and marked the boxes again, they would get another installment of Susie's money. This was the easiest money and first hand out many had received in their lives; and the pauper people were more than thrilled to do just that.

Johnny was forever fighting a losing battle in saving enough money to marry Peggy and leave this lousy town. Between all his citations and his meager wages, Johnny found it hard to eat, let alone save. Now that Thomas's factory was closed, money was even tighter for Johnny who had found minimum wage work at the "No Purpose" Store. He had been taught to work hard for his earnings and to stand on his own two feet, and he was more than happy to try and do that.

Ben Lazybutt was an average person with average looks. His curly brown hair hung down to his slender shoulders. He was too lazy to shave, so he had a full grown brown beard. He thought it was a waste of time to keep up on his oral hygiene and consequently most of his yellow teeth had been pulled or rotted and fallen out on their own. Ben had been out of work for a rather long time. He had haphazardly looked for work, but the jobs he could have taken he felt were far below his position in life. When Ben had checked the marks for free money and saw his new found fortune was from Charles, Ben had silently vowed to follow Charles in whatever endeavor he chose to pursue.

The money hand-outs from the governing trio of Liberty Town made Ben feel as though he had acquired a semi- fortune. Having not been healthfully fed in many months, this money allowed Ben to now grocery shop, and he was not shy about filling up his shopping boxes with consumable goods. As Ben shopped, he thought back to times before, when he was a respected owner of his own lemonade stand, he smiled as he filled his basket with item after item. He paid and went to the local NPS, No Purpose Store. There he spent more money on a new card game and magic tricks. When Johnny gave Ben his change, he wondered, *"Where did Ben get money to waste?"* Ben then stopped by the local liquor store and spent the rest of his "Susie money" on whiskey.

Shortly after spending his Susie money, Ben Lazybutt was sitting at the kitchen table ignoring the noise of his eight children, his mind was elsewhere. He sat day dreaming of his own version of an American dream, in his dream he didn't have to work for a single part of it. His once lovely wife was frantically scurrying about trying to get dinner on the table and the children and house cleaned "I could use a little help" she politely said. "I'm a tad busy if you don't mind. I don't want to live in this rat trap forever." Came his cranky response. "Did you find a job today?" His wife excitedly asked, knowing that Ben had been out looking for work an hour or two that morning. Ben had already fulfilled his weekly quota of job searching in order to receive his bimonthly pay from

the BFC as Ben referred to them.   "No one is hiring." he
answered, all the while thinking, *"Why work? The 'Big Federal
Corporation' is giving me money just to look for work and check a
couple of boxes."* "Well, I saw ads for a cook and a dishwasher at
the local tavern," Bens wife sweetly said. "Seriously?!" Ben
snapped as he slammed his fist on the table, "What would our
neighbors and friends think if they saw me working there? We
have a reputation to uphold, you know." "REPUTATION!" She
roared "We live off the government!? How much lower can we
sink!?" she yelled. Ben calmly answered, "If you ask me, we are
living rather nicely, and if we put that little money making womb
of yours to work, we are set for another couple years." Ben had
learned that Susie was now giving money away for each child a
family had to care for. Frustrated and so angry, Ben's wife could
barely speak, "If you think I'm having another baby, just so the
government keeps us fed, you're crazy. I'm done popping out
babies!" "But my dearest, it's so perfect. If I get a job, I lose all
this." Ben stated as he spread his arms to indicate their small
rented apartment. "Where is your dignity, you senseless ASS!" she
shrieked. "Dignity? DIGNITY!?" Ben roared, "I lost my dignity
when the government taxed my business more than it earned.
Damn bastards, made me lose everything I ever worked for. As
far as I'm concerned, they can damn well take care of me!" Ben
sat fuming as he thought back to the price of sugar and lemons
doubling with tax. Then he remembered Oshna coming each week
and taking all the money in his tin as a penalty, until he built a
public restroom. How was he supposed to do that with no
money? *"Screw the government"* he thought.

Ben's wife glared at him as she uttered, "Well you better figure
out another loophole, cause it'll be a cold day in hell before I let
you touch me again." Just then little five year old Mary jumped off

the bed loft thinking she was a bird and could fly - only to fall on the floor landing hard on her arm. Her mom quickly saw that the little arm was twisted unnaturally. "Go get the doc!!" Ben's wife yelled to no one in particular.

The oldest two, tired of the yelling, quickly donned their coats and bolted outside and ran up the street. 6 blocks from the Lazy butt household was the mansion of Doc Dogooder. The children rapped on the Doc's door and eagerly gave him 2 simultaneous but different answers of what had happened. The doc immediately hitched his horse and the three went zipping down the brick road in the Doc's buggy to the Lazybutt's house.

Upon entering the cramped apartment, the doc was taken aback at seeing the amount of people crammed into this tiny abode. After reigning in his disbelief, Doc went to work on Mary's arm. Her mother was horrified at seeing her daughter undergo the setting of the arm without any medication for pain. Ben was too concerned about the cost of the doc's visit to merit any thought towards Mary and her discomfort.

When the doc had set Mary's arm and splinted it best he could with the resources provided and made his way to the door, he paused at the table to write out the bill. Ben stopped him and said, "Doc, I don't know how I'm going to pay for this." The doc put away his pen and took a card from his coat pocket and presented it to Ben. "Call on this man in the morning, he will help" Doc said. Ben took the card, politely thanked the Doc and bid him good night. Before he retired himself, Ben took another look at the card and the name printed on it - **Futureano Americass**. Ben smiled to himself.

The following morning at about ten o'clock, Ben rolled out of bed, donned his clothes and headed outside to go see Mr. Americass. Futureano was well known around town, he was head of the school board as well as the town's community organizer. Ben found him in the BFC's lobby, drinking tea and munching on fruits and vegetables. Ben immediately took a liking to Mr. Futureano, finding him even more grotesque than himself. Ben somewhat explained what had transpired in his home the night before and concluded with the Doc giving him Futureano's card. Futureano took the card and said, "No problem, consider the situation solved." He sent Ben home. Futureano was whistling as he approached one of Susie's newer buildings. Hung in huge bold letters above its massive doors was MAMACARES. Futureano studied his figure in the mirror glass window, straightened a few loose hanging hairs, and walked inside. He marched directly to collections and explained the circumstances of Ben Lazybutt. Two Mamacare officials visited the Doc and was told the sum of the Docs services. They quickly calculated in another 10% for their services and left the Doc, saying, "We'll be back with your money." They knew exactly where to go.

Years earlier a man by the name of Bill Money had moved to town. Bill Money had made his money on improvements to the round wheel. No one knows exactly what Bill did to the wheel to make it better, but through his business savvy, every wheel ever sold after his "improvement," Bill received a percentage of. Thomas, owner of the largest wagon company in the area, respected Bill for his business savvy and as a person.

As the Mamacare's officials approached Bill Money's house, they were a little intimidated and it irked them that someone could actually have more than they themselves had. Mamacare officials loved their jobs, taking money from the wealthy and distributing it to those who really needed it. "Morning, Bill." Official 1 said.

"What can I do you for?" Bill answered, all the while inwardly cringing to find Mamacare on his doorstep. "There was an incident at Lazybutt's last night and the doc had to provide services." Official 2 stated. "What's that to do with me?" asked Bill. Official 1 stated, "You have much, Lazybutt has nothing. Everyone deserves the Doc's services. It's only logical you pay Lazybutt's bill. Please make me a check for this sum." Official 1 handed Bill a bill in which the doc's services and the 10% fee for Mamacare's consultation had been added. Bill stared at Mamacare and slowly said, "And if I don't pay?" "Well, the BFC I work for will put you in jail and fine you what they wish. It's easier just to pay the bill, Bill." Stated official 2. Bill cussed, took out his check book and wrote Mamacare a check and slammed the door in their faces. As the door closed, Mamacare officials yelled, "You can claim this on your taxes, Bill. You should be thankful!"

Later that week, Ben went and checked his boxes and grabbed his Susie's money for the week. Ben was in the grocery store where he saw the Doc. Doc smiled and said, "I see you used that card I gave you. Your bill was paid in full just an hour ago." Ben grinned and threw six one and a half inch thick Porterhouse steaks into his cart. *"This was cause for celebration,"* Ben silently thought.

Ben was waiting in line to pay for his eight boxes of goods he was about to purchase when Johnny came up carrying a single half-filled box. Ben glanced inside Johnny's box and saw a bag of beans, a bag of rice, and a small pouch of salt. Johnny gazed over Ben's boxes, his eyes widening in astonishment. Ben's boxes contained steaks, candy, vegetables, more candy, poultry and even more candy. Johnny casually asked, "Throwing a party Ben?" Ben answered, "No, just stocking up a tad." "Can't keep all that meat fresh forever." Johnny said. Ben answered, "Figured the dogs need a little treat." Johnny was astounded and horrified at Ben's wasteful comment. Johnny walked home wondering why his life seemed to be nothing but disappointment after disappointment, and Ben Lazybutt seemed to be prospering, in spite of living up to his last name. He compared his lifestyle to that of Ben's and concluded that he would be better off being a dog at Ben's house then working like a dog like he was doing now.

15 - **Work Safely per Company Policy**

Susie's money changed the economic downward spiral of Liberty Town. People had money to spend, and spend they did. They brought groceries which started the farm's prosperity gear. Farms needed feed, seed and weed poison which started a few refinery gears. The refineries drew their needed help from the bread lines and Liberty Town's prosperity gears started to turn once again. Susie happily told Charles, "I knew the money machine would fix everything."

Susie lent money to the saw mills for the needed safety upgrades and their doors reopened. The price of lumber dropped which made construction affordable to the public once again, people could now afford to buy a new house or upgrade their current home. Jobs opened up and the bread line shortened even more. Thomas opened back up his factory and hired Johnny back as a foreman.

Susie saw an increase in her, or the towns, revenue. Businesses were again paying taxes, the taxes on commodities started rolling in, taxes from business income started flowing and the taxes from pauper people started their trip upstream to her as well. Susie's money making machine continued to crank out money seven days a week, around the clock. For the first time in months Susie let her brain shut down for a much needed rest, she was happy and that made Charles happy which in turn made Futureano and the rest of the town happy.

The joyful attitude brought back the spirit of the people. They wanted to spread their creativity and talk of the dam was once again on everyone's mind. After much deliberation from the town, Susie finally let Charles agree to build a dam at a different location - a mile upstream from her ranch house. Amazingly, the protection of the malaria mosquitoes was somehow forgotten now that Susie didn't have to have the dam in view of her back yard.

WBIC was the successful bidder for the construction of the dam. They had sent Murphy West, searching for new building projects, secretly hoping he would be captured by Apache Indians. The bids for this new dam were five times the original dam estimates after all of Oshna's and Marshna regulations were factored in, but Susie didn't care, she simply hired younger men to crank the handle on the money making machine faster in order to pay for the dam project. She did not want the working class in Liberty Town unemployed and she had decided a lake close by her house would not be all that bad.

The turning prosperity gears drew more people to the area and the population of Liberty Town once again grew at an alarming rate. People from everywhere had heard of its greatness and flocked to its borders; the town finally had enough citizens to be called a city. More schools had to be built, the sheriff's department grew, Susie's governing grew and it demanded more luxurious buildings.

Thomas was cranking out fancy wagons at a record pace. Johnny with his new position was now making enough money to survive and save. He once again saw the possibility of marrying Peggy and moving away. Thomas also added a new position of 'watchman,' he did nothing but stand watch for Oshna or

Marshna. If the watchman saw either of the two, an alarm was sounded and the flood gate was sealed, stopping the machines inside the factory from being energized and Thomas's employees would quickly dress in their PPE, personal protective equipment.

Red was back to working full time at the docks shipping more exports then he was unloading imports while Peggy and Sue spent most of their free time together handling the daily chores of Red's ranch. Sue was really taking a liking to Peggy and was inwardly wishing her son and Peggy would tie the knot. Peggy would come over early in the morning and work all day long for nothing more than a mere meal. Sue felt a little guilty over this, Red would simply smile and tell Peggy, "We're indebted to you." Peggy would tease back saying, "Yes you are and I promise I will collect one day." She would flash a smile that Red suspected held a little playful plan behind her intentions.

The Neon Twins had become a popular favorite, spreading cheer wherever they went. They were not prejudiced towards any color or race of person, they simply enjoyed life and were too naive to understand that there were good and bad people in this world. Their smiles were genuine and consequently everyone they passed smiled at them. They took those received smiles as an indication that they were loved and consequently their smiles would broaden. Charlotte would try talking to them about their seductive dress, but the two would laugh at Charlotte and basically say, "Oh Miss C, you're so cute and innocent. But women just don't dress like you do anymore, it's too outrageous."

Charles was wanting to gain independence from his sister, Susie would gladly let him try just so she could laugh at the predicaments he ended up in. She would watch him blush into a deep red crimson and then come to his rescue. Charles would thank her and treat her like the most loved sibling ever until another occasion would arise that he thought he could handle on his own. Susie let him handle tonight's Q and A with no 3x5's.

Reporter 1: Mr. Governor...

Charles: Please call me Charles

Reporter 1: Charles, Please tell us in your words why Liberty Town is prospering above other towns.

Charles: Hard work and long hours at the job. If I and my crew hadn't worked so hard, we wouldn't be where we are today.

Reporter 1: "So the work of the working class didn't contribute to this town's success?"

Charles: "No, not really. You have hard workers everywhere, but only one Liberty Town"

Reporter 1: "So you're saying, without you we would be just another average town?"

Charles: "Exactly, well, not exactly, but yes."

Reporter 2: "What makes you more special than other Governors?"

Charles: "My looks."

There was quiet throughout the conference, Charles had been expecting laughter. So he continued, "and my dedication to the job."

Reporter 2: "What exactly is your job?"

Charles: "To make life better for all of you."

Reporter 2: "And how do you do that?"

Charles: "I do my job."

    This retort continued until Susie stepped up and said, "We all do our best to ensure laws are in place to govern the people, making your life safe. Excuse us, we have an important meeting we need to be at." Susie drug her brother away to her penthouse.

    Susie sat in her new skyscraper penthouse overlooking the city. She stared out the window in awe, she was inwardly happy, she had learned how to make Liberty Town a great city whose name was highly spoken of throughout the world. People from all of the new nation were seeking her advice on how to make their towns prosper as well.

    Gusto Constructo had ended up constructing a marvelous house. It was a very efficient house and was built with never before seen architectural design. People from the city would ride past it just to admire its beauty. When Jimmy rode past Gusto's house, he was not content just admiring it, he wanted to see the inside as well. Jimmy knocked on Gusto's door and with a large smile, explained his visit. Gusto gladly showed his workmanship and took to liking Jimmy who naturally took to liking Gusto.

    Jimmy and Gusto's friendship was cemented the day that both went horseback riding alongside their spouses in an open meadow. Gusto's wife's horse was startled by a very large nasty slimy snake and the horse sprinted through the meadow into a very large thick growth of wild rose bushes where it stopped. Regina took to crying, Jimmy, not caring about the many scrapes and cuts he would receive, took to rescuing Regina Contriour, Gusto's wife. Through that one incident, Jimmy and Gusto became great friends.

Jimmy valued the friendship and admired Gusto for a number of reasons. He was an excellent builder, he was honest and fair, and he despised the governing of Liberty Town. Because Jimmy knew the kind of work Gusto could do, Jimmy requested Gusto be hired on as a consultant for the dam and WBIC consented.

WBIC was rapidly becoming a huge corporation. They were the first ones to adhere to all of Oshna's and Marshna's safety rules and regulations. When other building businesses were bankrupted by citations, WBIC would be hired to finish the project. Since Oshna's and Marshna's rules and regulations were the base of WBIC's success, WBIC adopted their standards as their own. WBIC was adamant about safety. If an employee was seen shortcutting a safety standard, that employee was immediately terminated, because at WBIC, safety truly came first.

Gusto and Jimmy worked alongside WBIC's crew. They enjoyed the physical exertion and gained some warped since of pride for having worked and sweated all day. Moreover, they both believed in never having their crews do something that they themselves would not. Once again Jimmy found his crew greatly respecting him, and Gusto found a few new friends.

The money counters at WBIC greatly appreciated Gusto and Jimmy. In profit comparison analyses, the two doubled or tripled the profit of any other supervisor of WBIC. If there were to exist an employee of the month, Jimmy and Gusto would consistently share that award, the two also enjoyed working for WBIC who gave them freedom to get their work done.

On one particular Monday, the dam workers were all a little sluggish. They had just come off the 4th of July weekend and were feeling the effects of a little too much celebrating. Surprisingly, the machinery of WBIC was empathizing with the workers and was behaving sluggish as well.

Big Cutter was a portable saw mill built specifically for the making of this dam. It was powered by eight oxen turning a wooden shank which in turn moved a series of belts and pulleys of varying sizes. The end result was an 8 foot diameter saw blade moving with amazing speed and power, Big Cutter would saw any timber shoved into its blade. However, because of simple physics, if the blade was not moving before the tree was fed into Big Cutter, the belts would burn and brake as the oxen powering the mill started moving. Jimmy, Gusto, and Earl had witnessed this countless times.

Jimmy and Gusto both teased about how the portable saw mill was behaving. "Looks like Big Cutter drank too much whisky this weekend." Gusto said. Jimmy looked at Earl, the operator of Big Cutter, and replied. "I think Earl and Cutter celebrated together". Gusto looked down at Earl and teased, "That man Earl needs to find a girl. I do not think Big Cutter appreciates all of Earl's love."

Before WBIC's safety regulations were put into place, Big Cutter would have maimed, amputated limbs, and killed many men. With the safety regulations in place, including not placing oneself within five feet of any moving part, Big Cutter didn't have a chance to even scratch an employee, naturally the employees and supervisors were happy about many of the new safeguards.

This particular Monday, Big Cutters power driving oxen were

walking out of time. The wooden pulleys and belts were damp with dew, making the whole belt system slip. Jimmy and Gusto noticed steam coming off the 3rd and 4th belt at the wooden pulley junction, indicating severe heat and probably machine failure. At that time, a three foot diameter tree was being cut and the blade of Big Cutter stopped because the belt powering the blade burned in two. Big Cutter could not and would not physically start until the blade had been thoroughly cleared and a new belt installed.

When the 3rd and 4th belt junction failed, more power was given to the wooden contraption that fed huge trees into big cutters massive blade.   The large tree continued to be shoved into the unmoving saw blade until the tree feeding contraption snapped and broke. Pieces of large wood went flying everywhere, one landed on Earl, all this happened within about 5 seconds.

Jimmy and Gusto both immediately set out to help Earl. Jimmy jumped down the platform to the ground, Gusto, being older, took the stairs. Jimmy crossed directly through the workings of Big Cutter, grabbing a long limb from beneath the cutting platform that had splintered off the tree. Jimmy arrived where Earl rested and immediately started removing the trees weight off Earl via prying leverage; this simple action saved Earl's life. Gusto ran around the workings of Big Cutter and arrived by Earl's side a few minute after Jimmy arrived. With Gusto's help, the two were able to remove Earl from any further harm.

A WBIC courier jumped on his horse and rode to town. He simply told a paper pusher that an accident had occurred at the dam construction site. Word spread as fast as lightning and in fifteen minutes time a safety committee from WBIC was at the job site. Work at the dam immediately ceased, the safety team from

WBIC investigated the accident along with Oshna and Marshna. After all witnesses were questioned, the team concluded that Jimmy had saved Earl's life, but Since Jimmy had crossed through the inner workings of belts and pulleys of Big Cutter without first removing the oxen from the machinery's drive system per company safety policy, the safety team concluded that Jimmy was to be immediately terminated for breaking company safety policy.

He was told by a large shareholder of WBIC that he had saved Earl's life, but since he did not adhere to the strict safety mandate, company policy forced him to be terminated. Jimmy was confused and asked the WBIC investor, "So, if you were trapped under that wood, you would want me to take the time to unhitch the oxen before I saved your life"? The investor simply answered, "You have to ensure your own safety first before helping someone else". Jimmy reiterated, "You would have died." The investor re-read the safety policy to Jimmy. "Any employee who purposefully violates any WBIC safety rule, shall be immediately terminated without question".

Jimmy left wishing he could see that investors face as he unhitched the oxen while he laid there and his life bled out if he were in that situation. The blue collar workers were furious at learning Jimmy was terminated for saving Earl's life. Their view of the company was forever changed and Gusto quit as soon as he learned the story.

The following day Jimmy found himself at the town hall marking his mark in the boxes beside the statements "I am currently not working," and "I have looked for work". After seeing the sum of money given him for not working, Jimmy wondered *if he would ever work again.* As he was leaving he saw Charles and thought a man to man talk about all his concerns might be helpful. "Care to join me for lunch?" Jimmy casually asked Charles. Charles took in the comical look of Jimmy and his dress and quickly calculated that the hulk of this man could have nothing of value for himself. Charles rudely replied, "I don't think so," and he raised his head as he left. Jimmy thought, "*Snob*."

With Gusto and Jimmy both unemployed, progression of the dam almost stopped, WBIC seemed not to care. Moreover, after the incident with Earl, a safety team was created at the WBIC dam worksite. For an hour each morning the workers would meet and discuss work safety. Then the workers would divide up and walk the project, looking for work hazards and Marshna violations. They would meet back for lunch, eat, and then discuss any safety issues that might arise. They then had a safety tool box talk and then held another meeting to discuss upcoming meetings and any new meetings that should be held. Finally the workers were given their daily work assignments. The workers then gathered their tools, walked to their designated areas, noted that it was only fifteen minutes until quitting time. They would turn and slowly walk back, put their tools away, and then go home. Working at the WBIC dam site was truly safe.

16 - **Save Us Susie**

It was a beautiful Saturday afternoon when Jimmy, Red, Johnny and Gusto found themselves sitting outside the local tavern playing checkers. They each had a beer and a BIG chew of tobacco stuck between their cheek and gum. Red, being the biggest, spit the biggest. There was not an ant in sight safe from Red's spit. In fact, Red would collect the spit in his mouth and wait to spit until he saw a six legged Apache with antennas. He would then unload his spit on the ant and laugh as the ant trudged through gooey brown spit sludge. If Red missed his six legged enemy, Jimmy, Johnny or Gusto would have their spit ready for back up. What spit that did not drool through the planking slats, puddled. Charlotte knew the men's routine well and would make a mental note to hop, skip, and jump through the insect battlefield, to loose and let your feet touch the spit was suicidal, for one would slip and fall backwards into stagnant brown spit slime.

The Neon Twins were not as wise as Charlotte. They were hand in hand, giggling and dancing as they entered the spit insecticide battlefield. Neon One's left foot skidded on spit pile four, she faltered and grabbed Neon Two. This action caused Neon Two's right foot to solidly plant itself into spit pile seven, the two were now arm and arm fixed together as if they were in a three legged race. Unfortunately, two of their three feet were now very slippery with dark brown spit. The two slid arm in arm onto their butts into spit piles three, five, six, nine and twelve. Their hands then released each other and found brown spit piles one and two. They looked at each other, analyzed what they were sitting in, and each threw up. Not wanting to be sickened with the twins' throw up, the four men gathered their checkers and moved to another, soon not to be, battle free spit vs. ant war zone.

The twins ran to Futureano who was in an important meeting with the other town leaders. Seeing their teary eyes and filthy clothing, Futureano sent Jaerk to rectify the situation. Jaerk listened to the story patiently as the twins sobbed and raged against the wrong done to them. Jaerk tried to inconspicuously plug his nose against the strong odor emanating from the twins as they told their story. He was having a very hard time containing himself, but as an officer of the law, he decided he could not embarrass himself by doing what he wanted to do the most and so he waited until he had sent them home. Jaerk could not get the awful smell and sight to leave him, it was so bad that he threw up on his way to Town Hall. When he reached Town Hall, he filled out a new ordinance, number 1,645. A few minutes later, the four checker players each held a freshly issued ticket from Jaerk. "Ordinance 1,645, No spitting on the sidewalk," Jaerk said, "Pay your fine within thirty days". Johnny asked no one in particular, "I wonder why it's called a ticket?"

The four took their preposterous tickets and angrily pushed them into their pants. Red looked at the slimy puddle of brown slime and decided maybe the new ordinance might have some merits, he said, "I suppose we did create a rather nasty splooge pile." Jimmy chuckled saying, "Probably wouldn't need the new ordinance if our regard for others was dominant in our minds."

Johnny stated, "I think we used to think like that, but now we don't cause of things like this." He pulled out his ticket and threw it on the table. Jimmy said, "I think Johnny's right, I wouldn't spit on any of yours doorsteps, but I honestly want to spit on the Americasses." Gusto chimed in, "I think our inward spirit is being stripped away, follow me here. America was built on adventure and risk. Now we can't take risks, even to save a life, look at Jimmy's situation. So I presume that the more of our freedoms or rights or whatever you want to call them are tricked away from us, the more of our awareness to others is lost." Red said as he released more spit, "That might be a valued point. I never would have spit on the sidewalk 6 months ago." Johnny said, "I'm not sure, but I do agree with Gusto. I'm not allowed to take any of the risks you all grew up with." Jimmy said, "No, you're not, partially because we as parents won't let you. I wouldn't let my daughters do some of the things Tammy did growing up." Johnny got mad, "It's not right. We have rules being placed on us from the government and our parents. We are growing up with half the freedoms you grew up with. What's it going to be like 100 years from now?" Gusto responded, "Probably less freedom than there is now, but you'll be much safer." Johnny stood and thumped his hand on the table making the checkers bounce, "I DON'T WANT SAFE, I WANT FREEDOM!" Red, sensing the conversation about to become overheated, said, "Johnny, you're loved. We just want to see you happy and safe." Johnny responds, "I'm sure every parent does. But at what cost to our freedom?" The three older men ponder this and finally Gusto said, "I don't know. Just like Susie wants to keep us safe, parents want to keep their children safe." Red disagreed, "I assume Susie makes laws for control, I make laws to show my love." Johnny ended the conversation by saying, "The forefathers should have made a constitution for parents as well."

After the twins were escorted out of the important meeting, Susie asked the president of WBIC "How much money do you need from us to keep your company operational?"

The president of WBIC had prepared for this meeting for some time. The money counters had come to him a few months after Jimmy and Gusto were no longer working for the company. The counters had seen the decline in amount owed them vs. what they owed in labor, social security tax, income tax, liability insurance, workman's comp, employee health insurance, officer Chief Executive Officer (CEO) bonuses, vacation funds, exotic company conferences, and luxury buggies for its CEOs. We Build It construction was going bankrupt quick, and if its doors closed, thousands of workers would find themselves without work.

Sessiff Lee Paid, the president of WBIC, said to Susie, "Miss. Powers, your association gathers excessive revenue from all costs associated with our operation. The yearly income you make from the taxes on our employees pay is enough to run your organization for a couple of minutes. Moreover, the money the employees spend on commodities, sends even more money your direction. Personally, I have enough saved for me, my children, and their children to live happily. But if you let all of our employees become unemployed, you're doing this great country great injustice".

Susie asked again, "How much money do you need in order to keep your doors open?"

Over Lee Paid, Sessiff's brother and vice president of WBIC, casually answered after taking a sip of coffee, "It's not a matter of how much we need, it's a matter of how much are you willing to give in order to keep this town of yours economy booming.

Without us, your town will shrivel up and die." Sessiff continued, "We really do not want this money Miss Powers, we are just trying to help you out."

Charles, seeing their point, discarded Susie's prewritten 3 x 5 card and spoke, "They have a very valid point Susie, and we should give them the money."

Susie glared at Charles and asked the Paid brothers one final time, "How much money do you need?"

Charles, annoyed at Susie's glare and knowing his say was the ultimate power, blurted out, "We shall give you ten times the revenue of the sum of your last ten years. That should keep everyone happy."

Sessiff Lee and Over Lee Paid stood up and said, "You're welcome," they then walked out of the meeting room. Susie then excused Futureano and all others except Charles. "What the hell are you thinking Charles?" Susie loudly asked. Charles responded, "Great, the first time I think on my own, you yell at me." Susie calmly asked, "Where are we going to get that type of money?" Charles simply and happily answered, "Our money machine." Susie asked further, "Do you not realize our money machine is continuously running, it never shuts down. When will it have time to make extra money for your promise to WBIC?"

Charles had forgotten that the money machine was already behind on other promises. The continued growth of Susie's new and established organizations was taking most of their revenue, to the extent that the unemployed were having to wait an extra week for their money. The producers of babies were having to wait an extra four weeks for their money, Mamacares was not an efficient operation at all. Doctors had to raise their prices, hospitals had to follow suit. 65 percent of Susie's total income was being divided among several socialistic revenue leeches. Charles could not believe that Susie was nearly broke again. He cursed at her and asked, "Why can't you be content to leave things be? The people have enough governing their lives without you adding more governing to them. You're taking my money and giving it away." Susie was taken back that actual words worth merit came from Charles's mouth. She laughed and answered, "That's the beauty of it Charles, we don't want the citizens doing any act on their own without our approval. It keeps them safe and in line. It keeps them doing more and more of what we ask them to do and not what they themselves actually want to do. No longer can the people race their horses unless we allow them. They can't build a house unless we allow them. They can't efficiently run a business unless we allow them. People are not free anymore Charles," she walked to her brother and hugged him, "people are under my, I mean, our control" Susie finished saying.

17 - **The Unstoppable**

Susie's and Charlie's town was still prospering. Most everyone was working and those that were not were being subsidized with Susie's money collected by taxes from the working people's income, taxes from making goods and commodities, taxes from selling goods and commodities, taxes on imports, taxes on exports, taxes on business gains, fees collected from people for various acts, fees from damages to the government, citations and Susie's money making machines.

News of the town's growth spread to other colonies in the New Nation and from there to all the foreign countries. Consequently, the small town had become a large city. Susie had Charles call for a gathering to all interested citizens concerning many new demands that were arising daily from the old and new masses.

The town hall was overflowing. As was normal, Charles, Susie and Futureano sat at a spacious table on stage up front. Charles slammed down his gavel and spoke. "First order of business, we need a new name for our growing city." The native Liberty Town folks came unglued. First the morals and ethics of their town were changed, now their town's name? Their voice wouldn't count, too many foreigners had come in and had taken to Charles. Red sarcastically yelled, "Libertyless." Susie kept quiet as she let that sweet word roll over the minds of the gathering. Then she stood and said, "I love it." The new city folks clapped in agreement. Red slumped in his chair, amazed that his sarcastic suggestion was now the name of the city he resided in.

Charles then read the remainder of items needing covered that night.

1) Traffic is so compacted that walking and riding through town is now hazardous.

2) The town buildings for official business are overcrowded.

3) A Disciplinary system needs installed for those who have broken the law.

Again, after reading the first order of business, jabber and chatter broke out. By the time Charles read item number three, not one of his spoken words were heard, he was perturbed and stopped reading.

At last a motion was spoken that since everyone was slightly in disagreement about everything, that it would be all right for the town leaders to do as they saw necessary for the good of the people. The notion was seconded and the citizens left town hall having voiced over any future say in the growth of Libertyless to Futureano and his family.

Susie was delighted, the people had just given her more power to govern their lives even more than she already was. She silently thought, "*The little sheep. They have no idea what it is they do.*" She stood and walked out the back door down the street to her private restaurant. It was a restaurant she had built especially for her. It was built with the taxpayer's money, but they couldn't use it, it was a restaurant made special for only her and whatever guest she might want to take in its doors. The restaurant was fully staffed by eight employees who were paid by taxpayer's money, but they rarely got to serve the public, only on occasions Susie brought guests to her restaurant. There was a chef from France and a doorman. The restaurant was stocked with the highest quality of enzyme free meat, chicken and seafood all of which was paid for by the taxpayers, but they were never offered a chance to eat what they had paid for.

Susie was dressed in a navy blue woman's suit and her hair was tightly bound to the back of her head as was usual for her. The doorman opened the door and Susie walked in. She took off her suit jacket and a waiter was there to receive it. Susie unbound her golden hair and let it fall past her shoulders, it had grown to where it fell below her waist. A waiter asked her if there would be any guests tonight. She shook her head "No" and the restaurant door was locked.

Susie was seated at a luxurious table covered in a white silk linen, paid for by the taxpayers. Her seat was covered in a red silk cloth imported from Egypt and paid for by the taxpayers. A waiter brought her a bottle of wine. Susie shook her head no and said, "Whiskey." She ordered the lobster and prime rib. There wouldn't be a bill, the taxpayers would once again pick up tonight's balance.

Susie ate and drank until she was light headed. The French cook came and sat by her, he put his hand on her smooth bare leg. She smiled at him and said, "Not tonight, I have a headache." So the cook sat and admired Susie's beauty, but Susie paid him no attention, her mind was swirling with grand thoughts of a bigger and better Libertyless city.

Susie did not waste any time in putting her dreams down on paper proposing the progress she wanted completed already.

Engineers and architects were brought in to design a bigger better Libertyless America. At days' end, it was decided that for future Libertyless' growth and development, it would be best to build new official buildings at a new location. And, since they represented all that Libertyless represented, these buildings should be built at and on the prettiest surrounding area. The perfect place would have been on Susie Power's land; however, she was not willing to sacrifice any of her assets for the benefit of the city.

The next practical and logical area was to build the buildings on Red's ranch. Here they would have plenty of room for future growth, and the scenery was spectacular. It wasn't far away from town, but far enough away that Susie could be segregated from the city. Charles was promoted to governor and Futureano instantly became mayor. The two promoted Jaerk to be the chief of police.

When the new buildings were built, the old ones could be torn down which would allow area for a park and better traffic control. Additional land would be bought in a secluded area for building of a penal system. It seemed as though all items discussed in the city meeting were on their way to being solved.

Red had inherited the ranch from Sue's mom. It was close to town and had areas of spectacular scenery. Half of Red's land was a meadow with a stream, this made excellent ranch land. A quarter of Red's land was mountains which made for excellent hunting, the remaining quarter of Red's land had once been a delta. This made for excellent farming.

Libertyless powers that rule, hired by Susie, had spent hours analyzing Red's ranch. Being close to town they could easily annex it into city limits. The buildings could be designed and built to complement the scenery. The meadow was flat enough to build all the buildings needed. The stream running through Libertyless' future new governing branch, would complement the theme Susie Powers wanted to achieve. The part of Reds land unusable to Little America was the mountains and the little piece of farm land where Red's new home resided.

Red had bought the meadow land bordering his ranch from a friend and the deal was sealed with a simple handshake. The loan for the house, undersigned by the only bank remaining in the city, Higher Interested Bank, had taken the signing of a name and signature affidavit, a settlement statement, a certification addendum to settlement statement, a notice of right to cancel, an owner's affidavit, a deed of trust, a transfer of rights in the property, a compliance and quality control authorization and agreement, an itemization of amount financed, a payment letter to borrower, and 30 other documents meaningless to Red.

Red was and would be making payments to HIB for the next 29 years of his life. He figured by ranching the meadow he could earn enough extra money to pay the land off in fifteen years. Moreover, even if Red could not earn more money, the meadow view with the stream was well worth any price Red had to pay.

Mayor Futureano and newly appointed Chief of Police Jaerk were found knocking on Red's door Monday morning. Futureano happily greeted Red, "Morning Red, we are here with some exciting news."

Red, hating Jaerk for all the citations and false publicity Jaerk had given Johnny, asked Futureano while pointing at Jaerk, "What the hell is he doing on my doorstep?"

Futureano smiled and answered, "Glad you asked, I asked him to come along, everyone else was unavailable this morning. I wanted someone with me to share this exciting news."

Red, hating small talk, drove right to the point. "What news is that?"

Futureano said, "Glad you asked, Remember all the issues at town hall the other evening?"

Red answered, "Vaguely." Then asked, "What can I do to help?"

Futureano answered, "Glad you asked. You're going to sell Libertyless some of your land." Futureano wiped his long silver hair back over his head and tucked his dirty shirt back into his pants.

Red turned red and stated. "I love my land and I used to love my town. But you and the likes of you have slowly stripped every value of this town that I loved away." Then angrily asked, "Why would I sell this town anything anymore?"

Futureano responded, his smile was gone. "Glad you asked. Remember the other night the town gave us authority to do as was necessary for the benefit of the town. After much deliberation, we found it necessary to buy some of your land."

Red cut Futureano off. Slammed the door in Futureano and Jaerk's face, and went to his kitchen where he sat down. He was seething.

Jaerk opened the door and the two followed Red inside.

"GET OUT OF MY HOUSE!" Red yelled.

Futureano calmly said, "Look, we either take the land or buy the land. Either way, the town has already deemed the land as theirs. If you want financial compensation, you better talk to us." Red listened to Jaerk and Futureano explain that the government had the right to take land from land owners whenever they deemed it necessary, they referred to it as eminent domain. When Futureano was done, Red asked, "You're buying half my land, the meadow portion?"

Futureano answered, "Yes."

Red asked, "You're only paying half of my loan amount?"

Futureano answered, "Yes, you still owe for the portion of your land that Libertyless does not need. We're not warlords."

Red sighed, "You're taking my prime land."

Futureano corrected, "Buying, not taking."

Red stated. "So, I'm stuck making 30 years of payments for land that is basically useless to me."

Futureano explained, "We only buy what we need. No need in wasting any of the taxpayer's money."

When Jaerk and Futureano left, Red, who never cried, cried. He was now stuck working the next many years of his life to pay for land he no longer wanted. Each morning he would wake up and see the heart of the working city that had ripped his heart away. He wondered how he could tell Sue that the government just came and paid the bottom dollar for her grandparents' prime land. He threw up.

The new buildings were built. The best of the best from around the world were hired to do the engineering and construction, which resulted the creation of magnificent and spectacular constructed office mansions. There were big buildings and small buildings, there were buildings built for other buildings. There was a building for each town administration and buildings built for needs that might arise in the future. Even Marshna and Oshna were given their own separate buildings.There was an army building and a navy building. There was a building for when the two met. All the buildings were different but each carried a similar architectural theme.

Beautiful artwork and landscaping decorated the space between the buildings and the buildings themselves. Most of all, there was plenty of space left vacant between and around the buildings, just in case some other building needed built. Looking at the governing buildings of Libertyless city was spectacular. Of course, the taxpayers paid for these buildings but we're only allowed to visit portions of some and none of many others.

Susie made sure her building was the largest and most spectacular. It was pure bright white from top to bottom. The window frames, doors and roof were layered in thin gold leaf. Pure silver art decorations hung on the buildings spacious walls between the Windows and doors which were solid copper.

After Susie moved her whole administration, all the old town government buildings were torn down. All the salvageable material from the buildings that could be used in other projects, was hauled to the dump and was there buried. Johnny inwardly thought of the beautiful wagon he could build with some of the destroyed buildings. He even asked if he could salvage some materials, but was denied because this here material was government material not meant for the public even though it was bought by the public.

New parks and new roads were built where the old buildings once were. With the new park and new roads came new legislation to help govern the heavy traffic. The left hand extends straight left before turning left. The left hand extends up at a 90 degree right angle before turning right. Stop signs were placed randomly on all major roadways and sporadically on roads perpendicular to those roads. The following day over one thousand horseplay traffic tickets were issued by Jaerk and his police force. Many complained that the regulatory signs were never in place before, but their complaining found only deaf ears.

Johnny found himself headed home very late one evening after spending time with Peggy. The town was asleep, the streets were vacant. The only life Johnny heard was a hooting owl somewhere in the distance and the click of his horse's hoofs. Johnny made a left, then a right. He then proceeded to slow down as he passed through three stop signs. At the end of town, Jaerk rode through three different stop signs in pursuit of Johnny, he was waving a reflective red and a reflective blue strips of leather, compliments of the Neon Twins.

Jaerk happily greeted, "Howdy Partner." Johnny angrily asked, "What?" Jaerk said, "Failed to use your signal hand twice and you did not stop at two stop signs." Johnny asked, "Who am I signaling to? The streets are empty." Jaerk responded, "Law is the law. No need to ever break it son." "Even you didn't see me run a third stop sign." Johnny argued. Jaerk smiled, "Thank for bringing that to my attention." Jaerk then gave Johnny five traffic violations. Johnny pleaded, "You ran three stop signs in pursuit of me." Jaerk was annoyed, "We've discussed this. We are here to serve and protect you. Please pay the fines within thirty days." Jaerk rode away. Johnny thought. *"What a dickhead, doesn't that man ever sleep?"*

Later that month Susie sat alongside her newly delegated figureheads. There was a financial advisor, a head of city security, a head of commerce, an animal and plant advisor, a Corp of Engineer representative, the Chief of Police, a Census Bureau rep, Food Safety Nutrition Analysis rep, a Flood Emergency rep, and literally hundreds more, even a weather service counsel. Susie was a big believer in big government, and she now had the basis for governing every aspect of any citizen's life.

Charles started the meeting, "The issue today is crime. With all the new citizens of Libertyless, crime has drastically risen." Debate launched out and at the end of the discussion, Susie concluded that there were two types of crime. Any crime against her was considered BIG crime. Most crimes against the ordinary people would be considered small crime. After the crimes were divided, debate again launched about what should be done with the criminals.   In times past, the housing for a criminal was jail, there the offender was locked away accomplishing nothing other than serving time. But these were new times with new thoughts. The consensus was that while the criminals were being housed, their mental thinking should be changed. "We are going to change the way a criminal thinks" Susie had said, forgetting that she had removed moral teaching from the schools. So began another debate whether this could actually be done and if so, how. The end result was that the BIG crime offenders would be housed separately from the small crime offenders. The former would be treated spectacularly, conditioning them positively to change their stinking thinking. The latter would be treated harshly, conditioning them negatively into changing their criminal thinking. Eventually the two penal systems were named, Former

Philosophy Structure (FPS) and Systematic Public Safety (SPS).

So two of the vacant buildings on Red's past land were put to use. The FPS building was quickly staffed and the team set out stating standards that they would like to see set at their penal facility that would be built far far away. "A humans rights should be protected at all times" no one in particular said. It was therefore agreed that even though a felon had committed BIG crime, he should retain his rights. Susie's FPS prison was constructed many miles outside of town with protecting the inmates rights used as the foundational cornerstone.

The SPS penal system building was also manned. The officials of this building also thought that rights of law violators should be protected. This prison was built many miles outside the other side of town. The two prisons wanted complete animosity between one another.

Susie once again sat down with the leaders of each to discuss which law breakers would reside in which prison. Susie loved her money. Susie loved making money with her money making machine. Since Susie was a great money maker, only she could manufacture money. Anyone else who made money committed BIG crime and would be sent to FPS prison. Susie however could manufacture as much money as she wanted under no penalty of the law. Moreover, anyone who did not pay their taxes should be sent to the FPS system as well.

Susie also loved her privacy and protecting the privacy of others. However, if a threat to her might exist, then prying into an individual's privacy was tolerated. To open another's personal mail would be considered BIG crime. If an individual murdered or raped another, that would be small crime.

The distinction between BIG and small crime continued and after the facilities were built, both sat empty awaiting their first guests.

Earl was on his way to visit Jimmy and Gusto where the two had started breeding horses. Earl was an older man who operated Big Cutter at the saw mill at the dam site. With years of hard drinking behind him, Earl had few remaining years left.

Rudy and Bobby were out joy riding when they happened upon Earl and the two immediately set out teasing the older man. Then Bobby pushed Earl off his horse. Rudy quickly grabbed Earl's horse and the boys rode off.

It took Earl six hours to walk to the ranch of Jimmy and Gusto. With only whisky in his canteen to drink, Earl was nearly dead when Jimmy and Gusto rescued him. This was the second time the two had saved his life and Earl was very grateful.

The following day Earl retold his story to Jimmy and Gusto who talked of it with Red and Johnny. Johnny and Red quickly identified the boys and the five set out to the home of Bobby and Rudy. When Earl confirmed that Rudy and Bobby were the ones who had stolen his horse, and when Jimmy found Earl's horse in the back yard, the boys were grabbed and noosed to the closest tree. They sat the boys on Earl's horse and noosed their necks using Futureano's big oak tree that grew in his front yard. Rudy sat straight and proud on the horse, he inwardly didn't believe anyone would hang him today. Bobby was extremely scared and tried bobbing his head, but the noose wouldn't allow his head to move. The nervous energy, having nowhere to release itself, grew inside Bobby and when Red started tugging on the horses bit,

Bobby felt his noose tighten and wet his trousers.

Futureano came running to the scene yelling "STOP! STOP!"

Red said, "Your boys are horse thieves, round here we hang em for that."

Futureano said, "Round here? You mean my front yard?"

Gusto stated, "Was the closest hanging tree."

Futureano said, "These are just boys, you have no right..."

Red interrupted and said, "Done it all the time before you showed up. Never had any horse thieving either."

Futureano said, "This is not your town anymore to do as you up and think you ought to do. "

Johnny said, "My parents were original settlers here. They helped establish this town, this is mine and their town."

Futureano said while raising his hands, "Maybe so, but majority vote left in our hands to govern this town. You gave up you're right to govern to people like me."

Jaerk came up and Futureano had the five placed in custody for attempted murder while he untied his boys. The five sat in jail for four days awaiting a hearing. At court, Earl, Jimmy, Gusto, Red and Johnny each explained what had transpired over the last day. Bobby and Rudy were released with two days probation because they were minors. Due to the fact that this was attempted murder, it was deemed a small crime and the five found themselves the first guests at the SPS penal facility.

Peggy, Johnny's girlfriend, Regina, Gusto's wife, Sue, Red's wife, and Tammy, Jimmy's wife, found themselves discussing over tea how best to free their loved ones. They all concluded that information from the higher powers was needed. The following day Peggy asked the Neon Twins to join them, which they gladly did. Peggy asked the florescent blue dressed Neon One, "We need some information from some men, and how would we start?" Fluorescent purple dressed Neon Two laughed and said, "Oh, that's easy. We thought you wanted something else." Neon One laughed and agreed saying "Yea, we thought you wanted help in the bedroom." The two laughed together and then studied the four girls. Sue and Tammy they guessed were very old, at least twenty-four, they thought. They had lived hard lives and were a little on the heavy side, so the twins focused on Regina and Peggy. They studied their bodies and ran their hands through their hair. Finally Neon One said, "We can work with you two." They grabbed Regina and Peggy, dragging them to their apartment. There the two native Libertyless girls began their training in man espionage.

Neon One, the blonde one, asked, "What type of information are you wanting?" Regina simply said, "We need Charles to spill his guts." Neon 2, the brunette, whistled and said, "Difficult, but achievable." Peggy and Regina listened to the Neon Twins as they lectured on a man's weakness. Many times Peggy and Regina were bright red with embarrassment, but the twins never noticed. They continued talking and rearranging Peggy and Regina's hair.

When the twins asked Regina and Peggy to strip, the two natives nearly cried and held tight to their many layers of dress. Neon Two said, "Oh quit, you two have striking figures and for the information you seek, you're gonna have to use every ounce of lady charm you have." Neon One agreed. Regina and Peggy, for the love of Gusto and Johnny, let the twins dress them.

Regina walked down the stairs in a short, very very short, bright red dress, her face was the color of that dress. Regina's raven hair was curled and wavy, half of her black wavy hair covered half her face, the rest flowed down her body. She could barely see and she walked funny. Regina looked down and saw the top half of her bosom and her face turned a darker red than the dress. Peggy couldn't stop laughing at Regina as she followed her down the stairs of the Neon Twins' apartment. Peggy too was as red as an Indian. Her golden blonde hair was curled and it flowed over her body as Regina's hair did. Her very bright blue dress was every bit as short as Regina's and it was difficult walking in these very weird shoes that made her six inches taller than she normally was. Peggy looked at her bosom and turned as red as a sun burned apache. She noticed her bodies every detail was fitting to the dress. Peggy cried and said to Regina, "I can't do this." Regina turned and hugged Peggy, calming her down. She dramatically said as she covered her heart with her hands, "For the love of our loved ones, we will do this. It is only one day, we can do anything once for one day." The two walked outside and ignored the whistles of men as they crawled into the coach Sue had waiting for them. Tammy innocently looked at Regina and Peggy and briefly saw their bikini French under garments. Tammy said, "I thought one set of Neon Twins in this town was enough." Peggy pushed her hand over Tammy's mouth and harshly said, "Shut up".

They rode to Red's old ranch, they stopped and asked a security guard for directions to Charlotte's office. The guard stated, "No-one sees Charles." Regina bent out the back window exposing part of her cleavage and asked, "Even me?" Most of her

cleavage was exposed to the guard, and the guard looked at
Regina's bosom, then her sexy face. He coughed and said, "It's the
18th building on the left, the 2nd biggest building you'll see."
Peggy started sweating as they rode to Charles's building. She
followed Regina into the huge white bricked building. The doors
swung closed very slowly, as if once locked, they could not be
unlocked. The two were met by 5 security guards pointing rifles at
them, adding to their fear. Peggy's sweat increased and her dress
started becoming transparent. She yelled, "Charles wants to see
us now." The guards looked at Peggy and Regina, then they
lowered their rifles and a security guard led them up six flights of
stairs to Charles's office where he, the scared guard, knocked
lightly on the door.

Charles was looking across the road at Susie's office. He
wondered why he was looking up and not down. His mind flashed
back to that night he and Susie had explored each other's bodies,
his sister was a looker. Charles was sweating as he was thinking
about his sister, he despised her yet loved her. He loathed her yet
respected her. He wanted to hit her and hold her. He yelled at
the knock at his door, "WHAT!" Charles didn't wait for a
response, he stomped to the door and swung it opened, prepared
to fire whoever was disturbing him. The guard having knocked,
hid behind Regina and Peggy.

Charles was sweating and fuming. His eyes fixed on Peggy's
bright red face then traveled down her body, pausing and taking
in her every detail. He sweated more. Regina pushed herself
between Peggy and Charles and kindly asked, "Can we enter in?"
Charles stammered at Regina's dark brown eye glaring into his
face. He stepped back, allowing them in, "Certainly ladies."
Regina and Peggy marched into Charles's office just as the Neon

Twins had taught them. Regina walked to Charles's desk and sat, plopping her legs up onto his desk. Charles was upset that someone else was sitting on his chair with their legs on his desk, but he took in the sight and ignored his building anger, trading it for more perspiration.

Peggy grabbed Charles from behind, just as she had been taught by the twins, and said, "We want to know how to free the men at FPS." Charles broke free of Peggy's grip and pointed at the door, "Get out." The twins had warned of this. Regina got off of Charles's chair and said, "Fine." She and Peggy started strutting away, just as the twins had taught. Charles watched them leaving and yelled, "WAIT." Regina and Peggy smiled at each other knowing it was only a matter of time and persuasion before they had the information they needed.

The two sat Charles at his desk and interrogated him as they stood this way and that. The girls would bend and move in ways seductive to a man, just as the Neon Twins had taught. Charles was more concerned with watching the show then he was about the answers he was spilling to the girls. When Peggy and Regina had all the information they needed, they left, leaving Charles drenched in his own sweat soaked clothes. Charles wondered if he was really in love or was it infatuation? He decided he loved Peggy, Regina and his sister Susie.

Peggy, Regina, Sue and Tammy met and talked over tea. Tammy looked at Regina's plain plaid shirt and her long skirt and said, "I rather think the attire of the Neon Twins is quite flattering. I do hope you wear that red dress to church on Sunday." Regina gave Tammy a snarl and the four discussed what they knew. The bottom line was a considerable amount of money needed to be given to the warden, the judge, and Futureano to free their loved ones. The four tallied their net worth and concluded if they sold everything, they would have 1/100th of the sum needed to free their loved ones. Regina stated, "Gusto designed and built Susie's money making building. If we could smash in there, we could make us money we need like Susie always does." The four giggled and gawked at the insanity of it and made their way to Regina's house in search of Guess' plans to Susie's money making building. They passed Charles giving a speech to a large gathering in front of the old school. They stopped and listened to Charles's say,

"This school is the last representation of who we once were. We were a dead little town with no possibility of a brighter future. Now we have a great future because great change has come to this great city. Today we destroy the last of what once was, never again shall we be reminded of the harsh times we walked." Charles lit a stick of dynamite and threw it into a broken school glass. A few seconds later the school exploded and fell. The crowd cheered. Regina could not stop gazing at Charlotte as she was continuously wiping tears from her beautiful eyes.

The following day the four women were allowed visitation to the five men. They all immediately excluded Earl from their plans because they were unsure of Earl's loose lips. So the eight planned and schemed and planned some more. Finally a practically fool proof plan was established to break in and make the money needed to free the incarcerated men.

Gusto was sickened at his meticulousness. Every detail of the money making housing was built to perfection. The security was designed and then built over specifications. The team learned that the only reasonable way in to the building was through the piping that let the city's waste out. Yes, the women were going to take a trip up the sewer system. Gusto had given Regina instructions on building masks that would filter out the methane waste gasses. Regina, the ever improving one of Gusto's ideas, doubled the contents of the special plant used in lining the masks; however, she conveniently forgot to share this with anyone.

The women found the sewer pipe with little difficulty. They then drilled a hole through the wooden pipe and widened the hole with a saw. The four donned their seal skin suits and masks. One by one they entered the sewage pipe, then one by one they exited, gagged, threw up, put their masks back on and entered back in. They used for light two chemicals combined together in glass containers.

At the sewage Y that Gusto had told them to go to, the four turned and counted their crawls to fifty four. Here they stopped, drilled and cut a hole in the pipe, and tunneled upwards. After three hours they had cleared the dirt beneath the floor planking of Susie's special money making house.

The women were happy and giggly, the chemical used in filtering the gasses, when taken in excessive amounts, would aid the brains responses to happiness and giddiness. When the four saw 4 money making machines, they were quadrupily happy and giddy, for they had believed only 1 money making machine existed. Each grabbed a handle of a money making machine and cranked for thirty minutes. They then calculated they had enough money to buy the freedom of their men.

After sealing the money in sealskins, they dropped the money into the sewer, as some women often do. They themselves dropped back down into the sewage pipe and slid back in place the flooring of the money making room from underneath. They wedged it tight, then entered the sewer pipe. Then they placed a layer of seal skin over the pipe opening from underneath. Each then broke an egg filled with other chemicals onto the sealskin from a lifted corner. When the chemicals combined, they would create a gel that expanded 180 times its original size. "Hopefully" Gusto had said, "This will seal the opening and prevent any sewer gasses from rising into the money making machine room." The four then wedged back in place the wooden pipe opening as best they could. All this took the four women four times as long as Gusto had calculated. By the time the women had exited the sewer pipe with the money, they had breathed twenty times more chemical then they were supposed to. Consequently, by the time the women were on their way home, they were in no condition to be doing anything other than sitting at home Facelooking one another.

It was three am when they passed through town. They failed to signal their turns and failed to stop at the regulatory signs. What Jaerk did at this ungodly hour no one knows, but he had sighted the infractions and stopped the women while waving his red and blue strips of leather. As he was writing the citations, the overly giddy brain of Red's wife Sue, said, "You sure know how to spoil a woman's fun". Regina had to chime in, "Yes, no one home to play with you? So you take it out on any pretty ladies you feel like?" Tammy, who by nature was already a wild lady, said, "Jaerk, I think you like kissing other men and that's why you don't have any lady friends." Having struck a true nerve in Jaerk's body, Jaerk deemed them all overly inebriated and searched their wagon and bags. Upon finding stacks of newly printed money, Jaerk hauled them all to jail, he had never before seen so many joyfully walk into the police holding cell.

Having heard that her money machines were handled by

someone other than she had authorized, Susie immediately set the four in a courtroom. The trial took all but ten minutes and the four women soon found themselves being the first guests at the FPS penitentiary.

18 - **Uh OH**

Futureano had the Bible removed from the school's teaching curriculum. After that, it took a full day before the children's moral behavior rapidly declined. Charlotte, having her old school blown up by Charles, was now teaching at one of his new and improved schools.   She continuously saw the girls wearing shorter and shorter skirts and she was more amazed at seeing the young girls wear shorts that did not even cover their buttocks. Charlotte herself could not withstand not looking at the writing on these girls' shorts, "PINK," WATCH," "Stare at my ASS." The Neon Twins were in glamour heaven and soon the majority of the girls were counseling with the Twins on how to dress to attract a man's eye. Charlotte's eyes were a color they had never been, she was very confused.

The boys could not resist the arousing apple the girls were now advertising. They would stare up the girl's thighs and down the girl's cleavage. Charlotte could not get the boy's attention no matter what she tried.   When a boy stood staring at a girl's breast, the girl being gazed upon would laughingly say, "Excuse me, my eyes are up here" as she pointed two fingers to her eyes. Consequently, most of the children's conscience was not on learning, it was solely focused on teasing and flirting. Kaley, one of the few remaining students with any scruples about modesty remaining, found herself sitting beside Charlotte watching the youngsters sexually flirt one with another.

Kaley asked Charlotte, "Have these girls any shame?"

Charlotte replied, "I'm sure they do, but somewhere it's been lost".

Kaley gazed at a classmate wearing bright red shorts that had "Party Girl" written on the back and said, "I could never dress like that. I would be too embarrassed."

Charlotte thought and said, "I don't think it's a matter of being embarrassed as much as it's a matter of not wanting to advertise your private goods."

Just then a boy named Kevin came up and grabbed at a girl's red shorts. Having never been grabbed there before, the girl turned around and slapped Kevin. Kevin, stunned, said, "Sorry, I couldn't resist." She turned around while inwardly smiling that Kevin had taken notice of her.

Kaley said, "If he grabbed me like that, I would of kicked him hard as I could between his legs."

Charlotte said, "Exactly. But he would never grab you like that because you present yourself as being respectable."

Kevin was a handsome young man. Normally he was kind, polite, and good humored. Kevin worked hard at his father's farm and consequently had excellent muscle tone. Kaley had an unannounced crush on him and temporarily thought. "I wish he would grab me."

Charlotte asked, "What?" Kaley stunned, asked, "What?"

Charlotte stated, "You wish Kevin would grab you like that?"

Kaley turned red, she had truly spoken aloud her thought. She embarrassingly said, "I didn't mean to speak that aloud."

Charlotte reached over and gave Kaley a caring, "I love you," parental hug.

Kaley was the daughter that every father wanted. She was sweet, kind, caring, responsible and respectful. She was the oldest in a rather large family and at a young age was given motherly duties. Kaley never complained and kept a reasonably good attitude. Sometimes she would silently find herself vowing never to put her children in a similar situation as she had grown up in. Kaley was also very beautiful with sandy red hair, blue green eyes, and a voluptuous body. With her flamboyant character, her disciplined attitude concerning her feelings, and her looks, any young man would have gladly courted and married her.

Charlotte released Kaley and said, "Kaley, you know I love you and many times I have dreamt of you being my daughter." Charlotte laughed a little and continued. "I didn't know you had feelings for Kevin."

Kaley was happy to be sharing her feelings, "I don't want to, he makes me so mad when he pulls my hair. But my heart flutters every time I think of him."

Charlotte laughed some more and said, "Kaley, you do not have to dress and behave like these girls to get Kevin's attention. Kevin learned from Johnny that pulling a girls hair is the simplest way for them to say, 'I like you.'"

Kaley said as she rolled her eyes, "That's pretty stupid. Why doesn't he just tell me?"

Charlotte replied. "Men talk and think differently from women."

Kaley was confused, "Well I don't understand them."

Charlotte said, "Me either, I'm sure someday a man from Mars and a woman from Venus will explain it all to us." Kaley looked at Charlotte with an odd expression, but Charlotte ignored the look and the two continued talking. Kevin walked by the two and pulled Kaley's hair. Kaley turned as red as her hair asked, "Where is Peggy? She should be here helping sort and straighten out this screwed up mess." Kevin smiled at Kaley. She, still being mad at Kevin for pulling her hair, yelled to him, "Go away." Kevin sadly left, he wondered where Johnny was, he sure could use his friends advice right now.

Peggy at that time was sitting inside the FPS for having been caught being part of a team manufacturing money on Susie's money making machine. Susie was getting ready to eat her morning brunch. Peggy, having eaten steak and eggs for breakfast, doubted she could eat another bite, but she figured she needed her energy for today's activities.

Peggy had immaculate teeth. Since FPS wanted its inmates to be humanly treated, Peggy was scheduled for a 10:30 am teeth cleaning and checkup. At 11:00 she had Biology 101. At 12:00 was lunch. Since her options in correcting her thinking was to either be a doctor, Lawyer, accountant, or actor, Peggy had a 1:30 PM drama class. Peggy then was to meet up with her other three friends at 4:00 for their health and Beauty spa session. She was thinking life in the FPS prison was not so bad.

Regina, who was determined to be too old to be able to benefit society with a profession, was in a debate with a quilting instructor over point setting. Years later Regina would sue FPS over age discrimination and would be awarded a large sum of money.

Tammy, who had refused any mind changing tricks of FPS, was happily enjoying the melodrama brought in by Susie at the taxpayers' expense. Tammy could not wait to tell her three friends what had happened when they met for Health and Beauty. Naturally the three friends would be upset because the melodrama was their evening's entertainment.

Sue was busy talking to the warden about getting conjugal rights. Through letters of correspondence to Charlotte and others, it was not long before life inside FPS was known throughout Libertyless.

Kaley's sister, Kaleidoscope, from the age of three was always in trouble. But she was so cute and adorable that she never got punished. Having red hair the color of Charlotte, hazel eyes, and a big pouty lip, Kaleidescope learned to get her way very easily. She was as skinny as a fence post but ate like an elephant, had dropped out of school at an early age and was now living a hard life on the streets. When Kaleidoscope learned from her sister Kaley the lifestyle inside FPS, Kaleidascope decided she wanted to live there until she could get her life together. Kaleidoscope, sitting alone on the street eating out of the bakeries trash, decided to break into FPS.

It took a month of preparation before Kaleidoscope was ready to start her new lifestyle inside FPS. First she had made a suit identical to the ones worn by the women on the inside. She put this on. Then she put over that a full body suit painted to match the outside of the FPS housing. She then calmly started crawling towards the buildings. When she saw a guard, she stopped until the guard was out of sight. When she came to a fence, she simply crawled under it.

Little by little Kaleidoscope closed the distance to the buildings. When she was alongside one of the buildings, she stood up and slowly moved to the side towards a door she had seen. When she saw a guard, she stopped and waited until he was long past. She opened the door and saw that it was a warehouse. She made her way to the next building.

When she opened that door, there stood two guards. Upon seeing Kaleidoscope they took off running to catch her. Kaleidescope took off running as though she was trying to escape. When she saw she was out running the guards, she slowed down and let them tackle her. She screamed and hollered all the way to her cell and once inside, she thought *"That was easy."*

The following day none of Kaleidoscope papers could be found. The office assistants kept this quiet lest they be found inefficient at their job. That morning Kaleidoscope found herself eating better then she had in years. By that evening, Kaleidoscope was living better than she ever had before.

When Regina, Peggy, Sue and Tammy saw Kaleidoscope they greeted her with a friendly hug. When asked, "What are you doing inside FPS?" Kaleidoscope smiled and said, "Enjoying living off the tax dollars of the citizens."

Charlotte's class continued being more and more unruly. Discipline was no longer an option per Futureano's zero tolerance laws. A teacher was not allowed to touch a student under any circumstances. A teacher was not allowed to discipline a student in any way. Charlotte was at a loss as to how to take back control of her classroom.

A new foreign exchange student was admitted whose name was Osama Bin BlowUup. Easter was approaching and because of Osama's belief, none of the students or faculty members could celebrate Easter, or any other holiday. Kaley and Charlotte often questioned each other as to why the belief of one controlled the many? Kaley asked Charlotte during lunch, "Why can't we celebrate Easter?" Charlotte answered, "Easter is supposedly a Christian holiday. Osama feels Christianity is being forced upon him. Since we can't force our religion on anyone, we can't celebrate Easter." Kaley was confused, she said, "It's a free country, we should be able to celebrate whatever holiday we want". Charlotte stated, "It used to be a free country, now we have laws keeping us from being free." Kaley said, "I think the majority should rule. If the majority of us want to celebrate Easter, we should. Screw the beliefs of Osama BlowUup". Charlotte replied, "Legally I can't agree with you, but my heart and mind stand behind you 110 percent.

19 - **Pay Back**

Life for Gusto, Red, Johnny, Jimmy and Earl was not as luxurious as it was for their women locked away at FPS. The warden at SPS was old school and believed crime deserved punishment. It mattered not to the warden if you might be innocent or were guilty, if you were in his prison, you served hard labor. Thus, the five found themselves waking up before dawn and eating a piece of bread and butter for breakfast, then they would go break rocks for no apparent reason. At lunch they were served green slop that Johnny swore actually moved. Then they would break more rocks for the remainder of the day.

Those that behaved well were sometimes rewarded by being taken to FPS where they would set up pins and retrieve bowling balls for those bowling at FPS, but those times were few and the warden had his favorites that were always sent to set up bowling pins at FPS. None of the five were any of the warden's favorites.

There was also much fighting between the inmates at SPS. Red and Jimmy were too big to ever offend, but Johnny, Gusto and Earl often found themselves going to bed with bruised ribs and black eyes, life inside SPS stunk.

Susie was happy, things were ahead of her masterminded schedule. She hadn't taken a real days rest since she walked off that ship, she was tired and wanted a break. She remembered that none of this would ever have happened without Futureano's lovely letter, so she had her helpers track him down.

The two went out joyriding on their horses looking at land far away from Libertyless and dreaming of what they would someday be doing with that land. Futureano was very uncomfortable riding a horse, but having time with the great Susie Powers was worth the agony. They had ridden for 3 hours when a tribe of Apache Indians found their trail and hunted them down. Sensing that the innards of these two would contaminate the Apache lifestyle, the Apaches did nothing more than tie the two up beside an ant pile. They took the two fine horses of Futureano and Susie and then rode away, except for a young Apache who stayed behind to watch the show.

Getting bored that the ants were not making any progress past Futureano and Susie's feet, the young Apache stuck some pine leaves in various parts of their exposed bodies and lit them on fire. The Apache then hurried off to join his tribe.

Futureano and Susie struggled for hours and more furiously as the ants neared their privates and faces. When an ant bit Futureano where the sun doesn't shine, he screamed. This screaming was heard by Charlotte and Kaley who themselves were out joyriding a few minutes from town. Charlotte and Kaley galloped to the horrendous noise and saw their town leaders stripped naked and staked to the ground by an ant pile, the two broke out in gut wrenching laughter.

Susie looked up and saw the two and said, "Thank God. We are rescued." Kaley immediately stepped down from her horse to free Futureano and Susie when Charlotte said, "Stop Kaley. Why should we free them? They've done nothing but bring misery to our way of life." Kaley thought and responded saying, "We can't just leave them, we're not that inhumane." Charlotte spoke her thoughts, "Maybe not, but they can free our friends." Kaley spoke,

"That's a wonderful idea." Futureano angered, "Like hell we will, free us now or you'll join your friends." Charlotte looked at Futureano, ants looked like they were trying to make a new home on his big belly. His head was covered in stray ants and his hair he used to comb over his bald head was lying flat on the ground. Charlotte happened to glance at his shrunken organ and broke out laughing again. Futureano saw Charlotte's eyes looking at him and he started crying, he still had a strong crush on this red head beauty. Charlotte said to Kaley, "Come on Kaley, we're out of here. Can't help those who want something for nothing."

The two mounted their horses and slowly started riding away, Susie looked at Futureano scowled, "You blubbering idiot, if those two leave, we shall die." Then she pleaded to Charlotte, "We will do whatever you ask, please free us." Charlotte turned around and approached, then said, "We want full pardons for Regina, Sue, Peggy, Tammy, Jimmy, Red, Johnny, Gusto, and Earl."

Futureano screamed, "That's bull crap, they tried hanging my boys." Charlotte and Kaley turned, mounted their horses, and again started riding off. Susie said, "Shut up Futureano." Susie yelled to Kaley and Charlotte, "We will give your friends their pardons." Charlotte returned and said, "We want it in writing, I can't trust you or your companion." Susie said, "Fine, when we get back to town I'll have it written up." Charlotte her head, "No, I want it before you are freed. Kaley, go to town and bring back some ink and paper."

Kaley rode off and Charlotte enjoyed the show with the ants like the young apache had. Susie and Futureano were wiggling, screaming, and crying. Charlotte inwardly wished she had some of Red's chew to play ant war. Kaley returned fifteen minutes later and the documents were written and signed, then Charlotte had Kaley untie the two.

Futureano and Susie danced around naked a while brushing ants away from all areas of their bodies. They then asked Charlotte for some water and food but Charlotte simply said, "You're on your own." The two smiled as they rode back to town thinking of the misery their city's leaders were in.

Futureano and Susie found themselves wandering the wooded mountains naked. By now they were totally disoriented and thought they should surely die, both wishing they hadn't ridden hours away from town, neither thought to wonder how Kaley returned with pen and paper so quickly. Futureano looked at his bloody feet, then at Susie and said, "I wish we had a horse." Susie sighed, "I think we should die without a horse." Futureano adamantly said, "Horse thieves should be hung." Susie called her nephew on the irony, "That's funny, coming from you who freed your two horse thieves and imprisoned the ones doing the hanging." Futureano responded, "That's a totally different circumstance." Susie calmly asked, "Is it?" Futureano was quiet.

The two wandered naked hours more, it was near dusk, they found their way to the top of a hilltop. Upon looking down, they saw that they were only minutes away from the outskirts of Libertyless. Their bodies were bruised and covered in ant bites, their feet had deep cuts, they were a sore sight.

20 - **The Outraged**

Susie and Futureano snuck into town, they found some clothes hanging out to dry, and permanently borrowed them to cover themselves, figuring taking someone else's belongings was alright if it protected and allowed higher officials to continue their governing. Large red swellings spotted their bodies where the ants had bitten them. Futureano tried covering his red swollen bald head with his long remaining hairs, which were full of twigs and debris, it made his face look like it was decorated for a Halloween party. Susie's smooth white skin was riddled in red bumps, her skinny long perfect face was swollen and red, and her golden blonde silk hair was brown and grungy.

They immediately made their way to Doc Dogooder who broke out in laughter having heard their story, Susie and Futureano could not see the humor. The doc cleaned them up and put bread and milk over their ant wounds, the two took a week off to heal. The following day after recovery, as they sat at the Libertyless governing conference table, the first topic of business was writing a near miss report, since the two had taken a week off of work, the near miss report soon turned into a Lost Time Accident report.

The report was lengthy, it covered why the accident occurred, then it covered every conceivable way to avoid this accident in the future. The conclusion of the report was that when any important official traveled, they could only do so while being escorted with a small army of heavily armed men.

Charles asked, "How shall we explain to the people that we should be protected with firearms, yet we do not want them carrying or firing firearms?

Futureano said, "The people will understand that we are important and need guns protecting us. Their protection and safety is insignificant."

Susie silently reflected back to when she had first arrived in "LIBERTY TOWN," the day she walked down that dock, how Futureano had asked her to come help protect the citizens. So far she was proud of herself, she believed she was progressing well in developing organizations that the Founding Fathers of this New Nation would be proud of because the people were daily becoming more protected. She then thought of the 2nd Amendment, *the right of the people to keep and bear arms.*

Susie said, "We cannot take the people's guns away from them and yet use them for our own protection. They have a right to bear arms. However, that does not mean that people can use their guns."

Charles said, "We're getting various poll results from the people. Those that appreciate us feeding, clothing, providing medical services and giving them messengers to communicate with each other, are happy with our administration. The ones that are paying for all those services by taking their money through taxes, strongly disagree with our governing." Then Charles asked, "What if those that do not like us use their guns on us?"

Susie then reflected to what Thomas Jefferson argued. "*When governments fear the people, there is liberty. When the people fear the government, there is tyranny. The strongest reason for the people to retain the right to keep and bear arms is, as a last resort, to protect themselves against tyranny in government."*

They all pondered Charles thought for a while, Susie herself had heard talk of her being too big for her britches. Just over 75 years ago the people showed their resolution in the Revolution. Susie feared, rightfully so, that the conditions for the revolution were very similar today. She needed to think and said, "We will meet again to discuss this. As for now, all people in position of authority will carry guns and be escorted by a security detail armed with guns." The group adjourned.

Later that week Susie and Charles were playing ROFL. It was a game where they would hit a white little ball with various sticks into a hole far away. It was named ROFL because every time Charles would strike the ball, it would fly off sideways and Susie would find herself rolling on the floor laughing.

Susie hit the ball and asked Charles, "Are the people really that upset with us?"

Charles answered, "The ones that we give things to, love us. The others, yes, they are very unhappy."

Susie said as they leisurely walked towards their little white balls, "I do not understand, we have made them safe."

Charles said, "Yes, but every time we invoke a law of safety, a little more of their freedom is taken away."

Susie swung and turned to Charles's asking, "When did you get so smart?" Charles inwardly smiled, he had said words that had made his sister proud of him. He figured he was on the right track to freeing himself from her control.

Bill Money

Bill Money was on a two week vacation at the Bahamas, he was sickened every time he would see one of Susie's representatives. Nine out of ten times they wanted more of his money to pay for the needs of those less fortunate then himself. Fortunately, Bill had learned to hide most of his money so Susie and her minions could not collect nearly as much. What sickened Bill further, was all the money Susie wanted in taxes, Bill was paying nearly fifty percent of his earnings directly to Susie. If Bill had not learned to hide his money, Bill himself would now be needing Susie's handouts.

Taxes were to be paid in full by April 15th, Bill's vacation was not scheduled to return to Libertyless until April 16th. When Bill arrived home, there was an official looking letter awaiting him, it simply stated that Bill now owed Susie four times more in taxes because of penalties and interest on taxes unpaid.

Bill was furious and went to the building on Red's former land that had the sign reading "Donations To Your Town." It read "Donations" because income taxes in reality would not be briefly imposed until 10 years later during the civil war and permanently 60 some years in the future in 1913, currently taxes were considered donations. Bill silently choked and thought, "*Donations my ass, that's bull crap.*" Bill entered and found the appropriate representative to discuss this ungodly amount he now owed.

"We're sorry sir," the representative had said, "but you are late in paying your donations. If we excuse you, we have to excuse everyone."

Bill said, "The penalties and interest are insane."

The representative said, "We just want to encourage everyone to pay what is owed, on time."

Bill said, "I'm just one day late."

The representatishoshone his head, "Does not matter, Susie needs her money on time."

Bill angrily paid his donation and the penalties and the interest. Later on, the money counters of Susie would wonder where Bill so quickly came up with that much money. They would send more representatives, hired and paid for with Bills money, to find out where Bill hid his stash of cash. Susie had made it clear that "Not one Buffalo Nickel owed me shall be left uncollected,"

Bill went home and hired his own money counters with intent of finding more ways of hiding his money and more ways to pay Susie less. After a week of continuous working, they had calculated that Bill overpaid Susie a considerable sum, a deduction Bill could have claimed for ecofriendly wheel research had not been claimed.

Bill submitted the proper paperwork for his refund and after a week went by, Bill went back to Susie's donation building and asked where his refund money was. The representative said, "Well sir, we will get to it as soon as we can."

Bill said, "I will have to charge you penalties and interest as you have done to me."

Susie's money counter said, "Sorry sir, but it does not work that way. You cannot charge us penalties and interest on money we owe you."

Bill was confused, "I don't understand, I'm one day late and I get charged a huge sum in penalties and interest. Your seven days late in refunding my money and I get no compensation for your delay?"

Susie's Representative said, "Sir, we must wait at least thirty days before processing any returns. We need that time to collect interest."

Bill asked, "Let me see if I got this right. The way I see it, Susie needs lots of money. She doesn't earn her own money, so she takes the money she needs from people like me. She can use that money to make interest money and therefore she holds onto any money over collected. It sounds like Susie really does not care for the good of the people, only what is good for her."

The representative sadly said, "I'm sorry you look at Susie that way, and you are wrong. Susie does make her own money." Bill thought, "*WHAT? Susie makes her own money? Since when?* "

Bill left outraged. The days passed and he would continuously check in on the progress of his refund. Each time the representative would tell Bill, "I'm sorry sir, we are processing your refund as fast as we can." Three months would pass before Bill received his money back from Susie with absolutely no penalties or interest.

Red

Red had built his house on a delta, and where his house was erected, water had not rested there for over a thousand years. Red's house sat at least fifty feet higher than the land Susie had basically confiscated and built her buildings.

Red had been pardoned from prison and was entering his

door when a letter dropped down that had been slid between the frame and Reds door. He opened the letter and read that since his house resided in a flood zone, and since his house had a mortgage, Red was required to pay flood insurance. Red thought that it was literally impossible for his house to ever flood and discarded the letter. He was happy to be home and did not want to deal with junk mail, *"freedom is better than prison"* he thought.

Red made his next mortgage payment and a day later while riding his horse in town, his banker stopped him telling Red that more money was owed. Red was confused, "Why?"

The banker then told Red that additional money was required to pay for flood insurance. Red, getting perturbed, said, "I do not need nor want flood insurance."

The banker replied, "It's not up to you to decide. The government determines the flood zones and your house resides inside a flood zone.

Red said, "I built this house with flooding in mind. I built it far from where any flood water will ever be. I say again, I do not need nor want flood insurance."

The banker said, "Since you did not buy your own flood insurance, we were required to purchase it for you. The cost of your mortgage has been increased. Moreover, you owe for the flood insurance you have not had since the mortgage on your home began."

Red madly asked, "What?"

The banker answered. "Since your house now resides in a flood zone, it is required that it always was and will be flood insured."

Red was totally confused. He asked, "Why do I need flood insurance for months past?" The banker simply stated, "It's the law." Red's house had been built not in a flood zone, now some government official had drawn imaginary lines of where flooding could occur and Red's house resided inside one of those lines. Now Red owed for flood insurance he never had and was required to pay for flood insurance he would never need. He said, "This is totally insane."

The banker said, "Sorry sir, but the laws deciding all of this have been written for your protection."

Red wondered if a Susie flood zone expertise individual had even looked at his land and the absurdity of his house ever flooding. He asked, "Is there anything I can do to cancel this flood insurance?"

The banker answered, "That is not my level of expertise, but I believe there is something called a LOMA you can look into."

Red thanked the banker and spent the next month looking into a LOMA. One year and six months later, Red had completed all the LOMA requirements and paper work associated with it. During this time Red was forced to continue paying for flood insurance he never wanted nor needed. The cost of this insurance was one tenth of Red's total mortgage payment. Each month Red paid his mortgage, he grew more and more sickened with the workings of the government and what they required of their citizens all under the pose of protection.

When it was all said and done, Red and Sue had gotten the government to admit that their house was not in a literal flood zone. Since the house was now determined not to be in a flood zone, it was basic logic that the house never needed flood insurance. Since Red never wanted nor needed flood insurance, then all the money paid in insurance should be refunded.

Red went to the bank to get his money back. The banker said that he did not have that money, the insurance company held that money. Red proceeded to the insurance company to get his money back and was told that yes, since Red did not need flood insurance he was no longer required to pay for insurance and could get six months' worth of payments to the insurance company back.

Red said to the insurance agent. "Let me get this straight. If I become an insurance agent, I can then charge people living in the desert flood insurance even though they do not want nor need it. I can make them pay for this insurance for several years and then when it is determined that they do not need insurance, I only have to give them six months' worth of their payments back?"

The insurance agent replied, "We do not look at it that way, we look at it as protecting the banks investment in individuals homes."

Red left thinking, "*That's a perfect way to screw people out of their money*." The more he thought about it, the more irritated he became, this was his land and his house, and at least he was making faithful payments to deserve the right to call it his land and home. Maybe that's where the line crossed, between what one actually owned and what the bank owned. Either way, the government was the cause and stood behind the insurance company literally stealing one year of insurance payments from him. Red was outraged.

He flung his door open and was happy to no longer be paying flood insurance premiums to the insurance company. A letter flew and dropped at Red's feet, he tore the letter open and saw his home insurance rates were again raising for higher fire insurance. Red sat and wondered why he was even trying to buy a house, it would be much easier to go and live in government housing.

Charlotte

Charlotte's eyes were a darker green then they ever had been. Her old school had been blown down, removing the last of what remained of the old town's heritage. She was now teaching in this new and improved school.

Charlotte was asked to pick up the day's lessons each morning before class. She had asked "Why?" and was told. "THAT'S exactly the type of attitude we don't want. If I could fire you, I would." It was almost as though the powers that be wanted the children to be taught nothing more than what was given to the teachers to teach. She wasn't given a chance to prepare her lessons, each morning she was simply told, "This is what you teach today." She would look the class schedule over, roll her eyes, and then try to teach.

Today when she picked up her schedule and saw she was teaching on sex, she nearly fainted. She herself had not yet had sex and now she was supposed to teach teenaged children all about it. Charlotte slowly walked the long hall to her class.

Charlotte's class room was beyond any resemblance of the class she once taught. The children that were undisciplined, unruly, and disrespectful were controlling her class and she was not allowed to correct the disruptiveness. She saw at least eight teenagers nearly on top of each other. She wondered "*If they shouldn't be teaching today's lesson instead of herself?*" She wondered "*how boys and girls can behave this way being*

187

unmarried?" She saw another group circled around a lonely rag dressed girl, she was in tears as the children teased her about her looks and clothing. Another group was building a fort out of their desks. Then there was Kaley and Kevin, looking at her, ready to take notes on today's lesson. Charlotte remembered Kaley's crush on Kevin, she remembered Kevin pulling on Kaley's hair indicating, "I really like you." Charlotte turned red as she silently read the first line of the lesson. "Children, in today's society, having sexual intercourse is perfectly fine as long as you use protection." Charlotte stood and said, "I'm sorry class, I have a migraine. I've got to go home." She left and thought on her walk home how each day brought more misery into her life than joy.

Thomas

Thomas had built his factory from the ground up. He had literally given of his own blood in the building of his company through cuts, scrapes, and wrongfully driven nails. Through hard work and sweat, Thomas now ran and owned a very successful factory.

Thomas was also a very firm God fearing man. He lived his life and ran his business on Biblical standards set forth found in his Bible. God had told Adam, "Be fruitful and multiply." Thomas believed what God had told Adam was good enough for him. To think of killing an unborn baby was as near an unpardonable sin as one could get, in Thomas's eyes. In God's eyes, it was forgivable.

The American Constitution went into effect on March 4, 1789. In that complex lengthy remarkable piece of paper, only once did the writers vaguely refer to religious freedom. Article 6 near the end of the third clause it reads "No religious Test shall ever be required as a Qualification to any Office or public Trust under the

United States." Or as Red would explain, "It means that any individual can be a public official regardless of their religious beliefs."

The writers of the Constitution then had a quarrelsome debate over the Bill of Rights. Many believed that a bill of rights would limit the rights of the people. Imagine that? Other Founding Forefathers believed that certain thoughts written and not written in the Constitution needed to be part of the New Nations paper heart. On June 8, 1789 James Madison introduced the articles of amendments to the Constitution. The first of these rights was the Freedom of Religion.

Red explained the First Amendment in conjunction with the Constitution as follows: "The government shall not interfere with any religious group and no religious group shall ever run the government." The leaders and lawmakers of the new nation did a fairly good job of adhering to this for the past 60 years. Then when the Americass family line took office in Liberty Town America, they set a match to a fuse of the bomb, "Separation of Church and state" which amazingly, that phrase, is not in the Constitution or found in any of the Bill of Rights.

The Sixteenth Amendment, that which allowed Congress to levy an income tax, would not come into effect for another 45 years. Being that the Americass family held the morals and belief structure of those roughly 162 years in the future, they believed that the taxes collected from any individual could be used in any fashion they desired. Susie collected the money from the people and would use it as she deemed fit.

One of the things Susie and Charles wanted to use the collected tax money for was the killing of unwanted babies.

Charles despised children, who wouldn't after fathering Jaerk? Consequently, Charles supported a group called "Childless Families." It was a group that willingly eliminated any unborn child regardless of reason.

When Thomas learned his taxes were supporting Childless Families, he was outraged. This was definitely crossing the line of government not interfering with one's religious beliefs.

Johnny and Peggy

Johnny sat at the meadow holding hands with Peggy, he said, "I really want to marry you Peggy, I love you so much. But every time I come close to having enough money saved to marry and start a family with you, it's taken away by Jaerk and these damnable citations." Peggy was touched that Johnny wanted to marry her, she was more thrilled that Johnny wanted children, she too wanted children. She said, "I love you too Johnny. And just marry me, we'll figure things out as we go. But I don't think I want to bring children into this world. Don't get me wrong, I love and want children. But I can't imagine them trying to live a biblical standard in a world like this. It would be too much of a battle for them. Gosh Johnny, it's hard enough for us".

Johnny thought about Peggy's words, she was right. Johnny said, "I can't believe it's come to this so quickly. Just a short period ago life was hard, but it was good. Now life is easy, if you leech off Susie, but it's bad, very bad." Peggy said, "Charlotte was asked to teach about sex the other day in class, she left. I wonder how much longer they'll keep her around?" Johnny grabbed Peggy and rolled on top of her, Peggy giggled. Johnny asked, "Why do kids need taught about sex, I know everything I want to do to you." Peggy lightly slapped Johnny and said, "Hush Johnny, you have to marry me first." Johnny sat up, he looked at Peggy and said "Fine, you win." He pulled her hair and flipped a cricket into her bosom, then took off running yelling, "Peggy, I love you, let's get married."

Jimmy

Jimmy sat drinking coffee with Red. Jimmy was still upset at having been fired for saving Earl's life. He showed Red the last page of the paper. Red read that a young girl was arrested for giving her drunk friend a ride home, although the girl giving the ride was totally free of any alcohol, she was arrested for being in the vicinity of other children drinking. Red said, "Guess she should have let her friend ride her horse home being intoxicated. In today's society it's self-perseverance first. Don't ever consider being a kind and helpful neighbor." Jimmy looked his brother in the eye, "That's not in my blood." Red acknowledged his consent, "Guess that's why we won't make it much further than where we already are."

Murphy

Murphy was riding west. Every town he came to he was escorted out a few days later after several accidents occurred, not at his hand, but he was in the vicinity. He stood at the Pacific ocean admiring the beauty, "Nice." He turned around and headed back East.

Kaleidoscope:

Kaleidoscope sat eating steak and potatoes inside the FPS. A guard sat beside her and said, "We're getting a little crowded, you're gonna have to share your cell." Kaleidoscope finished her last bite of steak and threw her tray on the guard yelling, "This is bull crap." She took off running down the hall, slammed her cell door, and locked herself in.

Sheriff Wright

The sheriff found himself so bogged down in paperwork that he rarely had a chance to ever leave his office. Often he thought his life would be better being a deputy again. The paperwork required of him was so much that he had to hire 3 secretaries. He looked at the pile of papers still requiring his attention, it would be a year before he got caught up and by then another bigger pile of papers would be resting where the current pile now sat. Sheriff Wright cussed and grabbed another paper from the top of the stack.

The Neon Twins

Neon One yelled, "I hate you" to Neon Two. Neon Two asked "Why?" Neon One said, "I don't know." Neon Two said "Fine, I hate you too." Neon One asked "Why?" Neon Two answered, "Cause you hate me." Neon One grabbed Neon Two and hugged her. She said, "I love you." Neon Two hugged Neon One back and said, "I love you too." Neon One said, "I like making up." Neon Two said "Me too." The two grabbed hands and went running down the stairs in their jean short shorts, cowgirl boots, white t-shirts and cowgirl hats. When they stepped outside Regina saw Gusto look at the twins. She slapped his face and kicked him in the crotch. Gusto asked, "WHAT?" Gina said nothing and stormed away.

The native Liberty Town folk numbered about a fourth of Libertyless. The immigrants who migrated to the city were of mixed morals and had differences in governing principles. A quarter of the immigrants held true to the constitution and morals set forth in the bible. This left half the city enjoying Charles's and Susie's governing style, the other half were sickened to their bone marrow. Susie was looking at the current poll results, she showed a 97 percent approval rating for the way her and Charles were running Libertyless. She asked Charles, "How upset are these 3 percent?" Charles distorted the truth, he answered, "Not very, it's just taking them a bit to accept change."

21 - Osama MeBlowMeUp

Osama BlowUup had a brother named Obams MeBlowMeUp. Osama greeted his brother happily at the ocean dock, the two hugged and then laid down their mats, lowered their heads, and said their prayers. Johnny, who was visiting his father at work, watched the two pray. Johnny turned directions and knelt, raising his head towards heaven, Johnny started giving God thanks for his life, and Red joined his son. Jaerk tapped them both on the shoulders and wrote them a citation for openly praying in public view. Johnny pointed to the BlowUup brothers and asked, "What about them?" Jaerk answered, "Their not citizens of the US, they can do whatever they want."

When finished praying, Osama said, "I'm so glad you are here my brother," as he silently thought, "*I'm glad you're blowing yourself up today, sucks to be you.*" MeBlowMeUp responded. "I shall do what you ask of me and shall be rewarded with many virgins very soon," as he silently thought, "I'*m happy with the girls down here. You should go meet the virgins.*" The two partook in many preparation rituals that day and by midafternoon, MeBlowMeUp was loaded down with many sticks of dynamite and a single fuse.

It was midafternoon and the annual Rodeo was just starting, since entertainment was difficult to come by, pretty much everyone in town was coming to see the sporting event. Charles, Susie and Futureano were seated center of the arena at box seats near the top of the arena. These box seats were surrounded by men, all dressed in black, all carrying six shooters and rifles.

Below sat many of the Americass family, none of which carried a gun. Dissension between Libertyless citizens was at an extreme high; consequently, the other half of the arena was filled with citizens like Red, Charlotte, Kaley, Jimmy and Johnny, each carried a gun. MeBlowMeUp entered the arena, calmly walked while inwardly shaking to the center, threw off his trench coat and yelled, "I shall soon get my virgins." Silently he thought, "*I think this is the biggest mistake of my life.*" MeBlowMeUp then struck a match and lit the fuse leading to the dynamite strapped around his waist.

The Americass Citizens all stared in amazement at hoping to see something spectacular. Some of the others on the opposite side of the auditorium, seeing the danger of flame and explosives, drew their guns and shot the fire out of the fuse, they cared not for any new type of show that possibly could bring harm to any of their loved ones.

Susie, Charlie and Futureano all ducked down in their box. Futureano said, "See, I told you they wanted to shoot us." Red went to MeBlowMeUp and pulled his hands free from the fuse he was frantically trying to relight, Jaerk came to Red and stated, "How dare you spoil the show." Red simply replied, "No show I want to see." Jaerk put his arm around MeBlowMeUp and walked him out of the arena explaining how he was sorry for Red's actions. As they exited the arena, the fuse smoldered and reignited as they rarely but sometimes do. Three seconds later the whole rodeo crowd heard a noise shattering BOOM! and then felt a slight vibration, a portion of the Americass side of the stadium was disintegrated. Those closest to the explosion immediately died, those a little further away were seriously injured. Red, Johnny, and most of the native town folk immediately ran across the arena and started administering first aid to the wounded. The Americass side started trampling each other trying to escape any further danger, and consequently more people were seriously injured under the barrage of people exiting the stadium.

Susie stood and watched the crowd, noticing those who helped others and those who were concerned only about themselves. She looked at the ten men standing guard over her and Charles, they were unmoving and watching for danger coming towards them. Charles hid between the ten, he was kneeling on the ground, a little concerned that his blue suit and white shirt had gotten dusty. Futureano was hiding under the bleachers crying, his hair was fallen down his shoulders, and his belly wouldn't fit under the seat.

Osama watched the whole scene, sitting safely some distance away, he cursed that only a few imbeciles had been blown dead. The rest of the crowd swarmed the scene, looking for Jaerk and MeBlowMeUp, escaping further danger, and helping the wounded. Susie and Charlie quickly gleamed that the entertainment was miscalculated and unfortunately their son had died. Red and Thomas both believed that MeBlowMeUp might have intended to kill them all and fortunately most had survived.

In the weeks that followed a thorough safety investigation was conducted. Not leaving any thought unturned, Red's and Thomas' statements were taken into consideration. The conclusion was, that since no one from the rodeo had orchestrated MeBlowMeUp's act, it was therefore possible that he had intended terrorist activity. Susie, sworn to provide safety to the public, quickly set up another division to guard against terrorists. This division soon had many safeguards in place and life in Libertyless resumed. Thank you Susie.

One of the safeguarding divisions Susie's terrorist division created was the searching of those traveling into and out of Libertyless. With all the other safeguards, Osama found it impossible to obtain any more explosives, he decided to search elsewhere for what he needed. Leaving Libertyless, he patiently waited in line to be searched. He stood beside a war veteran with a prosthetic wooden leg and an old woman who could barely walk. The random searching of those entering the coach continued. When the searches saw the old lady, they let her by, when they saw Osama, wearing a white cloth around his head and a fifteen year old growth of facial hair, the searchers thought, "This is probably a terrorist," but not wanting to be accused of stereotyping, they let Osama pass as well. Then they saw the man with the wooden leg. "NOW there's a terrorist if we ever saw one," a searcher said. They took the man to a private tent, stripped him totally naked, and searched him. Having found nothing of any danger, they presumed the explosives must be hidden in the wooden leg. They removed his leg, went one hundred yards out, and lit his wooden leg afire. Noting happened.

The two searches then concluded the war veteran was safe to travel with other Libertyless citizens. Life in Libertyless was surely safe. Osama was angered that his brother had died for only a few imbeciles. *"They would surely pay for their transgressions,"* Osama thought. Osama then thought of the virgins he would soon have because he had no other brothers to have blown themselves up. *"Damn,"* he thought. *"I must tell my uncles to have big families."*

It took a couple weeks for Osama to find more explosives. He wrapped them around his body and then dressed himself as a very fat young man. He then bought a ticket back to Libertyless and stood in line, waiting to see if he would be randomly searched. Osama found himself standing behind a very pregnant woman and in front of a father and his two boys. The woman in front was definitely pregnant and Osama thought he would witness a birth on his way back to the city. The searchers saw her and led her to a room where she was thoroughly searched by two other women. The searchers saw Osama and thought he looked similar to a drawing that Susie's terrorist division had given them, but this individual was way too fat. They then saw the father and the two boys and thought, "*What a clever disguise for a terrorist,*" they had the man and his boys searched.

Osama dreamed of his revenge on the coach trip back to Libertyless. He would walk into the donations building and blow the whole financial structure of those imbeciles up, and with it, the many many many ungodly along with it. He smiled.

When the coach arrived, Osama made a straight path down the valley to where Red used to own his beautiful land. He marched straight into the main entrance, yelled whatever it is that terrorists yell, and lit his fuse to his dynamite. Nothing happened.

He was apprehended, tried, and sent to FPS.

Another safeguarding division of Susie's anti-terrorist division was that of stopping terrorist by destroying their communication. This infringed on the public's constitutional rights, but in the name of "safety" it was allowed. Letters of private citizens were opened and read, any indication of a possible common terrorist word being used caused an immediate flag on that individual of possibly being a terrorist. When Johnny wrote Peggy a simple letter saying, "I can't wait until we leave this city. You and I are going to leave this town in smoke," they both were tagged as possible terrorist. When Gusto wrote home telling his brother, "Possible gold mine. Will need to blow up a few more craters to be sure," he was tagged as a possible terrorist. Letter after letter was opened and read, citizen after citizen was tagged as a possible terrorist. Susie had to allocate more funds to the growing anti-terrorist division. When a letter was placed on her desk reading, "can't stand the politicians forcing their lack of God down my throat. Something must give, possibly another revolution," Susie quadrupled the anti-terrorist staff. She demanded to know who the sender and receiver of that letter was. Since it was sent to a false address, the hunters of the receiver were stopped at a dead end. Susie sat steaming at her desk having learned someone was really upset about the current government. "UNFUCKING believable" she had said.

Trent Smith

22 - **The Election**

Red soon learned that many others of the town were as outraged as he over the workings of Libertyless' government. Bill Money had the biggest house in Libertyless, Susie often found herself staring at Bill's house wondering how she could someday own it. Charles hated all the land surrounding Bill's house and would state to Susie, "Too many mosquitoes and gnats. You can have it Susie, I'll stay in town".

Bill had a huge ranch as well. Not that he enjoyed ranching, he enjoyed his solitude. With more of his money being taken away by Susie, Bill Money offered his property up for meetings and soon Red and others were venting their frustrations one to another each Friday night around a campfire at Bill's ranch.

Bill said, "I can't be paying any more taxes."

Jimmy chided, "For the first time in my life, I am glad I'm not as rich as you, Bill."

Regina said, "I can't believe prisoners live better than us."

Gusto asked, "Do the leaders know that their making us Commies?"

Charlotte asked, "Commies? I think they have more freedom than us, and what they're making me teach at school?"

Johnny interrupted, "Now there trying to take our guns. And the citations I've received, I think I bought them their new ROLF course."

200

Kaley said, "I'm tired of looking at everyone's underwear."

Regina asked Kaley, "How is Kaleidoscope doing?" Kaley replied, "She's taking college courses to be a brain surgeon."

Jimmy said, "Now they've taken any common sense out of working labor. Our every move is governed by some policy."

The talk would continue for hours, nothing ever being settled. When election time rolled around, things changed.

Bill said, "Red, you should run for Charles's office. Make things right down there on your old land. I'll back you."

Red answered, "I think I will." Then added, "I'll need someone to run against Futureano."

Gusto said, "I think Thomas should run." Thomas argued, "I haven't the time for my responsibilities as it is."

Red squared his shoulders to Thomas, "Thomas, this is more important than your current responsibilities. Four more years of what we got, you ain't gonna have no factory. Way things going now, Ben Lazybutt gonna own everything you own." Thomas thought about it and decided Red was right.

Charlotte inquired, "Who's going to run against Susie?"

Red answered, "Ain't no one can touch Susie, she ain't no elected official, but the essence of the common people and those elected to represent us. She just happened to place herself in the right place at the right time and those who have risen to power have fueled her pride and the result is something that few are proud of anymore. But maybe we get enough of us sitting in them their power offices down there, we can control her a bit, starting with Charles's office, that office that is supposed to represent all of us."

The founders of Liberty Town were going to take their city back.

The election process started, Red and Thomas were going to run against Charles and Futureano. The great and powerful Susie sat back and watched with interest.

The polls indicated a close race between the two parties then Charles started promising more food, more clothing, more medical, better housing, and a free new entertainment gadget that had yet to be invented. Anyone who voted for him and Futureano would get lots of free stuff. When Red confronted Charles as to how all this stuff was going to be paid, Charles pointed at the wealthy side of town where Gusto and Bill had houses, and said, "LOOK at all that wasted wealth. They should share it with you. They'll pay for your free stuff." The pauper people roared and cheered. Gusto and Bill left, both discussing how to further hide more money.

The campaigning continued, those that were unemployed or needed more government help, found themselves siding with Charles's ticket. Those who thought government was big enough and that they should learn to manage and survive with the money they've taken rather than increase taxes as their governing grew, found themselves siding with Red and Thomas's ticket.

Red and Charles ended up on opposite street corners yelling their promises to the public. Red looked at his red flannel shirt and blue jeans with holes in the knees, they were his best pair. He glanced at Charles with a dark blue suit, white shirt and red tie, Charles looked almost girlish. Red gave Charles the point on looks. Red listened to Charles's speak, always reading those damn 3x5 cards, he wondered what Charles would say without them. Red gave Charles another point for speech and thought himself already behind in the election.

Red offered the promise of lower taxes, this would put more spendable money into the hands of the people and would help create more jobs because people would buy more stuff. Charles countered by throwing money in the air and saying, "What stuff can't you buy? I'll help you get it." Red promised to lower taxes on businesses so they could invest more in research and their employees. Charles replied, "How can a business compete in the research Susie provides? She has more capital than any one business will ever have. Furthermore," Charles thumbed through his 3x5 cards and couldn't find one dealing with investing in the people. Charles spoke on his own accord saying, "Furthermore, the people are a great asset to this country. They contribute a lot to this community and I'm great at organizing communities. Without me the people would be lost. I promise to give you more guidance and more direction on what to do with your life. I make your life better and I should be the one reelected."

Red listened to Charles's and wondered, "*Does anyone understand what he is saying*?" He glanced around and saw Susie on the tavern balcony watching the whole scene. Susie was dressed in a long green dress that exposed her right shoulder, she had a crown of white flowers placed on top of her loosely bound golden hair. On the table was a set of scales heavily weighted to one side, after Charles had spoken, Susie placed a large weight on the lighter side. She glared at Charles and picked up another medium sized weight. She sat listening to Charles, the more he spoke, the angrier she got. "*How dare he use her name to win this election*?" She had worked hard to get to her current position and could care less who won, she would control Red as easily as she controlled Charles. She controlled the money, she controlled the governing agencies, she controlled the businesses, and she controlled the people. Susie was not an elected official, her position could not be challenged, and she was untouchable. Red promised to make Susie quit making money, this would mean less money in circulation and its value would therefore increase. Susie added another weight to the heavier side of the scale. Charles laughed at Red and said, "Honestly, you good people are considering electing a citizen who thinks money is worthless," he laughed some more and some laughed with him. Charles said, "Good people of Libertyless, I promise, your money will never be worthless. I promise you new roads, better schools, bigger government keeping you more safe."

Red interjected, "You mean more government reading our private letters?" Susie added another weight to the heavier side and silently thought, "*We read your letter because we're trying to keep you safe stupid.*" Charles ignored the comment and continued, "Our parks will be bigger and better. You're horses will be faster, your food will taste better." Red sat shocked as he watched the people take in Charles's every word, they truly thought he would make their foods taste better if he were elected for another 4 years.

Red looked at the red, white and blue flag flying behind Charles. He watched the Neon Twins on stage behind his competitor, they were wearing white and blue skirts and crop tops colored the same. They were dancing with blue and white pom-poms chanting, "Charles, Charles, he's our man. It's red, red that we can't stand." Then they cheered, "Kick him in the left knee, kick him in the right knee, we need, we need, we need a touch down." Red thought, "*WHAT*?"

Red said, "I will put the bible back in the schools." Charles flipped through his cards and read, "bible in school? Why? That's a direct violation of separation of church and state." Red thought, "That's *so far out of context and those words should not be allowed to ever be used.*" Charles continued, saying, "The bible has no place in our schools or government, it's nothing more than a book. To think that that's even an electoral concern is pure craziness. I can't believe I'm debating with a crazy man." The Neon Twins chanted, "Red, Red, he's crazy in the head, he should be lying in a bed."

The campaign continued. Then the day before election, Charles accused Red of being an adulterer. He then had Futureano and his boys describe how Red had violated Domestica in Futureano's own house. He then accused Red and Thomas of associating themselves with a murderer and described how a helpless Native American was murdered by Charlotte, Reds and Thomas's good friend. Mr. Bias printed these "truths" in big bold letters on the front page of Election Day's paper.

23 -**Rights**

Susie sat in her luxurious office talking to Charles after he won the election. Susie had been reading the constitution and the bill of rights. She had promised Futureano a safe society and now a tiny bit of her was starting to feel that she might be taking away some of the people's rights in the name of safety. Susie asked Charles, "What do you think of Libertyless compared to when we first arrived?" Charles looked out the window at the small river running through the official buildings. He smiled at Susie and said, "Its wonderful sister." Susie simply asked, "Explain?" Charles stated, "To begin with, the children no longer have "morals" being shoved down their throats. The children are being taught to follow, which in time makes our job even easier." Susie said, "The classrooms are chaotic." Charles said, "Just like we make the adults behave with fear, we need to control the children with fear." Susie asked, "How? You took discipline out of the school." Charles answered, "Me and Futureano are working on that."

Susie grabbed her brother and squeezed him. She asked, "You miss him?" Charles asked, "Who?" Susie answered, "Our son Jaerk." Charles showed no emotion, "Not really. You?" A tear ran down Susie's cheek. She said, "All he ever did was try and please us." She sat and asked, "Are we stripping the citizens of their rights?" Charles stood taller, "Absolutely not. They are well protected, they are safe. Their needs are met, the environment is protected. If a few rights are lost giving the people that, so be it." Susie told her brother "Thanks" and then excused him.

Jimmy was out horse riding in the woods with his three daughters, Betty Lou, Bobbie Sue, and Becky Boo. She was named Boo, because Jimmy booed about not getting his son and his hair loss when Becky arrived. Before the Americass family came to town, Jimmy's family sat down to dinner together every night. Now, the girls were busy with their friends and activities, Jimmy rarely saw his family anymore. They all loved horse riding though, and to get time with his daughters, Jimmy took them riding whenever he could.

Charles would give money to anyone who had a research cause. Charles had given money to researching the sexual behavior of wild blue monkeys. Charles had given money to study dating habits of people. Charles had given money to fund jello wrestling in the Antarctic and to test exercise ability of shrimp on a treadmill. If someone had a cause, it seemed as though Charles would readily fund the study of that cause, using the tax payer's money of course.

In one of these studies, Charles learned that many deaths occurred because people fell off their horses. In the name of protecting the people, Susie soon had a law requiring saddle belts be worn while riding horses. Moreover, she made a law that all new saddles come equipped with a saddle belt.

It was not long out riding before Jimmy and his daughters passed a police officer. The officer chased Jimmy and his daughters down and wrote them a ticket for not wearing their saddle belt.

Bobbie Sue asked, "If I were George Washington, would you still be giving us these tickets?"

The officer answered, "Yes mam, the law is the law."

Betty Lou said, "George wanted us to be free. Forcing us to wear these safety saddle belts is not freedom."

The officer replied, "Just want you to be safe mam."

Jimmy asked, "So you fine us for being supposedly unsafe?"

The officer replied, "I just write the tickets, the courts set the fines."

Becky Boo said, "I don't understand."

Bobby Sue said, "Its simple Becky, The opening of the Constitution clearly states that one of the reasons it was written was to secure the blessings of liberty to ourselves. Yet in the name of safety, more laws are created, limiting our freedom." Becky continued. "And officers like this gent believe it is their duty to force the laws on us by penalizing us for not obeying their laws."

The officer said, "I don't make the laws."

Jimmy said, "Seriously, we are not harming anyone, yet here you are penalizing us. Then he asked, "Don't you have some real crime work to do, like finding out where all of Johnny's belongings made themselves off to?"

Bobbie asked, "Why was this law made?"

The officer answered, "A study was done and it was found that saddle safety belts save lives." The officer finished issuing the tickets and rode away. Jimmy and his daughters continued the discussion.

"That's a bunch of bologna," Becky Boo said. Then she asked, "Why can't we just be left alone?"

Jimmy answered, "I understand what it is the law makers are trying to do. However, with all these laws, we are no longer free."

Becky said, "I think they have made punishment too painless. If a horse thief is hung, there would be very few horse thieves."

Bobby said, "We used to hang em. Futureano put an end to that. Now horse thieven is everywhere."

Jimmy said, "I agree, however, paying these fines is not painless. Money is tight at our house if you haven't forgot."

They continued their discussion as they rode. It was a Catch 22, laws needed to be in place, yet laws condense ones freedom.

Becky Boo finally said, "If they are making all these laws for our safety, how long before they make laws telling us what we can and can't eat?"

Bobby Sue answered, "Probably when they make laws telling us how and when we can poo and when we can pee."

Jimmy wanted to scold his daughter's language but held his tongue because he knew she was right.

24 - **Happy Women**

Domestica received a letter that day from the Higher Interested Bank, the HIB. In the letter was a plastic card and letter saying she could use the card to purchase whatever she wanted as long as the company she bought from accepted the plastic card. Domestica skipped reading the rest of the fine print, including the line that said any unpaid balance at the end of the month would be charged a twenty percent interest.

Domestica thought, "*Free money. How wonderful.*" She took her new plastic card down to the store where a new shipment of dresses had just arrived from up North. She went inside and joyously shopped, trying on dress after dress wondering which would catch Red's eye. After an hour had passed, Domestica was undecided upon three new dresses, so she took all three to the counter. The cost of the dresses was tallied and for payment Domestica handed the clerk her new shiny piece of plastic. The clerk asked, "What's this?"

Domestica replied with a smile, "It's how all competent stores receive their money now days. ARE YOU NOT a competent store?"

The clerk took the card to the office of the owner in back. The owner then read the card and having learned it came from HIB, he went to the HIGHER INTERESTED BANK. There the owner of the store met Mr. Lenderlee who answered the store owner's questions of receiving funds, "Yes, we will pay you what receipts you turn in at the end of the month minus three percent for our services." The store owner thought about this and figured since accepting this form of payment would sell three dresses instead of just one, he agreed to Lenderlee's terms.

The store owner ran back to his store, had Domestica sign a paper, and Domestica left with three new dresses, she was overjoyed at how simple this new shopping process was. Domestica figured she needed new purses to match her new dresses and went through the whole process again at the purse store. Having such success with dresses and purses, she then figured she needed new shoes to match her new outfits. At the shoe store, during the preceding process, the shoe store owner was hesitant when making the agreement with Mr. Lenderlee. The shoe store Samaritan asked Lenderlee, "Why should I give you three percent of my sales?"

Lenderlee asked a question in reply. "Could you be making the sales without having use of the plastic card as payment?" In reply, Mr. Lenderlee heard "No." "There you are, " Mr. Lenderlee politely said, "Because of the plastic card, we shall call it a FR card indicating Fast Revenue, you are making sales you would previously not have." As the shoe store salesman swiftly hastened back to his store, Mr. Lenderlee was thinking "The FR card, Financial Ruin."

The shoe store owner went back and gave Domestica her shoes in return for her signature on a slip of paper. Now she was heavily burdened with new dresses, purses, and shoes. As she was struggling down the street, the Neon Twins saw her predicament and went to help. On the way to Domestica's house, she could not keep secret how easy it was to get her wants. After helping Domestica unload her stuff, the Neon Twins hurried to the

HIB.

Mr. Lenderlee was an oriental who heard about Libertyless through his father's aunt's brother. When Lenderlee heard the term "FREE money," he approached his father with a business proposition. Lenderlee's father was a shrewd businessman who was making thousands everyday with his business savvy, he had taught his son this same shrewdness. One did not waste a single ounce of tin, coffee, silver or gold in the Lenderlee family, all money was to be invested. Lenderlee's father understood the investing opportunity his son was talking about, so he sent his son to Libertyless with more than enough money to finance the biggest bank in the US.

Lenderlee built the prettiest and biggest bank the country would ever see. In that bank was a tiny bedroom and bathroom, Lenderlee had not the time to waste walking to and from work. Meals were nothing more than food for the brain to help figure more ways of making more money, they would be brought to him daily. Lenderlee's clothes were all a light blue green, his shoes matched, his socks matched, his pants matched, his shirts matched and his suit jackets matched. Lenderlee had not the time to waste deciding what to wear that day, that time was needed to figure out more ways to make more money.

Lenderlee was short and skinny. He wore large black rimmed glasses, he had a full head of thick black hair. He cared not for girls or boys, he cared not for people; however, he did care for everyone's money. He never looked anyone in the eye, the one time he did happen to glance up into an individual's eyes, it was the eyes of Susie glaring into his soul. He had quickly averted his eyes from Susie, but he knew she had seen him for who he was. At that time there was instantly a feud started between them,

Susie wanted to control all the money and she knew Lenderlee wanted to do the same. Lenderlee's bank, the HIB, opened the day that the Espinoza gang robbed the local bank. Later that day Mr. Lenderlee had met the gang outside of town and had given each a gold coin for a job well done.

Lenderlee stared straight ahead, looking directly at the Neon Twins' breasts and asked, "Why should I give you a FR card?" In which the twins giggly responded, "Because we have many wants." Mr. Lenderlee asked them how much stuff they owned and Neon One answered, "Our father will be very wealthy soon. He is working his way up at Safe Shipping to becoming a helmsman."

Lenderlee had them sign a piece of paper with very fine print in which some of it gave HIB the right to take whatever family assets necessary to pay the debt of the FR card. He sent the twins on their way with brand new FR cards from the HIB.

The Neon Twins wasted no time in spending money they did not possess. Their first stop was at the lingerie store where they filled three bags each from the new Lilac line from up North. They then went to the Uncommon Designs store and bought many more clothes. Soon they were home cutting and sewing their brand new clothes into brand new designs.

It didn't take long for news of the FR cards to spread around town. Soon all the women were requesting their own FR card and all the stores not accepting FR cards were rapidly applying to the HIB for acceptance into their FR card program, the stores new they were losing sales to businesses that accepted FR cards. In a short time, the stores were bought out of supplies save for the stuff no one wanted. Soon that stuff was purchased as well by buyers who just wanted to buy.

Lenderlee sat in his office calculating the money made from the store owners. He ran an analogy prospectus of proposed earnings from unpaid balances on the FR cards. He sealed his findings and gave it directly to his trusted personal assistant saying, "You give this to my father directly." When the father read the report, he immediately sent his other sons to America to start more HIB banks.

Domestica was slurping her coffee when Futureano opened a letter from the HIB bank the following month. It listed various stores and amounts that had been paid to those stores. Then Futureano noticed he was required to pay HIB a significant sum and if he did not pay the balance in full, he would be charged significant interest on the unpaid balance. Futureano asked Domestica if she knew anything about this and she responded by explaining the simple process of getting stuff. He started sweating, he did not have that kind of money. Domestica saw the concern in her husband's face. She pushed him onto a chair and sat on his lap, her bountiful breasts squashed into his face. She twirled the loose hair on his bald head and asked, "What's wrong honey?" Futureano removed his head from between his wife's bosom and said, "Nothing I can't handle." He went to his Uncle Charles and asked for a raise, in which Charles simply said, "Sure."

The Neon Twins received an identical letter from HIB with different names of stores and different amounts paid. The reality of actually having to pay for their goods dumped on them like a bad case of the flu. Neon One asked Neon Two, "You know the difference between the craps and the runs?" Neon Two asked "What?" Neon One answered as she ran to the toilet, "The runs is when you make it to the toilet." The twins had no idea how they were going to pay for their goods, so they simply threw away the HIB FR statement thinking that the issue would then go away.

Red opened his HIB statement and sat down with Sue. Fortunately for Red, Sue had only purchased necessities. The two hid the FR card and vowed never to use it again unless it was an emergency. Then he made a payment for the minimal amount.

Gusto opened his HIB statement and was happy he was wealthy. He paid the balance in full and told Regina to be a little wiser in her spending sprees. Regina twirled around in her new bright red floor length dress with a low cut front and split to her hip, she blew Gusto a kiss, flipped her long black hair, and danced around singing some unknown Spanish song. Gusto wished he hadn't said a word.

Kaley opened her HIB letter and was thankful she had read the fine print and had not used her card.

Jimmy opened his statement from HIB and silently wished he had the money to be able to buy his wife Tammy all of her needs and wants. He paid the minimum balance required with a little more going to the principle. This is what the majority of the Libertyless Americans did and as time would pass, each month they would find themselves owing more to the Higher Interested Bank.

25 - **Billy Justice Americass**

Billy Justice, the big brother of Susie and Charles, was a very huge man. He stood at least 7 feet tall and weighed about 385 pounds. Like his son Futureano, Billy had no hair, not even enough to grow a comb over. He dressed in a long black robe and wore nothing else. His face was circular and he had shallow squinting dark eyes. After fathering Futureano and raising Jaerk, Billy would sit and do nothing other than study the constitution and eat.

Billy was no dummy, in fact, Billy was very wise. Billy knew that bringing change in giant steps was never received as well as making changes little by little. Like in losing weight, it was always easier to continue having someone lose a quarter of a pound then to have those just up and lose ten pounds. The former most always produced results while the latter found little success.

Billy used this same philosophy in law. It was easier to make changes to the Constitution little by little over time rather than try to make huge changes overnight. Billy was very patient, methodical, and persistent. Billy used to believe that the constitution was inspired by a Higher power, then little by little his views changed as he grew up.

His classmates had printed a prank paper in which he was the subject of ridicule. Because of his size, they had claimed he was the product of two beached whales. Billy suddenly thought freedom of the press might not be such a good idea.   When it came to Religion, Bill was adamant that everyone should have the right to worship God as they wanted. Then a small sect of an unmentionable religion sat Billy down his freshman year in college. They threatened to cut off his big toe if he did not agree to worship their unmentionable god. After that dramatic experience, Bill thought maybe a few laws governing religion should be put into place. Bill's best and only friend was shot in a duel, Bill suddenly thought right to bear arms could use some adjusting. When Bill got the news that his son Jaerk was blown up by a terrorist, he adamantly changed his view, thinking that government should be able to do anything necessary to protect against terrorism. When Bill learned Osama BlowUup was sitting luxuriously inside the FPS walls, he vowed to rewrite the 8th Amendment. When he had completed that goal, he personally was going to be the first to visit Osama. Bill knew that he could not rewrite the Constitution without Big Government and he had many amendments he wanted to change. Bill was happy with his sister Susie and Charles, they were well on their way to making Government all powerful.

No one saw Billy Justice Americass exit that transport that bought the Americass family to Liberty Town. Late that night, when all were asleep, Bill made the unloading ramp creek and groan as his humongous heavy body slowly descended safely to land. He then made his way to the basement of the courthouse where he never left. His son and brother Charles would bring him the necessities of existence along with the changes to Little America they desired. They would exit with his waste. Through time, the stench of the basement of the courthouse was purely wretched.

Susie made sure that the new courthouse had

accommodations for her brother Billy. The lowest portion of the new courthouse had complete living quarters for him. Bill didn't take advantage of these accommodations, he sat day after day unmoving, studying the constitution and law, knowing he could rewrite the constitution little by little by adding law after law. Billy's existence continued to be hidden, and that portion of the basement Susie had built was feared by everyone and they avoided it at all costs. Something of the smell emanating from that area kept them away. Today Billy arose and found himself humming and mentally singing Dave Frishberg's song, "I'm Just a Bill, I'm only a bill, and I'm sitting here at Capital"

Susie, Charlie and Futureano had been coming to Billy for months wanting something immediately done concerning gun control. This was not easy for Bill because the forefathers clearly stated that citizens had the right to bear arms in the 2nd Amendment. Bill silently wished that the forefathers would have just said, "No one can carry arms except the people that the ones in authority want to have guns." "*Oh well,*" Billy thought, "*if I can't get this figured, the worst case scenario is Charles makes an executive order.*" Billy laughed, "We are so close to having a 'Dictatorial communal' government.

26 - **Bikinis and Belts**

The president of FSI, Feel Safe Insurance, was treating Susie and Charlie to a steak and lobster dinner. "What's up?" Charles asked as he dipped a healthy chunk of lobster into a vat of melted butter. FSI answered, "That flood up north cost my company millions." "How can we help?" asked Susie as she cut a piece of filet mignon. FSI answered, "I need more money coming in." Susie thought and chewed, then said, "I'll have Billy look into it. Maybe he can have the desert acres be included in the flood zones." FSI thanked Susie and Charles, he then dropped a large bag of gold onto the table and said, "Give that to your favorite charity for me would you?" Charles and Susie split the gold and left a 2 pence tip as they left the restaurant, leaving half of their meals on their plates. They started making their way to go see Bill, but upon thinking of the stench, decided to have Futureano explain to their brother what needed done tomorrow.

As they walked through town they passed by the Sheriff's office and saw through the crystal window that Jimmy and Mr. Wright were having a heated discussion. "Wonder what their arguing about?" asked Charles.

"We have to put a stop to this!!" Gusto stated strongly. "How?" Asked Jimmy. "I don't know," said Gusto, then asked Sheriff Wright, "Do you?" The Sheriff answered "I might, just don't have everything quite figured out yet."

Johnny was dressed in his blue jeans, spurs and a blue shirt. His cowboy hat was dusty, he'd been riding fence all day long. As he neared town, he stopped and picked up his manure box for his horse that he kept hidden in the bushes outside of town. He heard the low buzz of a rattlesnake in the bushes, his heart skipped a beat, instincts had him drawing his gun, but it was chained to his holster. He calmly backed away keeping an eye on the coiled snake, then tied the box to the butt end of his horse. He crawled in his saddle and belted himself safely to his saddle with his saddle safety belt, then rode uncomfortably on into town.

He rode calmly, it had been a long day riding fences. All he wanted to do was have a beer with Jimmy and then visit Peggy. He passed a group of girls headed to the river to go swim, he thought the new black and white striped cloth pants of one swim suit was rather nice, he visualized what it would look like with the white top of another. The sleeves of the suit were puffy and the top covered all of the girl's shoulders. Johnny thought his imaginary swimsuit outfit would be completed by the black bonnet swim cap worn by a third. He smiled and started riding again when he heard the Neon Twins yelling, "WAIT! WAIT FOR US!" He turned to see the Neon Twins running down the stairs of the apartment, both were wearing nothing more than a thin small neon green bustier that covered only the lower portion of their chests and a thin neon green triangular patch of cloth that covered just a tiny portion of their lower portion. Johnny coughed as he watched their body parts bouncing and unconsciously he spurred his horse and it took off galloping down the street. He had never before seen a girl in a bikini, as his horse was racing forward, he was looking backwards at the Neon Twins running to join the other girls to go swim. When he turned himself further backwards, being strapped to his saddle, his lower portion did nothing but slightly move with his upper half. The horse thought this meant slightly turn, so it did, and ran right into a police officer of Libertyless. The officer was drinking coffee and when he was hit by Johnny's horse, it spilled down his chest. This made the officer scream which scared the horse, the horse jerked away from the officer and ran faster through town. Johnny, being belted into his saddle, could not adjust his lower half to accommodate the rampant running, he was now in an awkward riding position. It was rather hilarious and the city folk thought so too, they watched Johnny and his horse running through town. The waste box, tied to the horses butt, was flopping up and down, the manure in the box was bouncing out. Johnny started screaming "WHOA" and pulling on the reigns which calmed the horse a bit and then suddenly brought the animal to a complete stop. Johnny was jerked forward and he heard cracking in his bones, the manure box, having its momentum suddenly halted, flew over Johnny's head and landed on the line of officers all pointing their guns at him. Johnny looked and sighed, he tilted his cowboy hat and said, "Evening officers. What's up?" The first officer was running to catch up with Johnny and his horse, the leading officer of the line approached Johnny and asked for his license, registration and proof of insurance. Johnny unbuckled his saddle belt and reached for his papers stuffed in his blue jeans.

Charlotte watched the scene, her eyes were a bright green as she was laughing at what she just saw. Then they started darkening as she watched Johnny dismount his horse, turn and face a wall. Kaley came outside on the patio and asked, "What's up?" Charlotte answered, "Johnny's in trouble again." Kaley asked, "Anyone hurt?" Charlotte answered, "Maybe everyone's pride, but other than that, I think everyone's ok." Charlotte then explained what had transpired, Kaley laughed and then stated, "I wonder if those bikinis are safer to swim in? I about drown every time I go swimming." Charlotte agreed and took off running up the street to catch the Neon Twins and the swim party, they caught them in a heated debate.

Neon One was saying, "So what if part of my body is exposed? It feels wonderful to have the sun hitting this much of my body and if people are offended by my body, that's their problem, not mine." Neon Two continued the debate, "And, I don't see how you can swim in those, those... whatever you call em. I can swim like a dolphin and I don't see dolphins covering themselves up." Kaley interjected, "Aren't you embarrassed?" They both laughed and looked at their sisters' shapely bodies, they turned to Kaley and asked, "Embarrassed about what?" Charlotte answered, "You're nearly naked. That's what." The twins looked at each other and then back to Charlotte, they ignored the question and Neon One said, "You two would look great in our green bikinis." Charlotte and Kaley looked at each other, then at the twins. Both loved the sun, both loved to swim, both couldn't swim in today's swim fashion, both were unknowingly considering slipping into a bikini. Kaley looked at Charlotte and smiled. Charlotte said, "NO. No no no." Kaley asked, "Why not? We simply pull our current swim wear off when we get to the river." It had been a hot day, this evening was just as hot. Charlotte said to the twins, "Alright, the stores are closed. Can we borrow your swim suits?" The twins joyously said "Sure." The girls started walking back to the twins' apartment, they turned around and saw three quarters of the other girls following. The twins laughed and said, "We might have to compromise, we don't have this many swim suits."

Johnny was looking at a handful of tickets, reckless driving, speeding, endangering an officer, endangering the public, not signaling, and littering streets with horse waste, a fine double all the others. He was sadder at having to tell Peggy that the wedding would be postponed again and wondered how the conversation would go. Peggy would ask, "Why weren't you paying attention Johnny?" Johnny couldn't lie to Peggy, he would say, "Cause I couldn't stop looking at the Neon Twins in their swim suits." He knew Peggy would be furious and storm away, so he tried thinking of other honest answers and decided he would simply say to Peggy, "I got distracted by some girls yelling." *She would certainly understand that girls yelling could be quite a distraction.* He mounted his horse and started riding to Jimmy's, it was only a couple blocks away to the bar where he was at. He no sooner took four steps when an officer handed him another citation for not buckling up. Johnny accepted the ticket, buckled up, and rode thirty more seconds to meet Jimmy at the bar, there he unbuckled and went inside for that long deserved beer.

Inside the Neon Twins' apartment was laughter and girls nearly naked everywhere, everyone was trying on what swim suits the twins had. The twins were a giving pair and they were enjoying watching the other girls laugh at their own modesty. Charlotte and Kaley tried on a suit and both said, "NO WAY!" The Neon Twins encouraged them and said, "We'll be alone, it's nothing different then what we're doing right now." Kaley and Charlotte laughed and consented, the other girls had their swim suits cut and tailored by the twins. When the twins had finished, the girl's all looked like they belonged on a foreign beach on a foreign planet where clothing had not yet been invented, no-one would dare dress so immodest anywhere else. By the time they exited the apartment, it was near dusk. They hurried to the river, stripped off their outer clothing, and jumped into the water hole in the cooling river. They all swam like never before, laughing and giggling. Without the extra water weighted clothing, they found themselves having more fun than any could ever have imagined. Charlotte's eyes were as light as earlier when she watched Johnny recklessly riding through town.

The sun started to set and Johnny left Jimmy at the bar, he started riding over to Peggy's. The swimming girls were starting to chill and decided they should get out and head home. They were crawling out of the river right above where Johnny crossed the river on the path to Peggy. He was crossing the river just as the girls were exiting the water, Johnny froze as he watched Charlotte come out, and his eyes widened as Kaley followed Charlotte. He sat back as the twins followed Kaley and he leaned forward as the remaining girls followed the twins. Johnny was dumb struck, he couldn't move, his jaw was wide open, he knew he should look away, but couldn't find that much self-control.

Charlotte glanced downstream and saw Johnny gawking at them, she screamed and covered herself with her hands. The other girls looked where Charlotte was looking, they saw Johnny, screamed and covered themselves up with their hands as well. Johnny screamed and unconsciously kicked his horse again.

The horse, being startled with all the screaming and then being kicked, took off running again. Johnny ducked under the first branch he came to, he sat up just in time to be smacked by a different branch. It knocked him backwards but not off his horse because he was buckled safely into his saddle. He felt pain shoot down his already hurting back. He righted himself, saw a branch quickly approaching, and ducked, he was in a daze and couldn't think straight. He peeked up, thought it was safe to sit up and take control of his horse. He sat up and a branch whacked his head, knocking his hat off and putting a large cut on his scalp.

Johnny cursed and fell over, his saddle belt kept him safely secured to his horse as his head was further scraped and cut by the lower branches beside the tail as the horse continued its run through the wooded path. Finally the horse slowed and stopped, Johnny slowly righted himself, and he felt blood trickle down his face. He unbuckled his safety belt cussing at its deathly grip, then let himself fall to the ground. He looked up into the angelic eyes of Peggy, he felt her comforting touch start comforting his wounds.

Johnny was taken into Peggy's house where he was administered first aid. Finally he became coherent and listened to Peggy rapidly talking and asking about his wellbeing. Johnny put a hand to her lips and said, "I'm all right." Peggy asked the dreaded question, "What happened?" Johnny started to answer but then thought better to plead the fifth, he answered, "It's a long story." Peggy sat back, "You're not going anywhere tonight Johnny, we have all night." Johnny sighed, "It all started with the Neon Twins wanting to swim with the other girls." Johnny was too tired and beat up to try and say anything other then what had transpired and Peggy patiently listened to Johnny's story. Then she stood and slapped Johnny on his bruised face, his wounds reopened and started bleeding. This time she didn't offer any more comfort.

Johnny said, "Peggy, please, understand. I didn't want to stare, it shocked me." Peggy sarcastically said, "Right, startled you so much that now we have to postpone our marriage." Johnny said, "It's not like that. I didn't plan this. It's just, I've never before seen anything like it." Peggy was fuming, she inwardly was thinking "*I'm no longer pretty or sexy enough to capture Johnny's attention. Hell, he never acted like that around her.*" Peggy asked, "Do you think I'm pretty?" Johnny answered, "Of course." Peggy simply said, "Well, you never before have ever lost your senses looking at me, now you've done it twice in a day, looking at someone else." Johnny answered, "I've never seen you in one of them swimsuits." Now Peggy was more furious, Johnny was indicating that she had to prance around like some skank to make him lose control of himself like he had today, she would not stoop to that level. She was also mad at Charlotte and Kaley for caving into the immorality of obscene swimwear. She stormed up to her bed in the loft and started crying. Johnny went to follow, but the pain in his head tripled as he tried to stand, he laid down and fell asleep.

The following morning Peggy left before Johnny got up. When Johnny did awake, he found himself alone in the house, he cleaned himself up and sat drinking cold coffee.

Charlotte watched Peggy speed through town. She went to Peggy's house to see if she could figure out what was wrong and maybe help. There she found Johnny laying in the grass outside, soaking up some sun and letting his body rest. Charlotte was at first too embarrassed to wake and visit Johnny, then she remembered the whole scene was probably no longer then a few short seconds. Charlotte sat and talked with Johnny, when they were done, Charlotte gave Johnny a comforting hug.

Peggy, having decided to go make things right with Johnny, had returned just in time to see Charlotte and Johnny hugging. She turned bright red, called Johnny an Americass, and took off once again. Johnny was again dumb founded.

27 - **Mr. Porntz**

Six months after HIB gave away the FR cards, the Neon Twins father found himself answering the door to Mr. Lenderlee and several low occupational workers of the Higher Interested Bank. Mr. Lenderlee had in his hands papers given to him from the basement of the courthouse, they allowed him to enter and confiscate all the possessions inside the Neon Twins' house. The father, having no choice in the matter, sadly watched all his earthly belongings become the property of HIB, Mr. Lenderlee calmly watched while inwardly smiling.

When HIB had left, the Neon Twins tried explaining to their father how the stuff was simply given to them and the bills, since they had been trashed, did not matter. The father, angered at his daughters' lack of sense, kicked the two out of his apartment, they found themselves wandering the streets in search of shelter and food. On the second day they were crying into one another's arms, Charlotte saw the twins crying and sat beside them on the street sidewalk. She simply asked, "What's wrong?" The twins respected and liked Charlotte and Kaley. Having lost the pride and respect of their father, the twins did not want to lose Charlotte's friendship or respect as well. Neon One simply said, "It's been a tough day, it's nothing we can't handle." Charlotte left being greatly concerned about the twins, she turned and said, "If you girls need anything, please don't hesitate to ask." Neon Two started to speak, but Neon One put a hand on her sisters' leg quieting her and Charlotte walked away.

A stranger approached wearing nine golden chains around his

neck and smiling a smile of golden diamond teeth. The twins saw sparking blue and silver pants, they looked up and saw a huge gold plated belt buckle. "What's wrong?" the stranger kindly asked. The twins broke out crying and struggled through their story. Thirty minutes later the stranger was taking the twins to his home, promising food and shelter.

On his way to his house, the stranger finally introduced himself as Mr. Porntz, or as the twins would later call him, Porn for short. Mr. Porntz had told the twins that they could stay at his house as long as they did what he asked of them, the twins, having never done anything adventurous, readily agreed. Mr. Porntz soon had the girls modeling in different nearly naked and totally naked poses. He would then capture those poses on film and they would be printed in mass on Porntz's printing press. The papers, filled with the Neon Twins in many various compromising positions, found themselves hidden in the homes of many men, even Sheriff Wright found himself embarrassingly purchasing Porntz's publications. The boys would find themselves taking longer baths while thumbing through the pages of Porn's paper, the men would find themselves working longer in the wood shed accomplishing nothing. The women would sense something wasn't exactly the same, but they had no clue as to what.

Mr. Porntz, seeing the success of his new Porn Paper, soon had a house erected that housed many homeless girls. In exchange for food, shelter, and a little money, all the girls had to do was pose for Porntz in various acts of seduction and/or sex. As time passed, Mr. Porntz learned that in order to keep his subscribers, he either had to bring in new girls or have the experienced girls do more vulgar things.

The moms who caught their boys looking at Porntz's papers,

tried scaring them by telling them that if they continued doing what it was they did, that they would soon find hairy warts growing out of the palms and backs of their hands. This scare did not stop the boys and they would often find themselves examining each other's hands looking for the dreaded deformity. The wives who caught their husbands looking at Porntz's paper, found themselves hurt, feeling unworthy, and in a divorceable fight with their spouse. Porntz's papers were definitely not healthy for the moral fiber of Libertyless. Those in higher authority knew this, but they themselves were not willing to give up their monthly subscription to Porntz's paper. Pastors and deacons of some of the churches found themselves digging in the trash for thrown away Porntz's publications, or they would order them under a false identity. Porntz's paper was a huge success in Libertyless and it found its way to other towns and cities in the US.

James and Jasmine had met in their late twenties, they instantly fell in love at first sight of one another and were later married. Jasmine was tall and skinny with dark skin and black hair, her eyes were a dark brown. She was very attractive but thought herself ugly. James was stocky with big arms, he was dark like Jasmine with sky blue eyes and dark black hair, he was always confident. The two were walking down the wooden sidewalk when the Neon Twins approached from the other way wearing black thigh high boots and black skirts that barely covered their upper thigh, their shirts were skin tight and a dull black. Why they dressed in black today nobody knows. James stopped mid stride and watched the twins approach, smile at him, pass, and then walk away. Jasmine watched her husband look at the twins and instantly got angry, she assumed James was wanting to sleep with the twins. The opposite was true, James did not want to sleep with the twins, but he did want Jasmine to dress like they did, he knew Jasmine would look very seductive in a short black skirt and black thigh high boots. He asked his wife Jasmine, "Why don't you dress like that?" Jasmine, being raised in church and being taught to dress modestly because men have weak eyes, replied, "Because I'm not a slut." After that day, sex between the two became more out of duty one to the other rather than from feelings of love for each other. They would find themselves jokingly arguing about who had to do the work this time. James knew he could and would never cheat on Jasmine, but he wished the sex in the bedroom was a little spicier. Jasmine, being raised as she was, thought it inappropriate to behave any other way then what she was and always would.

James was walking home from work when he saw Porntz's publication boldly displayed announcing 100 ways to please your lover. James looked around and seeing no-one he knew, bought the publication, he rushed home and started studying the article. Naturally while reading and seeing the different pictures of sexual positions, James got aroused. Jasmine came home and caught James looking at the Porntz paper. She came unglued, screamed at him, and immediately closed her inner self off to James, though she would still fulfill his needs. Thus the viscous whirlpool began, draining their sex life of any life. When they had sex, Jasmine would think James was thinking of other women, she knew this true because James was always trying different things with her. James was trying new things because he wanted to pleasure Jasmine more. The more Jasmine closed off to James, the more James felt he was incapable of pleasing his wife. The more James felt that, the more Porntz publications he purchased. He soon learned it was easier relieving the testosterone tension by thumbing through a Porntz publication then to try and get

Jasmine in the mood and then recuperate from the physical exertion. He also learned it sometimes felt better, Jasmine hadn't taken the time in their marriage to learn what really pleased him. James was too tired from the conflict and his work to care anymore. Jasmine would get angry at James for looking at any other women, she instinctively closed up more, being hurt because she felt betrayed. She felt there were more women in the bedroom then just her.

Then after two consecutive 84 hour work weeks, James made the mistake of telling Jasmine, "It's Halloween, you should dress up for me." Jasmine quickly responded, "That's not me, I don't feel like dressing up and I never will." James thought for a second and then felt his whole marriage slipping away. He knew if marriage was based on feelings, it would crumble. James said, "You just don't get it. Day after day I do things I don't want to do while you stay home free and yet you say, I don't want or like to do that, so I'm not going to. It Really has me upset, I just can't visualize us being very happy in the upcoming years when one says I'll do whatever is necessary, whether I like it or not and the other says, I don't feel like doing that, I don't like it, I'm not doing it. Had you of even said why. Like I find it morally wrong or it makes me feel cheap. But you say, I just don't want to. With that attitude, I don't ever see me ever wanting you to do anything special again. Even if you did dress up right now, I wouldn't even want to look at you. This is so much more than me not liking beans and you don't see it or are choosing to ignore it."

Jasmine responded, "I do get it, that you do so much, and I do appreciate it all. You also need to understand that there are certain things that you ask of me that literally hurt me inside by making me feel devalued and like trash. I know that is not your intent. You have never been able to accept this in me. There is far better in our marriage, and we do have a lot of happiness. I have been supportive of you to the best of my ability. I have told you many times in the past how it makes me feel. I can't believe you don't remember this."

James replied, "Maybe I can't comprehend that the clothing industry is a multimillion dollar market with clothes designed to attract a man's eyes. And I happen to get the one wife who dressing to attract my eye makes her feel devalued and like trash? Don't worry Jasmine, you never have to attract my eye again. I'm sorry liking looking at you makes you feel like dirt. Personally, I'm feeling a little shitty right now myself."

Jasmine sadly replied, "You want me to dress like a streetwalker, looking nice isn't the problem. The streetwalker dress mentality is what makes me feel that way."

James countered, saying, "You say, because I don't want to I'm not going to. It doesn't matter the beginning or end of the sentences, it's a crappy attitude to have with your spouse. Where would we be if every time I didn't feel or want to do something, I simply say, I'm not doing that? I give you house, food and freedom to not work at the sacrifice of doing crap I don't enjoy or feel like doing everyday. I didn't know we were basing our marriage on doing things based on how we feel. I was in the dark, but my eyes are open now."

Jasmine started crying and said, "I am still putting my applications in for work. I am sorry I didn't finish school, I am sorry I stayed home to take care of the kids instead of helping you make money. I am really really sorry your life is crap. There are few things that I have ever had that attitude about. Overall, I have supported you. I do a lot that I don't want to do. You do a lot that you don't want to do, its life, but the difference is if you are morally and emotionally opposed to something, I don't push you to go against your convictions."

James replied, "You know, I took an oath to take care of you. I laid pipe in live sewer to take care of you. I didn't feel like it and yes I felt shitty, but I did it to take care of you. I asked you once to dress up. Oh my God, forgive me. You said no, end of story. Now you decide you're basing what we do for each other on feelings? Now you hide behind convictions? At first it's feelings and now it's convictions? Whatever it is, you got your way, because I no longer feel like looking at you sexually.

Jasmine said, "James, it's always been both with me, I am sorry I have hurt you, truly, I am."

James said, "Jasmine, you are avoiding the issue. Are we basing our marriage on our feelings or on what we know we have to do to fulfill our duties and responsibilities? Even if we don't FEEL like it. Because if we are, our marriage has no future. And now we have deeper issues. Even if we solve the FEELING one, I have to go the remainder of my marriage knowing that my wife won't sacrifice her feelings for 30 minutes of play and yet I sacrifice my feelings 12 hours a day to take care of her. And then, knowing sex is so fucking disgusting to you, I no longer want sex, which is very important to me. Thank you so much for taking that desire out of my life."

Jasmine, completely destroyed, said, "Our marriage has always endured and come through stronger. I love you very much and I am willing to move mountains to keep you. You mean a lot to me, you always have. You are right, feelings come after responsibility and duty. I also agree we have to heal things."

James agreed with Jasmine, "Your right, our marriage is too strong to throw away over sex. I would toss it if remainder of years is based on feelings. The whole system crumbles. I don't feel like taking care of you today, therefore I don't work. So now we have sex issue. I take responsibility for that one. Since sex is a feeling issue, I don't want sex because it's your duty or responsibility. I've tried 20 plus years to get you to enjoy sex, evidentially I've failed terribly. I just have to make a conscious decision you hate sex and our marriage is put back together. I'll spend rest of day swallowing that pill, but we be ok."

Jasmine said, "I don't hate sex, I think my issue is more from knowing you view porn. I believe you know this based on what you wrote on that issue. Am I dressing up because you have some Porntz image you saw on your mind or do you see me? I don't want to play games where I have to be someone else. Not that you have asked for that, because it would make me wonder if you are thinking about an image. Pretty messed up huh?"

James said, "Swallowing pill, can't talk, lol, Jasmine, since we first been married sex with you is different. You've never really liked it. I can handle giving it up, just gonna take a bit to get accustomed to. And of course I'm looking at you and not imagining someone else. We've been through this and you won't even tease. That was one thing I asked for last weekend. Dang me, never mind, I'm giving it up, sorry and I really wish you make up your mind. First it's feelings, then convictions, now because I look at porn. Seriously, each pill taste different. Quit making me eat more please. I love you too much to make you have sex because it's your duty or responsibility. If your feelings aren't in it, fine. I can handle not having sex because you don't feel like it either. If it's

conviction, I can swallow that pill as well. I just have to realize I
married a nun. I can swallow that. If you don't want sex cause I
look at porn, I Can't swallow that pill."

Jasmine said, "I'm not trying to make you eat more, this is my
feelings which then connect to my convictions. I don't want to
give up sex, I would miss it. Honestly."

James and Jasmine were at a crossroads in their sex life.
James figured, as long as Jasmine knew a marriage could not be
based on feelings, the marriage would be worked out and come
out better. Jasmine knew that their marriage was not the issue,
their marriage was solid, and sex wasn't. Jasmine felt there had to
be a balance between feelings and sex. James felt Jasmine should
just do what he wanted because he did so much for her. Both
were very confused.

James started packing. He said, "You figure out why you really
not ever play dress up and then we talk. Until then, I've convinced
my big brain the little brain don't get any more ever. He's just got
to live with it because that's the way things are around the house
anymore. By the way, just a thought from a man's perspective.
Sometimes he just wants to make love, sometimes he wants his
woman a little on the trashy side, and sometimes he's curious
about new ways of pleasure."

Jasmine sat sad as James walked out the door. She repeated
an earlier argument, yelling, "James, porn is fantasy, it's not real."
James, knowing sex and porn were sweeping the nation, calmly
said, "Real or fantasy, it doesn't matter. What matters is I married
a wife that's not even willing to give a fantasy a try. I'm too tired
to give us a try anymore Jasmine." He quietly closed the door as
he walked uptown to the hotel. Jasmine sat quietly, staring into

the dark, wondering how truly clueless could he be?

Charlotte was teaching class when she noticed a bunch of young boys gathered in a circle sweating. She walked up and snatched away the paper they were looking at. When Charlotte saw the Neon Twins nakedly displayed, she ran to the trash and threw up. She dismissed class and ran to the twins' apartment. There she caught Earl Hurtz, the father of the twins, leaving to go board another overseas voyage. Charlotte threw the paper at Earl's feet where it opened and showed his daughters naked with several other older naked men.

Charlotte's eyes were a laser firing green, a color they had never been before. Earl was sickened and blamed himself for what it was that he now saw on paper his daughters do. Earl Hurtz, the father of the twins, soon found himself in the stinky courthouse basement debating the stench of Porntz's papers with Bill. "This Porntz magazine should be illegal," Earl said. "You're right Earl," Bill said, "it should be. But I must protect the constitutional right of Freedom of Press, it is the First Amendment you know?" "Our forefathers had no intention of that meaning freedom of exposing the nakedness of our youth." Earl shot back. "What they meant and what they wrote can often be interpreted in various ways," Bill replied. Then continued, "The courts should never jeopardize the rights of the people, even if we find some being hurt." "That's bull crap," Earl contradicted, "You're making laws daily stripping the rights of people out of the hands of the people claiming it's for their safety. Yet now, my daughters are truly being hurt and you say the constitution prevents you from protecting them." Bill said, "We try to make the laws that are best for the people while staying within the limits of the Constitution, ensuring everyone's freedom." Earl countered, "You make laws protecting animals while savagely stripping the rights of the citizens away, you care nothing for the Constitution unless it helps your agenda, whatever that might be."

"Whatever do you mean?" Bill innocently asked.

Earl shot back, "We can't open umbrellas on the street because we might spook the horses, yet we can photograph people naked." Bill, tiring of the conversation, asked Earl, "Would your daughters be in the Porntz paper had you not kicked them out of your house?" Hurting Hurtz where it hurt the most, Earl hung his head in shame and walked up from the stench in the courthouse basement. He didn't know what to do, so he went on his six month work voyage on the Charlotte Harrison. When Earl was gone, Bill, a devoted subscriber of Mr. Porntz's paper, pulled out the latest edition of the magazine and started paging through the pages.

Johnny saw his pastor suspiciously walking to the trash. The pastor looked around, thought no one was watching him, and buried something into the bottom of the can. Johnny waited until his pastor left and dug through the trash until he came to a Porntz publication. Johnny quickly looked at the paper, stuck it in his vest, and rode to the woods. There Johnny had thoughts that never in two lifetimes could he ever imagine. He tossed the publication into his saddle bag and rode to Peggy's.

Peggy was making dinner when Johnny grabbed her from behind like he never had before. Peggy felt the hands on her chest, turned and slapped Johnny, yelling, "Johnny, what has gotten into you?" Johnny said, "I can't wait any longer Peggy. I've got to have you." Peggy, confused, said "Johnny, you have me. I might be a little upset over your behavior, but my heart is yours."

Johnny grabbed Peggy on the shoulder and said, "Not like that, I want to be intimate with you." Johnny roughly kissed Peggy like Rudy had on that day long past. Peggy pushed Johnny back and said, "You know we can't do that until we're married. Besides, ever since you saw those twins nearly naked you've been acting really strange. I don't think I could do that with you right now. Even if we were married." At the name of the twins, Johnny remembered what he had seen them doing in the Porntz Paper, he turned red and yelled, "Well I can't wait any longer. I'm gone Miss Goody Two shoes." Johnny stormed out the door never giving Peggy another thought. He was headed to Mr. Porntz's in hopes of losing what he had been saving for Peggy. When he left, Peggy sat and cried. The dinner burnt and started filling the house with smoke, Peggy didn't notice, she was too concerned about having possibly lost Johnny for nothing other than sleeping with him.

James sat in his hotel lonely and feeling crappier then he had today while he was talking with Jasmine. Jasmine sat in the same place she'd been sitting when James left. She hadn't cleaned or ate since he walked out. She was thinking that this could be fixed, she just didn't know how. James left the hotel to go see Jasmine, he determined she was more important than sex. He walked in the house, picked Jasmine up, and then hugged her. Then he smelled her and said, "You stink." Jasmine hugged James back and said, "I missed you so much, don't ever leave me again or I'll kill you." James, fearing for his life, silently vowed to never leave again.

28 - **Abe Lincoln**

Throughout the beginning of time, man has fought for land and his home. After all, it is a basic responsibility of any good father to provide shelter and necessities for his family. In Libertyless, before the Americass family moved to town, the citizens understood that some could afford better dwellings then others.

Abe Lincoln was born February 12, 1809. He was now forty some odd years old living in Libertyless with his wife and two boys. Abe grew up in a log cabin and since a log cabin was good enough for him as a child, Abe figured it was good enough for his family as well. He had bought one and three quarter acres on the Northern side of town, at the base of the mountain range. It was an undeveloped parcel of land with just a few neighboring dwellings and the land was heavily wooded. Abe thought it was perfect, a perfect place where he could teach his boys the lessons of hard work and the satisfaction of a job well done, a place where Abe could build a simple dwelling and teach his boys about being humble.

Abe awoke his children early Monday morning from the rental house they were living at. Little Abe said, "Dad, its 4 am, are you crazy?" Big Abe said, "Dad's not crazy, he's got a mission." Big Abe and Little Abe sadly got up and dressed, they knew today would be a long day of hard work. By now Abe had coffee brewing and breakfast prepared. The two boys and Abe ate and drank, then loaded the wagon and rode to their new land with three axes and a day's supply of nourishment.

Abe sized up the land and discussed with his boys where best it would be to build their house, when all were in agreement, each set out to chop down their first tree. The neighbors, having heard some sort of large wood pecker annoyingly chopping, woke up and surveyed their surroundings. Nosey neighbor one gasped as she looked out her window and saw her favorite maple tree fall to the ground. That nosey neighbor immediately rode to town and triggered a new home inspection for Abe Lincoln when she voiced her complaint at City Hall.

Abe and his boys continued chopping and working. Mr. Tyler, Mr. Van Buren, and Mr. Buchanan all came with their families to help Abe with his log cabin and by mid-morning, Abe had quite a clearing on his land and the base of his cabin was complete. At lunch time the wives brought food and more help. By midafternoon Abe had a shanty shack, he was happy.

The house inspector, because a complaint was voiced, headed to Abe's land. Upon seeing the newly erected wooden shack, the inspector was horrified. "What is that?" inspector Smith questionably asked Abe. "That's my new house." Abe proudly replied while giving a huge smile. "You can't be serious?" Smith asked. "Yes sir, plan on moving in tomorrow," Abe excitedly said. "I can't let you do that, we have laws governing such living conditions," Smith said as he tried imagining a family living in such poor housing. "Last I checked," Abe said as he removed his black top hat and wiped sweat away, "This is America, the land of the Free, the home of the brave. I can do what I want." Then he asked, "Are you my new master of some sort?"

Smith tried explaining. "Look Abe, I know you're a good man." Smith continued after pulling out a rather large book and opening it to page 35, He read as he pointed out to Abe sections in the book, "We have laws governing housing. Dwelling unit must contain 1) Kitchen with a stove, sink, and refrigerator. 2) Bathroom with a toilet, basin, shower or tub. 3) Hot water. 4) House must be capable of being heated to 68 degrees F. 4) Sleep room must not pass through another sleep room." Abe interrupted Smith and pulled the large book from his hands. After skimming through the many pages, Abe said, "I studied law my whole life, never came across this here book. Where did it come from and who wrote it?"

Smith replied. "I don't know where the laws actually come from. All I know is I'm given this book and expected to make homes built follow its requirements." Abe angered, "It's no law I want to live under, you're taking away the freedom of the people in their pursuit of happiness, you're not allowing me to build my dream cabin." Smith argued, "All these laws are for the safety of you and others, we are making this country safe." Abe said, "Living where and how I want to live is my right, it's not your right or obligation to govern how I choose to live." Smith said, "I'm sorry Abe, that's just the way things are around here. You'll have to bring this home to current standards before I can let you live here."

The party at Abe's house was discouraged, they felt for Abe, knowing one of his dreams was his little log cabin. They all tried consoling him and left after all the food had been eaten and lemonade drank. Abe went home to his rental, contemplating the laws of man.

The following day Abe and his boys immediately went to the library where they started looking at the various books filled with an incredible amount of laws. Abe looked at a book with more than 54,846 pages of tax law, he was astounded, put that book aside and started studying construction building law. At the end of the day, Abe looked at the massive collection of law books and wondered if this was The Land of Law or The Land of the Free.

The following day Abe Lincoln dressed and left his rental while putting on his black top hat. He went to the building permit building where Red used to own his land. He then learned his building permit could not be bought without a considerable amount of money, which Abe did not have. He went to the HIB, there he met with Mr. Lenderlee. Lenderlee asked Abe, "And what assets do you offer in exchange for the loan?" Abe answered, "I give you my word, and I will repay you the money you loan me." Lenderlee replied, "Your word is worthless to me Mr. Lincoln, please leave, you're wasting my time." Abe left, the laws, regulations and conduct of man had cost Abe his pursuit of happiness.

The following day Abe went back to the library and started researching more. He wondered if the new country could be salvaged, if it could be changed to allow man to do what he wanted with his own property. The more he studied, the more sickened his heart became, law suits were a problem because people would sue for any minor or major wrong they felt had been done to them. Individuals were suing individuals and companies, companies were suing companies and individuals. For protection of their cash assets, companies had to place higher restrictions on how their company operated, Abe understood this. What Abe could not understand was the courts siding on the absurd side of some lawsuits. Abe choked as he read about the courts siding with the individual who sued and won because his coffee was too hot. No wonder companies and individuals were guarding themselves against individuals and companies. Abe also couldn't believe the courts often sided with the minority over the majority, it seemed the beliefs of one outweighed the belief structure of the many.

Abe spent the following day studying the court system. After 12 hours he decided that the courts were ruling primarily on the laws of man over the rights of man. Abe figured the quickest way to maybe right the lawsuits and the courts would be by the politicians. He kept considering that the Senate's main purpose is confirmations of judges and approving presidential appointments, such as the secretary of defense. Maybe they could start appointing judges who believed in the justice of man over the justice of the current court system. Abe soon learned that the majority of the Senate were self-serving and not people serving, the majority of the elect believed they were to be served by the people and not that they should serve the people. The majority of the Senate appointed judges, that met the Senate criteria and not the peoples, were judging Libertyless.

By the end of the week Abe was even more discouraged, he figured much of the current situation could be solved by people taking responsibility for their own stupid actions. Abe thought out loud, "Like that will ever happen." Abe continued his thought process. "As long as people wouldn't take responsibility for their own stupid actions, there would be frivolous law suits. As long as judges and their courts continued siding on Stupid's side, there would be more regulations from companies, cities, counties and even communities, like his own." Abe was starting to consider that the current law crazy crisis in Libertyless, and the future of Libertyless laid in the hands of the judges, not the politicians.

Abe went back to studying the courts. He sent his sons to take a survey from the general populace. Abe learned 98 percent of the people had no idea who the judges were they had voted into office. Abe wondered "Why knowledge concerning the judges running for office is kept so secret?" People had a right to know what character of judge they were voting into office. Was it a judge who believed the rights of one outweighed the rights of the many or vice versa?

Abe studied the laws of Susie. He understood Susie was making laws to protect the citizens. Then Abe remembered Ben Franklin saying, "**Men who trade their freedom for a little bit of safety, deserve neither**".

Abe wondered why religion couldn't be a basis for discrimination, he wouldn't want a Muslim teaching his Christian children. Then he remembered frivolous lawsuits and the courts would side with the one. "*It was too screwed up to save,*" Abe thought. He went home, packed up his family and moved into his cabin. "*It still is a free country,*" Abe thought. "*I should be able to live how and where I choose.*"

29 - **Life Goes On**

LIBERTYLESS

Cotton, Tobacco and Indigo were exported north. Textiles and machines that machined were imported from the North. Trade in Libertyless was booming and a ship building yard was constructed, this increased the need for more housing and food. Libertyless was at a record growth rate.

CHARLES and SUSIE

Charles's pride and dominance was growing as fast as Libertyless. Charles was no longer taking advice from Susie, he was concerned only about himself and his ideas. Susie was concerned about the safety for not only her family, but all the citizens of Libertyless. She had been studying the constitution and Bill of rights, she knew she could reach her masterminded plan quicker under the guise of safety which was clearly written in the constitution, that the people should be protected. Susie continued stretching her power by adding more safety to the populace. She strengthened the army and navy and continuously added more departments that would help keep the populace safe.

Charles had taken control of the money making machines, Susie had become so concerned about safety that she gladly let Charles run that administration and he was gaining more popularity with everyone who readily accepted his free money and goods Susie's money provided. The families who did not have jobs, were given money, the families that could not afford medical, were given medical, the families that could not afford food, were given food. The businesses that were going bankrupt, were given money to keep their doors open, the insurance companies were given more clients due to laws requiring mandated insurance. Foreign countries were given money just so they would like Charles and illegal immigrant's needs were provided for. Charles continued mass producing money on Susie's money machines and freely gave that money to everyone except those who continuously worked.

Susie didn't care who liked her, she did care about the wellbeing of the citizens and their safety. Her biggest problem was now her brother Charles, she was rapidly losing control of him, and he was operating on his own agenda and not hers. He was more politically powerful than Susie had ever intended.

Charles was daily becoming smarter, he used to have to rely on his sister Susie, but his position was daily adding to his intelligence, at least as to what to say to people. Because of his popularity, he was slowly cutting Susie off of their once shared power, Charles knew he could never have the army attack the citizens, he did determine that he could build a security detail that could attack the citizens. He knew Susie would buy into it because it concerned the safety of the people. He approached Susie with his Homeland Security idea, Susie readily accepted it and Charles left Susie's office smiling. He was going to build his homeland security team huge, big enough to withstand Susie's army and navy. The day Charles started giving money to, and selling high tech guns and other weapons to Iraq, Iran, Syria and Egypt was the day Susie unleashed on Charles. She Screamed, "YOU ARE CRAZY!" Charles taken off guard, "Why? Because I'm helping our friendly foreign countries?" Susie replied, "You're giving the

relatives of Osama BlowUup guns and money. That is crazy."
Charles said, "If I give them guns and money, they will like me and
not ever attack us." Susie, pulling her own hair, stated, "You are
insane, every weapon you give them will be used against us or on
one of our neighboring allies." Charles proudly said, "Believe what
you want, I know what I'm doing." Susie sat in her office watching
Charles spend money and dictate crazy orders. She wondered to
herself, "*What kind of monster did I help create?*"

SUSIE'S MINIONS

Oshna and Marshna had to continuously add to their staff to
accommodate the citations needing written to all private and
publicly owned businesses. They were given authority to shut any
business down that they deemed unsafe. Mr. Mental was also
given a great deal of authority, he had hundreds working under
him shutting any project or business down that might endanger
the safety of some biological organism. The security detail
ensuring the safety of the Libertyless politicians developed and
grew, she even gave them a name, Family Betterment Insurance,
or, the FBI. Susie, having decided foreigners could be a threat to
her citizens, started another bureau to gather Intel on foreign
countries. She named them the CIA, Catastrophic Intelligent
Assassins. Susie continued adding troops to her army and navy, no
one would dare strike against her and her citizens and the citizens
were readily accepting that Susie was untouchable, even if the
masses grouped together, they would not be able to overpower
her. Libertyless was quickly becoming a dominant city in the world
just as Susie had planned.

FUTUREANO

Futureano was the only binding left between Charles and Susie.

He played the two against each other and they both were clueless to his games. Charles thought Futureano always sided with him, Susie thought Futureano always sided with her. Both Charles and Susie always gave him his desires in hopes of keeping him on their side, he advanced to a high position in Libertyless and his spoiled nature grew. He became chief aid to both. He had more money than he knew what to do with and would visit Mr. Porntz's mansion 3 times a week, Domestica didn't care, and she loved her husband for his money, not his character. As long as she kept getting bigger and faster carriages, nicer clothing, bigger jewelry, she was happy.

Meanwhile:

 Osama BlowUup continued his luxurious living inside Susie's FPS. Osama would write letters daily to his uncles stressing the need for large families because just one brother blowing himself up would not be enough to destroy all the wicked in Libertyless. Osama would enjoy his meals and housing while also telling his uncles how corrupt this new nation was. He would page through Porntz's Publications and write home telling his uncles that they should be subscribers as well, so they could see the corruptness of the Americass women. Osama did this while inwardly seething that his brother BlowMeUp might now be enjoying virgins like the Neon Twins.

 Osama was enjoying the recreational facilities of FPS when Kaleidoscope came in for her morning exercise. Osama , being raised learning that woman are only good for sex, and being aroused by Porntz's papers, upon seeing Kaleidoscope exercise, made sexual advances towards her. Thinking, "*All American women are easy and submissive,*" Osama did this boldly, he walked up to her and grabbed her chest from behind.

Kaleidoscope, having lived through Apache attacks and having lived on the streets, instinctively elbowed her attacker in his ribs, then she quickly turned and kneed him in the groin. As Osama was falling to the ground, Kaleidoscope kneed his nose which immediately broke, as Osama reached to protect his nose, he exposed his ribs and Kaleidoscope kicked at them, breaking two. Then Kaleidoscope jumped on the wounded man and started throwing fists wherever they would land. It took four guards to pull her off Osama, he was taken to the doctor, and she was taken to solitaire confinement. When news of this reached Susie's ears, she set in motion the building of a separate FPS, one to house women and one to house men.

Meanwhile:

Johnny had ridden his horse across the river, up the trail behind the dam. He rode a mile up the lake to Porntz's huge white mansion nestled on a peninsula. Johnny's tempered testosterone was at a record high, he vowed he would have sex tonight, no matter the cost. Johnny knocked on the huge black Iron Gate, a huge muscled man came out and simply asked, "What?" Johnny embarrassingly answered, "I would like to come in." The muscle man asked Johnny if he had three hundred dollars. Johnny calculated that that was three years wages and said, "No." The muscle man turned his back on Johnny, "You have no business here," then he left. Johnny sat watching the pretty girls swim in their bikinis, he noted that none were really as pretty as Peggy. He wondered, "*Could I really give myself to some strange girl when I truly love Peggy?*" He decided he couldn't and mounted his horse, his direction set towards Peggy's house.

Peggy was hanging laundry when Johnny rode up. She looked at him and yelled, "Go away." Johnny dismounted and handed

Peggy the wild roses he had gathered on his way here. She grabbed the flowers and threw them on the ground as she said, "It's gonna take a lot more then flowers if you're wanting me to forgive you." Johnny replied, "Peggy, I am sorry. You're the only girl I love and want to be with." He walked to his horse, mounted it and rode away.

Peggy faltered and started crying, she loved Johnny, they had so much in common, their beliefs, interests, activities, and attraction one to the other. They belonged together and here she was not accepting Johnny's apology over sex. She ran and saddled her horse and took off after him, she was sure they could work this out.

Johnny's testosterone was out of control, he didn't know what to do. He had apologized and Peggy had spat in his face. He tied his horse to a tree, grabbed Porntz's publication out of his saddle bag, and started releasing the sexual tension inside of him, maybe then he could think straight. Peggy rode to Johnny's horse and stopped, she watched Johnny for a brief second wondering, "*What is he doing?*" and said, "Johnny, we need to talk." Johnny looked at Peggy and turned red, he couldn't believe he didn't hear her approach. Peggy said, "I'm sorry Johnny." She dismounted and walked towards him, she needed a hug. Johnny turned around and said "Just a sec." He dropped the Porntz publication as he covered himself up. Peggy asked "What's this?" as she picked up the paper. She looked at the front page with the exposed Neon Twins kissing one another, she looked at Johnny and nothing was making sense to her. What she did know was this, Johnny was looking at naked women while touching his private thing. She couldn't make sense of it, but she knew she was deeply hurt. She dropped the publication, looked at Johnny and said, "Go marry them, you're not marrying me." She mounted and rode away determined she would never speak to Johnny again.

Johnny was confused, Peggy wouldn't sleep with him, and he couldn't sleep with anyone other than Peggy. "*What am I supposed to do*?" Johnny wondered. Maybe it was better not being married to Peggy, he needed a sensible woman.

Peggy was a sensible woman, a little after leaving Johnny, she remembered the story of David and Bathsheba, she understood men were attracted to naked woman, she understood Johnny had needs although she had little idea of what exactly those needs were. It all came back to sex and she was throwing away a perfect relationship because of it. She turned her horse around and rode back to Johnny, praying he had finished that disgusting thing he was doing.

Johnny was mounting his horse when he heard branches rustling in the woods. He tried drawing his gun but found it chained to its holster. Then Johnny saw Peggy, she jumped off her horse, exposed her breasts to Johnny and asked, "Is this what you want from me?" Johnny turned his eyes and said, "NO." Peggy started crying because she thought she wasn't as attractive as the Neon Twins and consequently Johnny didn't desire her. Johnny pleaded to Peggy, "Please cover up." Peggy cried harder and said, "So I was right, you would rather look at the twins naked, you think they're prettier than me." Johnny said, "Absolutely not, I'm confused Peggy. All I know is I'm sick thinking we won't be together and I have needs that aren't being met right now." Peggy interrupted, and asked, "Why?" Johnny laughed and said, "I think it's a guy thing. He grabbed and hugged her, she hugged him back, they both were confused. Peggy asked, "Can you fulfill your needs looking at me?" Johnny turned red and answered, "Maybe, Heck Peggy, I don't know. I doubt I could do that in front of you." Peggy said, "Well I don't like you looking at naked women." Johnny gave Peggy his word that he wouldn't look at any more Porntz's publications and the two sat and held each other, both very confused but happy to be back together.

Meanwhile:

Billy sat in his own stink contemplating ways to remove "God" from all of America's currency and creeds. "*Screw God,*" Billy thought, a real god never would have let my nephew be blown up, a real god wouldn't let hunger and famine exist, and a real god would heal the sick and make life delightful.

Meanwhile:

Regina, Sue and Tammy were grocery shopping and all were contemplating why their three dollars used to buy three boxes of goods and now it only bought one. Tammy said, "Dang people, doing nothing more than making themselves rich off my last dollars." Regina said, "I think Susie and Charles have so many taxes in place that price of goods had to be increased to pay the taxes." Sue said, "I think there's so much money floating around that the value of the dollar just isn't what it used to be."

Meanwhile:

Charlotte continued teaching as best she could under the commands of those in more authority. She about quit teaching when she saw in her new history book that the American Revolution never happened. Charlotte caught Susie one day in the street and voiced her concern. Susie responded to Charlotte, saying, "Just teach, it's not that complicated carrot top." Charlotte was angered but had no idea how to fight the whole system alone.

Meanwhile:

Red continued working his job at the ranch, making his house and FR card payments, owing a little more at the end of each month. He constantly wondered, "*Is this battle really worth the fight.*"

Meanwhile:

Thomas was sitting in his office wondering, "*Why does it now take three people to do what used to only take one?*" He thought, "*Had I ever worked as lazily as some of my employees, my dad would have switched my hiney.*"

Meanwhile:

Abe continued making improvements on his log cabin with his boys. It was now going to take many months to accumulate the money so the kitchen, bathroom, utility room and extra sleeping room could be incorporated. Each drop of Abe's sweat made Abe think harder, specifically, the people needed to know more about the judges they elected. The people needed to know more about the Senate and the types of judges they would confirm. Nosey neighbor one silently cussed as she watched more of her favorite trees disappear one by one.

Meanwhile:

Jasmine and James learned more about each other even though they'd been married many years. James vowed to never look at Porntz's publications again, Jasmine vowed to be a more interesting spicy lover. She would give James his testosterone taming anytime he wanted, within reason, even if it meant her own hormones had to be put on hold.

30 - **War**

Ben Lazybutt was sitting home drinking beer, he had sent his wife and eight children out for more consumables and food so he could have some privacy while he paged through Porntz's new publication. Chastity, Ben's wife, was having a difficult time keeping the eight youngsters in reign. Marry was complaining of her arm hurting, Ben and Joe were playing with everything they could see and touch, Sherry and Samantha were running around playing hide and seek, Tom and Billy were teasing little Tim. Tim went crying to his mother and was frantically pulling on her dress, Sherry and Samantha ran into the display of eggs and broke the majority of them, Marry slipped in the scrambled eggs and landed on her injured arm, letting out a huge painful scream.

Chastity cussed and dragged them all outside where she one by one swatted their butts. Nosey Neighbor One, having never seen such discipline, immediately filed a complaint at Susie's Family Services. They, believing no child should ever be disciplined, immediately went and confiscated Chastity's eight children.

Chastity ran home and rushed through the door. Ben, having not completed what it was he was doing with Porntz's magazine, was caught with his pants down. Chastity, seeing Ben and understanding what she had just caught her husband doing, immediately turned and ran out the door. She had nowhere to go and no one to share her story with. She was found by Kaley, slumped in an alley corner, crying. Kaley helped her up and the two found themselves in Gusto's house talking with Regina.

"I don't know what to do," cried Chastity.

"Explain what you see happen once more." said Regina in her broken English. Chastity relayed the story. Regina said, "I fear for our youth when they are grown up. Having to live with a community of undisciplined, eh, people." Chastity said, "It was all too much. I had to make them behave." Kaley said, "I've been spanked many times and I turned out fine." Regina said, "Yes you have, but look where Kaleidoscope, eh, prisoned up." Kaley laughed and said, "Yes, but most of that was her choice." Regina agreed. "True." Chastity asked as she slumped defeated, "How can I get my children back?" Regina said, "I do not know, we speak to Gusto when he arrives home." Gusto came home and listened to the story. Having no idea how to fight Susie's System, he too was at a loss. They put Chastity up for the night with the promise of talking with Abe the following day, Abe was the best lawyer they knew.

The Indians were little by little being forced to leave their new homes. They had already been moved twice, now the white man was encroaching on their new land. As with most brave men whose homes and property are being taken, they gathered together in a decision to fight. The Apaches, Comanche, and Sioux all put aside their bitterness one towards another to stand together and fight the white man.

The Indians had planned for seven moons this battle against the white skins. Every one of five years of age and older were equipped with either a bow and arrow, war club, tomahawk or jawbone club. They kept themselves hidden in small groups, this morning they numbered over a thousand. They circled Libertyless and waited until high noon, the time to strike.

Chastity, Regina and Gusto could not find Abe, they had looked everywhere but he was not to be found. Near lunch time, they decided to rest and eat, then start their search again.

Susie was arguing with Charles. "Why did you send our army oversees?" Charles answered, "Because we need to protect them." Then offensively asked, "Are you really that stupid?" Susie answered, "Our duties of protection are to the citizens of this land. Not foreign countries." Charles said sarcastically, Susie, Susie, Susie. You need to open your eyes and see the big picture. It's not just us or them, we are all one big happy world and if I need to ship our troops to keep it that way, I will." Susie answered, "One day something catastrophic is going to happen, and I do not think any of the king's men or horses will even try to put you back together." Charles said, "Careful Susie, or I might have you go live with Billy." Susie left, slamming Charles's door in his face. She wondered, "*Since when did I start coming to Charles office and stop making him come to mine?*"

Peggy and Johnny were holding hands walking the isles of the No Purpose Store. Since Johnny believed he would never ever be able to afford a real diamond ring, they were searching for an imitation that Peggy could be content with, they found it in the gumball machine. Johnny traded in some of his saved dollars for coins and the two took turns dispensing gum balls, anxiously working towards the silver ring that should soon be dropping out.

The Neon Twins had been asked to do something that even they could never imagine. Mr. Porntz had said, "Girls, you must earn your room and board. If you're not willing to do certain things, I'm afraid I'm gonna have to ask you to leave." The twins had grabbed hands and marched out of Porntz's huge white mansion, they didn't need to speak their thoughts to each other, and both knew that swallowing their pride would be easier. They had started their march back to Libertyless being horseless and tearless, their tears had dried up many months ago. They were hand in hand marching directly to Charlotte.

Futureano was in the bottom of the library giving a speech to fifty unemployed citizens about violence being the destroyer of children, husband's and wife's, families, churches, communities, and even complete nations. Futureano had been dining at Susie's private restaurant, his stomach was now twice as big as it once was. Even the tailored shirts he now bought could not distort the huge pot belly. His green and pink tie would flow down from his neck, make an 80 degree angle, and end resting nearly horizontal by his belly button. His suit pants were 4 inches too short, Futureano never noticed because he could never see that portion of his body. He raised his hands and screamed, "Citizens, violence is never the answer to any conflict. **EVER**!"

High noon struck and thousands of Indians raced upon Libertyless. Citizen after citizen reached for their guns but found them chained useless to their holsters. The screaming and panic started, arrows flew into defenseless citizens. The police drew and fired their single shot loaded into their six shooter into the mass of Indians. They had and were allowed no other ammo to reload their revolvers. They fought as best they could, but they were no match for the trained warriors. Husbands hid their wives and children, then died trying to protect them.

The reserve army grouped and anxiously awaited orders to go defend their families. The captain had them "stand down," they were not permitted to war on Libertyless' soil. One soldier left to go fight, he was shot in the back by the Homeland Security agent standing watch. When the army turned their guns on him, several

hundred other Homeland Security agents emerged from hiding
and pointed their guns at the army.

Gusto, seeing what was transpiring, hid Chastity, Regina and
Kaley under a walkway. He made sure they understood to stay
hidden until the war was over. He then ran to the sporting goods
store, there he found Jimmy, Red and Sherriff Wright. "Damn
handcuffs on these guns." Sheriff Wright said. Red said, "When
I'm done with these Indians, I'm going after Susie and Charles.
This is insane." Jimmy and Mr. Wright agreed.

The three broke the chain securing the rifles, loaded them and
started shooting the Indians. As was common, Regina did not
obey Gusto by staying hid and Gusto soon found Regina and the
other two women loading rifles for the men.

Charlotte saw the Neon Twins running up her roadway yelling,
"Indians, Indians." Charlotte ran to the twins and tackled them
just before an arrow flew over their heads. She ran them to her
apartment, down the stairs, and hid them in the fireplace. She
then grabbed her rifles and went upstairs to protect the twins.

Abe was shooting Indians from the top of the library using his
guns he never reported to Susie. Abe was shocked when he saw
Futureano waving a white flag tied to a pole leading a large group
of citizens out from the library. Abe knew they wanted to talk
peace and started defending the group of peace talkers with
bullets.

Susie's buildings on Reds former land were easily defended by
the armed men of Susie's' Family Betterment Insurance, they had
rifles and unlimited ammunition. Susie stood watching the fight
on her rooftop, she looked over and saw Charles shooting his rifle
at the warring Indians. Susie noted that many of her protectors

were being accidentally shot in the back by Charles's poor aim. When the Indians on Reds former land were all dead, Charles pointed his rifle at Susie and pulled the trigger, but the chamber was empty. Charles smiled his bright white smile and waved at Susie as though he was just joking. Susie ordered the FBI to go help protect the Libertyless citizens.

A panting messenger told Susie the army was not helping in the war. Susie looked at her brother reloading his rifle and cussed. She sent several messengers to both the army and navy telling them to start protecting the citizens, she cared less what their orders had been.

As the war progressed, the Indians found themselves killing two to every one of their own that died. But the white men outnumbered the Indians one hundred to one.

Johnny was protecting Peggy with his body when an arrow hit the bubblegum glass. Gumballs dropped and rolled everywhere, making sounds like tiny gunfire, Johnny covered more of Peggy with his body.

Four messengers entered the standoff between the army and Homeland Security. One messenger simply said, "Your family's are being killed by savages. Susie says everyone helps fight." They all ran up the road to join the fight against the Indians. Within minutes the Indian war ended.

31 - **Post War, It's Expected**

When the fighting stopped there was mass confusion everywhere. A thousand dead Indians laid throughout the city, hundreds of Libertyless citizens laid dead beside them. Chastity's first concern was for her children, she ran to the houses her family had been housed in and started gathering them up one by one until she had all eight. There was no complaining, the housing parents were too concerned for their own children to be worried about Charlotte's. She marched home and found Ben drunken and naked with Porntz publications scattered around him. She dragged him outside and locked the door, then she burned the papers. She had no idea about the future and how she would survive, she didn't care, she had her children safely home, that's all that mattered right now.

Johnny sat down beside Peggy. They hugged each other tightly and Johnny said, "We're going to get married and go live somewhere where we can freely carry guns." They went to the gumball machine and pulled the arrow out that was stuck in its side, at the end of the arrow was the silver ring they had been trying to extract earlier. Johnny placed it on Peggy's finger and it fit perfectly. Peggy didn't care what ring she wore, she was now officially engaged, her inner self was dancing around on a mountain top joyously singing, "Going to the chapel and I'm gonna get married." Her physical mind was convinced that Johnny really did love her, heck, he was willing to sacrifice himself for her.

Abe looked over the scene and vowed to himself to forever

fight for all rights of all citizens, to never let the Constitution or rights be made a mockery again. As he was thinking this, Futureano walked in leading five Homeland Security agents, they surrounded Abe and took his undeclared guns. Futureano was yelling at Abe, "You stupid ignorant merciless killing jackass. We could have talked peace with those savages." Abe was too spent to argue, but inside he was seething mad and wondering, "*Are there really individuals running loose in Libertyless that truly believe like Futureano?*"

Gusto and Regina hugged as they had not in many years. Homeland Security agents swarmed the store and confiscated all the guns and ammunition from their hands and those unused still hanging in the store rack. Gusto and Regina didn't speak a word, but both were more afraid now then they had been during the Indian attack.

Charlotte dug the black sooty twins out of the fireplace. They looked at each other and started laughing, never had any seen the other so funny looking. Charlotte grabbed the two and said, "You're living with me now, no questions or debate." The twins' tear duct flood gates burst open and a month's worth of unshed tears came flooding out of all three.

Susie avoided Charles at all costs, she knew Charles would kill her if the opportunity ever arose. She immediately called together her most trusted friends, including Sybille Equity Liberance, and started talking about reigning in Charles's and his Homeland Security.

Charles sat in his office with his Homeland Security advisors talking about the war and who would side with who if a civil war ever broke out in Libertyless. Talk turned towards the army.

Charles inwardly thought, "*I will keep the troops overseas until I have leaders in place that will shoot their own family members at my command.*"

It took a month for the life in Libertyless to somewhat return to normal. Children had been lost, spouses had died and the mourning remained. Red and his group continued meeting at Bill's house to discuss taking back their land. They wanted their freedom back, they wanted their constitutional rights restored. No solution was ever reached and each week they would all leave a little more disgruntled.

Jordan was Red's youngest son, the brother of Johnny. He was tall and skinny with straight black hair and dark brown eyes. He was not talkative or social, but he was keenly intelligent. The character difference between Johnny and Jordan was Johnny was always in the foreground and Jordan felt overwhelmed in following his older brother's footsteps, Johnny was extroverted, Jordan introverted. The visual difference was Johnny looked mean and lean, Jordan looked more like a tree in the desert, no-one knew Jordan was twice as strong as Johnny. Jordan, spoke for the first time. "These people have been given so much for so long that they now expect, they now believe, we owe them. As long as we continue to give to them, they will continue to expect it from us."

This sparked serious jabber, for what Jordan had spoken seemed to be one of the pyramid bases of all that was wrong. Susie expected taxes from the citizens and their businesses, she expected to be given, or to take, whichever she thought necessary. And that that she took, she freely gave to those who gave her nothing. Those that she gave to now expected it to be given daily to them. Susie expected her city to grow and since its growth benefited the citizens, they were expected to finance her goals. Charles expected to be able to do as he pleased, not caring what was in the citizens' best interest. Charles expected respect from those he gave his sister's assets to, he expected to be the highest elected official in the world. Futureano expected that others believe and behave as he, that his morals and standards were good enough for him; therefore, they were good enough for all. He expected to receive a salary supportive of his lifestyle, it didn't matter that others had to live on less, he was a highly elected official who deserved his standard of living. Some of the pauper people expected Susie's money so they could continue their lifestyle. They expected more every week because they wanted to eat and live in better restaurants and homes. They expected free medical and dental, a few wanted a nice retirement plan. They weren't expected to give to society, exactly what was expected of them is still unclear. As long as the tax paying citizens continued giving these expectations, those expecting would continue to expect more. From the highest power of Susie to the lowest of the paupers with fifteen kids who said, "Someone needs to be feeding and clothing my family."

Abe said, "Good point Jordan. We also have to consider the political balance. Charles is no longer taking orders from Susie, he's a loose cannon. Susie is so safety conscious that freedom is lost. The judges are making a mockery of the courts and most of the Senate and Congress could care less about the people. I can't really decide what it is they care about other than money. I don't see anything changing for the good in politics anytime soon. I do know the balance between judicial, legislative and the presidency is a jumbled mess."

Red said, "Our firearms are nearly non-existent, we couldn't fight the government if we wanted to. Homeland security outnumbers our guns sixty to one. If we could depend on the armed forces backing us, we might stand a chance, but who knows how the generals really think?"

Neon One said, "Let's move." Charlotte hugged her and said, "We might have to, but this is our home, we have family buried on this land. If at all possible we would like to stay here. We just want it back to the way it was before all these weird ideas started maturing in the people who migrated here. They can have their ideas, but their forcing them down our throats and we don't like it."

32 - Say What?

Lovely little Kaleidoscope was tiring of solitude confinement. So the following day when breakfast was served, she put on her best 'Get me out of trouble pout' and said, "Lady, you know I don't belong in here." The prison guard, dressed in her wrinkle free blue suit, said, "Yes you do sweetie, you nearly killed Osama." Kaleidoscope giggled and responded, "Not here, but here in prison. I snuck in." The guard, not believing that tale, laughed and said, "Right, whatever you say." Kaleidoscope said, "Really, check with the warden and the office records. I bet you can't find any paperwork on me." The guard said, "You're so cute. Why must you lie?" Kaleidoscope gave her perfect, "I'm an angel look," and answered, "I'm not lying, honest, check it out."

Later that day, the guard, not knowing why, actually did go to check on Kaleidoscope's paperwork, having none to find, the guard pursued Kaleidoscope's story further. In a weeks' time it was concluded that Kaleidoscope did not belong in FPS.

Having never dealt with someone breaking into prison, there were no laws in place governing this, so Kaleidoscope was set free and she ran home to be with her sister Kaley. Kaley was overjoyed to see Kaleidoscope and when the greetings subsided, Kaley asked Kaleidoscope, "Why are you free?" Kaleidoscope smiled and answered, "Brain surgery classes were boring, figured I'd try something else for a while."

Susie's FPS lawmakers were soon debating over corrective action of this incident.

Lawyer 1 asked, "Why shouldn't someone have the right to live in prison if they want?"

Lawyer 2 answered: "If they want to live in prison, they need to break a law, be tried and found guilty."

Lawyer 1 said, "But then they're not FREELY living in prison."

Lawyer 2 said, "This is a stupid conversation."

Lawyer 1 asked, "If a prisoner has a right to live in prison, why should not a law abiding citizen? It is their tax dollars paying for it."

Lawyer two said, "Then some would want to live in prison."

Lawyer 1 said, "My point exactly. We have visitation, recreation, procreation, education, health, dental, vision and sometimes liberation."

Lawyer 2 said, "It makes no sense." Then asked, "A citizen should have a right to live in prison even though he has done no wrong?"

Lawyer 1 said, "Exactly, you got it. But here's the real question, why would a free citizen want to live in prison?"

Lawyer 2 answered, "Because life inside is better than life outside."

Lawyer 1 said, "Yes, that's the problem."

Lawyer 2 said, "I see. Now back to why we're here. We need to make laws ensuring that even though a citizen should have the right to freely live in prison, it is unlawful to do so."

33 - **WAR?**

Meetings at Bill's house were growing boring. Everyone basically had the same three major complaints: 1) they were tired of giving what they earned to those who did not earn, giving to the power head of Susie and Charles clear down to the paupers living in the allies. 2) They were tired of living amongst others that did not share their belief in One True God and therefore behaved and lived under a completely different constitution of morals and values. And 3) they were tired of the lack of freedom to build or do on their land as they pleased. Too many rules and regulations had been set in place by the Government, the state, the county, the city and the individual communities. The growth of these governing agencies was out of control.

Charlotte said, "I wish the Americasses never moved here." Regina and Kaley agreed. Red said, "I thought I could of made a difference had I been elected." Thomas said, "We would have, I think Susie would have listened to what we had to say."

Kaley said, "I like Susie, I think she just got caught up on an unstoppable train charging towards power and dominance, using safety as her trains fuel." Red said, "Maybe so." Becky Boo asked, "Why can't we move?" Jimmy answered his daughter. "This is where are roots are, dearest." Jordan said, "Our roots might be planted here, but the ground is fertile with poison. We continue living here, we shall die."

Bill Money asked, "Why don't we fight?" Abe, frustrated at the lack of organization and the mention of war, stood and said, "Let's run through our issues and solutions one last time before we start talking civil war." Then he asked, "How bad is the tax situation? Is it really so bad that we're willing to kill our neighbors over?" Thomas answered, "My business is taxed so heavily that I can't keep my doors open. Every time I start making profit, that profit is taxed away. I can't invest in research or my workers. The bottom line, I can't support my family as I once could. I worked hard to build my business so I could live a lifestyle of my choice. I can't do that anymore. Is that worth fighting for? Probably not. However, when I see my dollars being given to those who don't work and to organizations I don't believe in and are scripturally against God Almighty, then yes, I'm willing to fight." Red said, "I'm sick of working so hard for so little. I could buy Sue many of her desires, but I can't because Susie takes my money and gives it to those who don't work. Like Red, that's probably not worth fighting for. But crap Abe, when I see my money being spent to take God out of my country, being spent to take God out of our culture, being spent to rewrite our heritage and history, it makes my blood boil and I'm wanting to fight to get things back to the way they should be." Gusto said, "They take our money anyway they can. Taxes on commodities, building permits, citations. Our money is being stripped from us at every corner we take. They tax us directly and they tax us on the things required to live. Our forefathers fought for less, I think we owe it to them to preserve what they fought and died for." Bill Money said, "They play by two different sets of rules. One for them, one for us. It's not right. I think it's time to set things right".

Abe asked, "So it's worth fighting over money?" Regina stated, "It's not the money, it's what they're doing with the money." Tammy continued Regina's thought for her, "They make us live on a tighter budget while they just tax us more if they need more money." Charlotte interrupted Tammy saying, "Their making me teach bull crap, it's..." Kaley interrupted Charlotte, "Their using the money to make our lives..." Regina interrupted Kaley to finish her thought, "Their taking God and His morals out of our culture... "Becky Boo interrupted Regina saying, "I just want to ride my horse without a saddle belt..." Charlotte interrupted Becky boo finishing Becky Boos' sentence, "So many saddle belt citations have left the populace struggling for money, Johnny can't..." Regina spoke louder, "I love cherry pie and I can't afford to buy cherries anymore. I'm..." Kaley said, "Our neighbors don't work and they're living a better lifestyle thamoraln us..." Charlotte continued her thought, "Poor Johnny, I love that kid and he gets nothing but abuse from the officials. He..." Peggy jumped in and said, "I knew you loved Johnny. Because of..." Sue chimed in and said, "Our way of life isn't what it once was." Charlotte said to Peggy, "I don't love him that way." Becky Boo said again, "I want to go horse riding." Chastity quietly said, "I'm tired of Ben looking at Porntz's publications." Charlotte again said, "I don't love Johnny that way." Bobby Sue said, "We'll go horse riding tomorrow." Kaley said, "I don't like looking at everyone's underwear, just Kevin's." Kevin said, "What?" Abe yelled, "LADIES!" The talk quieted and then Regina blurted, "I want a cherry pie." All the women started speaking at once and Abe again had to yell, "LADIES, ENOUGH!" The chatter again quieted.

Abe said, "I've spent hours contemplating this. Does anyone have any suggestions to change the situation politically?"

No one spoke. After a minute of quiet, Red said, "Without money, we'll never win an election. Without winning the elections, we'll never change the political thinking. It's like their keeping us broke for a reason." Charlotte said, "If we could teach the children proper morals, virtues, and duties, we might change things in fifty years when those children take back the government." Red replied, "Maybe so, but even then, all of Susie's organizations she's created might be too far down their traveling road to ever return to where they started." The chatter quieted as they all absorbed that piece of information. Abe said, "I strongly believe much of our problems and issues lie in the courts. I don't see anything there changing anytime soon. Let's take a vote, those in favor of a civil war raise your hands." Everyone raised their hands except Becky Boo who asked her sister, "Should I raise my hand?"

Abe said, "Just the act of supplying our foreign enemies with weapons and money would give us just cause. What they've done by taking away our guns is even more cause. With your tax and moral concerns, it's beyond just cause. The minority is ruling the majority and every day they get stronger, things need set right."

They all brainstormed the possibility of having a Civil War and taking back the official offices to govern their homeland as they deemed fit. In the end, it was decided that since at least thirty five percent of the town worked for or indirectly for Susie, and fifty one percent of the others probably voiced their opinion for Charles in the election because Charles supplied their living money, they were outnumbered. The group now believed they were the minority.

Abe closed by saying, "I believe your numbers are off. I believe more Libertyless citizens think and believe like us, but they're not educated in their rights given to them in the constitution and Bill of rights. Moreover, the army can't fight against us, but Homeland Security can, their guns probably outnumber us by 10 to 1. When the right to bear arms was given to us, it was primarily given to keep the government in check by the citizens, those days are long past. Even if we all had guns, ammunition is now way too scarce. I see no other choice but to leave." Red said, "If you can't beat em, leave em."

And so it was decided that they would pull up their roots and plant them in poison free land. "Where are we going?" Bobby Sue asked. She was answered with over a hundred shouts as everyone yelled, "TEXAS!"

34 - **Prepared**

In the weeks that followed, Red and his gang calmly and quietly talked with their friends about their feelings of possibly moving. If a tiny doubt was heard in the conversation about not wanting to move, the conversation was innocently changed to a different topic. If great desire was heard about wanting to move, then those ones were filled in on the plan of Red and his gang. By the end of the third week Red had a good estimate of how many wanted and would move, it wasn't horse breaking science, most of the ones with a strong biblical background wanted to move. Of those that didn't, it was solely that they couldn't bring themselves to part with their home. A quarter of the business owners wanted to move, they were the ones not heavily subsidized by Susie or they were making so much money that they didn't want to start over, like Mr. Porntz and Mr. Bias. Most of the army and navy wanted to leave, they were sick of politics governing the way war was fought, and having to fight with rules while their opposition fought with no guidelines was insane. The people totally dependent on Charles' handouts wanted to stay. Most of the political office holders wanted to stay as did those who were directly working for Susie and Charles. As a whole, the bulk of the working class wanted to leave Libertyless, the pauper people and politicians liked things just the way they were.

Thomas refitted part of his factory to produce wagons made for rugged travel. They had heavier springs, stronger wheel bearings and sided with oak to help defend against attacks. Gusto and Bill bought all the horses and oxen they could find. By the end of the third month after the decision had been made to leave, transportation was ready.

Thomas and other factory or business owners who were moving slowly sold their assets. They then went to the Higher Interested Bank where they cashed their Susie money in for gold and silver. Bill, Jimmy and the other Libertyless leaving citizens then went to the HIB and traded their Susie money in for gold and silver as well, in a short time, all those leaving were free from owning any Susie money. Mr. Lenderlee was a little concerned when he opened the vault door and saw only a few gold and silver pieces remaining. Susie continued making money on her money making machines, she was happy to finally see a little surplus of her money.

Supplies were bought by Red and his crew, as new shipments arrived, they were bought as well. The Americass family had never been so happy, trade in Libertyless was still booming.

35 - **Peggy Gets Married**

Peggy awoke way before the crack of dawn. She was so excited, today she was finally getting married to Johnny. After the decision to head west had been made, Johnny had approached her and said, "Peggy, figure since we gonna be starting a new life, we might as well be starting it together. Peggy, if you would, would ya take this ticket gatherin hunk of a man as your husband?" Peggy threw her arms around Johnny and kissed him like there were no other man alive, then she reminded him that she had already said yes. Johnny blushed and slipped a chirping cricket down Peggy's s slacks, he tore off running saying, "Just wanted to propose properly, I sure do loves you Peggy Lysandra, I'm gonna make you the happiest wife ever."

Peggy screamed at Johnny as she dug the cricket out of her britches. Inside she was overjoyed, she had dreamed of marrying Johnny since the 2nd grade. The parents were informed and Red thought it might be a good idea for the groups morale to see the two married before their long trip west. So at the crack of dawn, wagons, horses, oxen and the Libertyless folks leaving Libertyless to find more liberty, gathered around and watched the two be given to each other to become one.

Red said to Johnny, "About time, now let's move before some of that poison blood decides to join us." They took with them everything of use that they could fit in their wagons, the farmers took all their stored crops, the ranchers took their cattle, and the city dwellers took any machine that would help start a new life elsewhere. Those that didn't have horses or wagons were given what they needed to help those needing help. Not a piece of Susie money left with them, but most carried at least a little silver and gold.   Never in the history of heading West was there seen such a large mass of wagons, people, and animals leaving a city.

Charlotte road her horse alongside Red asking, "Are you sure I can't bring the twins?" Red answered, "We can't. They'll bring their poisoned blood to our new home." Charlotte said, "They just don't know any better, we can teach them." Red said, "We've done lost most everything we own cause of that character, I can't let that happen again." Charlotte started crying, she said, "I love those girls. Their like my daughter's." Red said, "But they're not. Sorry Charlotte, it's the way things have to be. Now get back in line."

Charlotte dropped back to Gusto and Regina, she told her story of the twins. Regina said, "I just don't know Charlotte, what if Red is right and they contaminate our new society?" Charlotte's eyes were a translucent green, she was very sad. She said, "I promise they'll do our new home good." Gusto said, "I like em, but I'll be damned if I let that soiled blood ruin our new life." Charlotte dropped back to Kaley who was driving Charlotte's wagon sitting beside Kaleidoscope. Charlotte told Kaley, "I can't leave the twins, I'm headed back to Libertyless." Kaleidoscope said, "Go get em, we'll hide em until we're too far away to dump em off." Charlotte grabbed an extra horse and headed back to Libertyless.

36 - **Libertyless**

Futureano awoke a couple hours past the time Red's wagon train had started west. He showered and put on his best green and blue suit, he combed his hair over his bald head in a perfect motion. Although he was now holding many high titles, he still attended the monthly school staff meetings so he could see Charlotte, he really wanted to sleep with her and this morning was staff meeting at the school. Domestica asked, "Why are you so happy this morning?" Futureano replied, "Nothing that concerns you my dearest." He kissed her lightly on the cheek and headed out the door.

At the meeting he didn't notice any empty seats other than Charlotte's, even though there were many. He ran to Charlotte's house to make sure she was ok. On the seventh rampant knock, the Neon Twins opened the door in their skimpy colored underwear and looked at the sweaty figure of Futureano. They stood back and Neon One sharply asked, "What?" Futureano asked for Charlotte while looking at the attractive body. The twins searched the house but could not find her. Upon hearing the twins' reply, Futureano forced himself into the home saying, "I'll just wait for her return." The twins closed the door and sat worrying about Charlotte and the potbellied bald man sitting on their couch. The twins' talk turned to absurd ideas of what happened to Charlotte. Neon One said, "I can't believe the beast killing teach has been taken to be sacrificed." Neon Two, replied, "I didn't say sacrificed, I said martyrized." Neon One asked, "What's that?" Neon Two replied, "I don't know, but it's terrible, I'm sure." Futureano sat listening to the conversation and watching the twins. As their talk escalated, so did Futureano's concern. A couple hours later he finally left.

Charlotte waited at the corner of her house until she saw Futureano leave. Finally when he left, Charlotte went inside. The twins ran and greeted her with warm hugs, Charlotte's eyes were a bright green, she was extremely happy to be holding these two. Neon One said, "Thank goodness mom, I mean teach, we thought you'd been sanitized." Charlotte gave a questioning look and said, "Never mind, we don't have time. Put these on." Charlotte gave the twins each a brand new pair of blue slacks. She started packing clothes for the twins and when she turned back towards the girls, she saw they had cut horizontal slits throughout the new slacks from the thighs up to their butts, they both were twirling around, admiring their handiwork. Charlotte gasped as she saw their bare buttocks sticking out of the slacks, she shockingly asked, "What did you do to your new slacks?" Neon One gave Charlotte a hug and said, "Calm down mom, it's called fashion." Neon Two said, "Let me fix your jeans mom, you'll look totally fabulous." Charlotte started doubting her decision to return for the twins when Neon Two said, "Charlotte, thanks for everything. We'd be totally lost without you and we really hated Mr. Porntz. You're like the mother we wished we never had." Neon One corrected her sister saying, "She means, you're like a real mom and we love you." Neon Two said, "Yeah, what she said." Charlotte grabbed the two and rushed them outside. She helped Neon One onto the spare horse and couldn't help but notice the neon green panties sticking out of the new slacks flash across her eyes. She helped Neon Two up behind her sister and saw the neon pink panties. Charlotte sighed and said a prayer to God asking that this decision not be a mistake. The Neon Twins didn't ask Charlotte where they were going, they followed her like a happy puppy would its master. Charlotte started back to the wagon train following its tracks and the twins followed Charlotte.

Ben Lazybutt woke up to an empty house, Chastity had allowed Ben back in the house. She had even asked Ben if he would come with her to Texas. Ben, not wanting to miss the new edition of Porntz's paper, readily declined, he was happy to finally be alone.

Little by little Libertyless awoke and started their daily routine, very few noticed that others were missing, most were just too self-centered to care about anyone other than themselves. The clerk at the grocery store was shorthanded, he silently cussed at the insanity of all his best workers not showing up to work on the same day. The clerk sent an errand boy to go to Ben Lazybutt's house and immediately hire him at three times the errand boy's wages. The errand boy, sensing an opportunity for more wages, asked that his wages be increased. The clerk, overwhelmed with duties, reluctantly agreed.

The errand boy knocked on Ben's door. Ben, annoyed at being interrupted, clothed himself and answered the door. The errand boy laid the clerks offer out to Ben and Ben quickly calculated Susie's handouts, he determined he would be just fine without working. Ben sent the errand boy back with a reply to the clerk of, "No thank you." The clerk then sent the errand boy up the street, knocking door to door, to find help for the store. For every house the errand boy found occupied, he received a response of "No Thank you, Charles takes care of us just fine."

The Pointless Store owner was shocked at having to open his store alone, normally it was already up and running. Today his faithful assistant was gone, he surmised she was sick and cussed at having to work in his own store. The individual who had bought TFPW was amazed also that some of his best workers were all absent the same day. He thought about closing his doors, but instead closed down the portion making small wagons and moved them to the line creating large wagons. The workers from the small wagon line had not been tasked trained on the equipment making large wagons. When an employee dropped a 4x4 on his finger and it swelled, that injured employee ran up the street to the Wesoo brother's law firm. There the Wesoo brother's listened to the injury incident and immediately after the injured employee left, the Wesoo brother's started the paperwork for a lawsuit against the new owner of Thomas' old wagon factory.

Charlotte was passing the Porntz mansion as Mr. Porntz was riding out the huge black gate headed to town. Mr. Porntz tilted his hat to the girls and said "Morn ladies, bringing me new talent? She sure would sell a bunch of papers." Neon One said "Fuck you Mr. P, Miss C would die before she spread her legs for you." Neon Two said "That's right, Miss C is a proper lady." Mr. Porntz said,

"Give you five years wages for one hours work." Charlotte gasped out, "You call it work?" Neon Two said "Never mind him Miss C, he's nothing but dirt." The three ladies galloped away, Charlotte rode quietly thinking of the money. Neon One was right, she would die before she posed for Porntz, but she could easily see how many could give away their morals for the money.

Mr. Porntz rode to the HIB with a wad of Susie money. He wanted his 12th gold chain which took 2 ounces of gold. Mr. Lenderlee, upset that his best tellers hadn't shown up for work, gladly took Mr. Porntz's money and went back to the vault to trade the money for gold. Upon entering the vault and seeing that now only one gold coin remained, Mr. Lenderlee calmly returned to Porntz and returned his money saying, "I'm sorry Mr. Porntz, but we cannot accommodate you at this time." Mr. Porntz pulled out another wad of Susie money and asked Mr. Lenderlee if the two wads together would purchase the gold he desired. Mr. Lenderlee thought of the vault overflowing with Susie money and the vault with just one gold and one silver coin. He kindly responded to Mr. Porntz, "No, but I will give you twice that amount for each of your gold necklaces." Mr. Porntz, having excessive Susie money but no gold, kindly declined Mr. Lenderlee's offer and Mr. Lenderlee calmly turned and walked away. Mr. Porntz yelled, "How much money do you need? I got more." Mr. Lenderlee ignored the question and continued walking away. When Lenderlee rounded the corner, he ran to the ledgers and started tracing the selling of the gold in his vault.

Nosey Neighbor silently watched this whole transaction. She did not know what this all meant, but inwardly felt "*This can't be good.*" She asked Mr. Porntz what he wanted with that much cash and Mr. Porntz replied, "2 ounces of gold." Nosy neighbor wanted the stack of cash, she looked at her wedding ring and said, "I'll sell you this for half your cash." Porntz, not caring about cash, made the trade, he still needed another 1.75 ounces of gold.
Mr. Lenderlee quickly organized an armed coach filled top to bottom with Susie money, he was sending it north to trade for silver and gold.

Nosy neighbor ran home and proudly displayed to her husband the wad of Susie cash she got for selling her wedding ring. He was shocked that his wife would sell her wedding ring and gave her the cold shoulder the remainder of the day, she couldn't figure out why.

Kaley and Kaleidoscope were getting concerned about Charlotte not being back, but they kept quiet. Red and Jimmy kept a steady decent pace headed west, Mr. Wright scouted the way. When Wright saw a herd of antelope, he shot three so the travelers would eat well tonight.

Charlotte couldn't keep the twins moving. They were so intrigued by the wild forest, mountains and meadows, never had they been this far outside of town. They saw deer, antelope and even a bear. Charlotte about fainted as they galloped towards the bear wanting to pet it, fortunately the bear ran away. Charlotte spent hours teaching about survival safety and swore it went in and out of the Neon Twins' ears like vacant air. When dusk was approaching, Charlotte decided it best to make camp, they would try and catch the wagon train tomorrow.

Charlotte fed the twins and herself with beef jerky, wild strawberries and choke cherries. If she didn't catch the train by tomorrow, she knew she would be in serious trouble. They cleaned by the river and Charlotte threw her sleeping bag over all of them. Charlotte prayed, saying, "Please God, please keep us safe." Neon Two interrupted Charlotte and asked, "Who are you talking to?" Charlotte answered, "God." Neon One said, "I don't hear Him?" Charlotte directed their eyes to the stars and said, "The heavens declare the glory of God." They all three sat mesmerized by the stars shining brightly against the translucent moon, the sky was much more vividly visible in the open country than in town. One by one they happily fell asleep.

Red had the wagons make a huge circle. They built a fire and ate fresh antelope and other stored edibles. Still no-one noticed Charlotte gone other than Kaley and Kaleidoscope, both were getting very concerned. Kaleidoscope simply said, "Quit being a worry wart, she's fine."

37 - **After Liberty left Libertyless**

The following morning Charlotte arose to a rustling in the bushes, she saw a bull snake strangling a cotton tail. Charlotte killed the snake and was about to kill the rabbit when Neon One asked, "What's that?" Charlotte answered, "A rabbit." Neon Two asked, "What do they do?" Neon One answered, "Their cute and fuzzy silly. Sometimes I swear you don't know anything." Charlotte giggled and said, "They make good food." Neon Two was shocked, "You can't kill it." Neon One agreed and both stated tearing. Charlotte, a little annoyed, asked, "WHAT are we to eat?" When the twins had no response, Charlotte snapped the rabbit's neck and started skinning it, explaining the hierarchy of life. Then she explained that God had provided. Charlotte gathered tinder and started it with her flint. They roasted rabbit, packed, and were, on their way. No sooner had they started when Neon Two said, "I have to poo, what do I do?" Charlotte stopped and pointed at a tree and safe leaves to use. Neon Two gave her a snobbish look, but went anyway.

Red and the others crawled on their wagons and headed out. Kaley was now more concerned about Charlotte. Kaleidoscope simply said, "Ain't nothing I've seen she can't handle. She'll be fine," then she said a silent prayer asking for extra protection for Charlotte and the twins.

Day 2 After Liberty left Libertyless

Libertyless:

Mr. Lenderlee's iron coach returned with just one gold and one silver coin. The horses were sweaty from traveling long and hard. Mr. Lenderlee quietly asked, being astounded, "This is all the gold and silver you could buy with a coach full of Susie's money?" The account executive replied, "I was lucky to get the piece of silver. Every bank we visited was overflowing with Susie's money."

Mr. Lenderlee was immediately carried to Susie's office by Lenderlee's carriage. He rushed through the safety searches and ran upstairs, bursting through Susie's door, he said to Susie, "You must stop manufacturing money."

Susie suspiciously asked, "Why?" Then explained, "We must make the money to pay what we owe." Mr. Lenderlee replied, "Every piece of money you make, makes the previous piece of money less valuable. Right now your money is already worthless." Susie could not believe anything of hers being worthless and asked Mr. Lenderlee to explain. Mr. Lenderlee said, "I just sent an armored coach up north, it was loaded top to bottom with your money. That amount of your money bought one ounce of gold and barely one ounce of silver." Susie slumped in her chair and sighed, "What do you suggest I do?" Lenderlee answered, "Shut down the money machines now." Susie passed on the word and for the first time in a long time, Susie's money machines took a break and their cranks stopped turning. Susie, knowing Lenderlee's words were true, grabbed the key to the money making building after its gigantic steel doors were closed and locked.

Mr. Porntz, wanting his twelfth gold chain, set out through town in search of gold with his wads of cash. When the sellers of the gold saw the great sum of Susie's money being offered for the gold, they questioned Porntz as to why he did not trade his Susie money in for gold at the bank. Mr. Porntz would simply say, "That short bastard won't do business with me. I offered him twice what I'm giving you and he still wouldn't trade." This put fear in many about their trust in Lenderlee and the value of their Susie money. They ran to the bank to gather and trade their Susie money they had saved into gold and silver.

In the past, Mr. Lenderlee had used these people's savings for paying the stores their receipts of the FR cards and investments in prospering and non-prospering businesses. By midafternoon, Mr. Lenderlee could no longer give the people the money they had saved. He would not trade any amount of Susie money for his remaining two pieces of gold and the silver coin. His vault was empty of Susie money, his vault might as well of been said to be empty of gold and silver. He might have been able to continue giving people their saved Susie money until end of business day, but the armored coach had drained his resources of fast cash. Lenderlee went back to Susie and asked for a loan so he could open the bank the following day. Susie, figuring she could choke Lenderlee out of the financial gathering picture, sent him to her brother Charles.

Mr. Lenderlee ran across the street to Charles. After an hour wait, Charles saw Mr. Lenderlee. "What can I do you for, great friend?" Charles asked as he vigorously shook Mr. Lenderlee's hand. Mr. Lenderlee kindly asked Charles for a loan. Charles took Mr. Lenderlee to the money making building. He was telling Lenderlee, "I'll crank, you tell me when you have enough." Lenderlee was undecided if this was pointless or might help, his decision was made for him as Charles was unable to enter the locked money making building.

The people tried trading their Susie money for gold and silver with Charles and Susie, but neither brother nor sister had ever given thought to this ever happening. Susie and Charles had no trading store nor storage of gold and silver backing the Susie money.

The sense of panic was spreading like a virus throughout the city. People were yelling "It's the end of the world." Stores kept running lower and lower on goods and the store owners continued to drastically raise their prices trying to curtail the buying. By the end of the day, a loaf of bread was sold for forty times its morning price. When people learned that their life savings would only buy three or four loaves of bread, they were depressed.

Charlotte and the Neon Twins:

Charlotte tried riding fast to catch Red and her liberty family. Just as they started trotting on the trail, Charlotte would hear, "I have to pee." They would get going and the other would say, "I'm thirsty." She would get going and hear, "Now I have to pee." She would get going and hear, "My ass is sore." By lunch Charlotte was sure she had made the wrong choice in bringing the twins to the new homestead. Then Neon One yelled "Rabbit, I'm starving." Charlotte was too, she pulled out her swing shot and killed the rabbit. The fire was started and the rabbit roasted. Then Neon Two asked, "Can we thank God for providing us with another meal?"

Charlotte hugged her and gave thanks to God before they ate. They set out on a slow pace following Red's wagons wheel tracks. Again they never caught Red and had to camp, Charlotte found an enclosed area made of rocks by the river. They tied their horses by some tall grass and Neon Two said, "I'm starving again. How do the people survive outside the city?" Neon One said, "I don't think they do. That's why we never see country folk in the city, they're all dead." Charlotte said, "They live using a lot of prayer and common sense." Neon One laughed and said, "I don't think we got sense, maybe we need more prayer." Charlotte laughed and agreed saying, "You need more prayer then you realize." Neon One asked, "What are we going to eat?" Charlotte said, "I don't know, maybe you ought to ask God." Neon One looked up to the heavens and said, "God, I'm starving. What are you going to feed me?" They all heard a loud thunder boom in the distance and looked up at storm clouds gathering in the sky. Charlotte said, "Maybe next time you might be a little more polite." Charlotte quickly gathered branches to lay above the rocks, they didn't have time to build a good shelter and they all slept miserably wet and cold as they cuddled one another.

Red:

Red set a steady even pace, they didn't stop to eat, they ate on the go. They didn't stop to poo or pee, the person simply held it or caught back up to the wagon train when their business was finished. At days end Red made camp and said, "I need to see Charlotte." Charlotte, not being found and Red having heard what Charlotte had done, sent his boy Johnny to go find her. Peggy, feeling insecure when Johnny was around Charlotte and the twins, objected, saying to Red, "That's bull crap sending Johnny to go rescue Charlotte and the twins. Charlotte made her bed, let her lie in it. Johnny belongs here with me." Johnny, having never stood up to his father nor disobeying one of his commands, was at a loss as to what to do. Jordan saved his brother by saying, "I'll go dad." Red, concerned that Jordan might not be old enough to handle the rescue, was now at a loss. If he let Jordan go and something terrible happened to Jordan, he would never forgive himself. If he didn't let Jordan go, he would be instilling into his youngest son that he believed his youngest son incapable. If Red forced Johnny to go, Peggy would hate him and it would show Johnny's loyalty to him over Peggy. Red thought Johnny needed to man up to him and make this tough decision for him. Fortunately Johnny did, he said, "Dad, Peggy's right. I need to be with her here. Jordan's plenty capable of rescuing the other girls." Red patted his son Jordan on the shoulder and said to him, "Stick to the trail, Charlotte will be following our tracks. Proud of you, now get going." Jordan packed his horse with a few days' supplies and started back towards Libertyless. He was feeling a bit overwhelmed at taking on such a large task, but he also felt confident and happy that his dad had trusted him.

Day 3 After Liberty left Libertyless

The following morning Ben rolled out of bed, clothed himself and went to Susie's Building of Giveaway. Ben checked his box indicating he was not currently working and waited for his Susie money. A few moments later, Ben was informed that there was no money to be given away, Ben left moneyless. He had no money to buy food, it had been wasted at the Pointless Store, the liquor store, and on Porntz's publications. Ben went to the store where he had been offered a job the day before and was told they were no longer hiring, until more shipments of goods came in, the store was closed. For the first time Ben felt a little disgusted with himself for spending his last bit of money on Porntz's new paper.

News of Susie's valueless dollar spread throughout Libertyless, the New Nation and to the foreign countries. Overnight exports to Libertyless ceased, without prepayment of goods in gold or silver, no company would risk their assets for Susie money. Since Libertyless had no gold or silver, no goods were received.

The store owners hid what goods they had left, but their stores were raided, anything was taken and their shelves laid empty. Soon everyone was hoarding whatever they could steal from empty houses. They would leave their house to go steal from their neighbors, only to return to find their house had been raided. Neighbor turned against neighbor, no-one trusted anyone. People hid in their homes wishing they had a gun to protect themselves and whatever assets they still possessed.

Susie was escorted to her personal restaurant to find it vacant, she went in and found the pantries empty of any edible goods. The gold plated silverware was gone, the chandeliers were missing. Susie was escorted back to her house, there she found her security detail firing random shots at Libertyless citizens trying to rob her home.

The shipyard was filled with wandering people searching for any good of any sort. Finding nothing of value, they started destroying and vandalizing the machines surrounding the dock.

Thomas' old factory was sealed shut, but that did not stop the angry vandals. They broke through windows and destroyed whatever they could.

Susie's employees collected their pay, seeing that it was in Susie dollars, they asked for it to be exchanged for gold and silver, she, having no gold or silver, couldn't make the exchange. Her employees started quitting ten by tens. The army that hadn't left with Red quit, the navy that hadn't left with Red quit, Susie's FBI quit and Homeland security disbanded and went searching for other money and food.

Mr. Mental started eating his mosquito larva.

Charles and Susie were fighting like they hadn't done since they were kids. Susie screamed at Charles, "You tried to kill me." Charles responded, "I was playing." Susie said, "You lie and now your lies have us in a hell of a mess." Charles asked, "What did I do?" Susie answered, "You gave away money like it was candy. When you needed more, you simply made more or took from the working citizens." Charles argued, "You stole from them too." Susie said, "I took from them to keep them safe." Charles replied, "Well I gave to them to keep them living." Susie said, "They could have worked a bit for their money." Charles laughed and asked, "Have you ever seen any of them work? And those that do are just plain lazy. They wouldn't have survived without our help." Susie said, "Well, I'm at a loss of what to do, they'll probably all die anyway. Damn, where did all the working class go?" Charles answered, "I don't know, but I think I'll pack up and go with them." Susie stated, "Like hell you will. You wouldn't last an hour in the woods. Besides, you helped create this mess and you'll damn well help fix it."

Charles left wishing he were a tad bit smarter, he knew Susie was right, he wouldn't survive an hour in the woods alone. He chuckled as he thought about Futureano and his sister stark naked staked near an ant pile. Then he immediately saddened as he tried thinking of ways this situation could be fixed and found none. Charles stopped at his favorite restaurant to eat and found its doors closed. He knocked on the door, the owner asked "What?" Charles said, "I would like to eat please." The owner asked, "You paying with gold or silver?" Charles pulled out large sums of Susie money, the owner laughed and slammed the door in his face. Charles went to the bakery and found its doors closed, he went down Main Street and found every door closed. Charles walked the streets hungry and alone, for the first time in many years he started to be scared. He wished he hadn't fought against Susie, he wished he would have stayed close to her rather than try and kill her.

Jordan:

Jordan loved speed, Jordan's horse loved speed, and the two always went as fast as they could go wherever they went. Jordan was following the tracks of the wagon train back to Libertyless, he passed the little lake in the river where Charlotte and the twins were cooking, bathing and swimming for a brief period.

Charlotte saw that they were never going to catch Red anytime soon, they were tired, dirty and hungry. Charlotte saw a young deer drinking at a pool in the river, she drew her six shooter and shot the deer in the right eye. Neon One yelled, "You killed Bambi," and she started to cry. Neon Two said, "Maybe God is providing for us again. I'm starving." Charlotte gutted and bled the deer, she knew she couldn't camp here tonight because a bear might come rummaging at the smell of blood. Charlotte started another fire and had the twins help slice the meat into jerky strips. When the meat was drying, the Neon Twins stripped to their underwear and jumped in the cool water. Charlotte was hesitant, but seeing the twins swim nearly naked gave her the courage to swim in the same fashion. She knew Johnny was far away and they were miles from anyone. The three washed and played. When the meat was cooked, they ate, packed Charlotte's saddle bags up with jerky, and headed west chasing Red. A few minutes on the trail Charlotte noticed the horse tracks headed back to Libertyless. She studied them and instantly knew they were Jordan's. She stopped and contemplated heading back to Libertyless for Jordan or continuing to chase after Red.

Red was overly concerned about his son Jordan, this was the first time Jordan had been in the country alone. He knew his son was capable, but he wished he'd sent someone else with him as a riding companion, the woods could be a dangerous place. Red slowed the speed of his travel down a notch, Sheriff Wright traveled ahead continuing to scout the territory. Kalidescope had to keep calming Kaley concerning Charlotte's wellbeing. Regina kept telling Gusto all the things he was going to have to do at their new land and all the ideas she had for their new house he would build. Thomas was enjoying the freedom from the stress of his old wagon making company.

Day 4 After Liberty Left Libertyless

Charles again tried talking to his sister who was getting irritable because she was not getting the food she was accustomed to. Charles asked, "Why can't we start the money machines up and end this mess?" Susie said, "First, the money they make is worthless. Without gold and/or silver backing the currency, it's worth no more than toilet paper. Secondly, who's gonna crank the cranks for free?" Charles enthusiastically said, "I will, I'll crank them faster than anyone." Susie asked, "Don't you get it? The more you crank, the less each dollar is worth, the money has no value." Charles hung his head and almost started crying. Susie almost felt sorry for her brother, but then she remembered the SOB tried killing her. She kicked him out of her home, then she thought she might want a man around the house. Then she wished she hadn't destroyed all the confiscated guns.

Charles walked the streets alone. He passed Nosey Neighbor and she yelled, "There he is," and in seconds, out of nowhere, Charles found himself swarmed by people ripping and tearing at his clothes yelling at him the only words he heard, "Give me, give me, give me." Charles had nothing to give.

The local farms were raided, but the raiding was minimal, most of the farmers had picked up and left with Red. The farmers that

left with Red knew God was their Provider and had not doubted
the choice to leave Libertyless. They knew in their hearts it was the
right choice.

The Americass family found themselves debating solutions
while sipping on potato soup broth. Even Big Billy had come out
from the stench of the courthouse basement to offer his advice.
Susie said, "We must get the factories producing and sell the goods
for gold or silver." Futureano blurted, "Damn Red and his people,
this is all their fault." Billy asked, "Why so?" Futureano answered,
"Because they were the heart of this city, they were the working
class." Billy answered, "We still have workers here, and it doesn't
make any sense Futureano." Futureano responded, "It has to be
their fault, everything was fine until they left." Charles was angry,
he wanted a solution, "Futureano, shut up. I'm hungry and I want
food. We are here to find a solution, not place blame. Please
continue Susie." Susie continued. "If we could get gold coming in,
we can buy food. If we have food, we will have the strength to
rebuild." Futureano said, "You want me to work in the factories for
the promise of food? You won't find me working there." Susie
stated, "Then you shall die of starvation." Charles asked, "Will the
people work for free?" Susie answered, "If they do not, they will
die along with Futureano." Billy said, "There are many laws
written for Oshna and Marshna I fear we cannot uphold under
these circumstances." Susie was past all the laws, survival was
more important, "Then we shall break our own laws. I'm tired of
being hungry and I'm sick of potato soup."

Charlotte and the twins stopped studying Jordan's tracks,
Charlotte decided it was best to try catching Red because she had
no idea why Jordan was headed back to Libertyless. She mounted
up and tried hurrying the twins to keep up with her. Five minutes
later she glanced back and the twins were nowhere in sight. She
cursed and headed back, finding the twins dismounted, in the
woods, yards away from their horse left untied. Charlotte tied the
two horses and went to inspect what the twins had found this time.
She was screaming mad, she was going to tell them to mount up
and head back to Libertyless. They would never survive out in the
wilderness and Charlotte would not have their death on her hands.
When she got closer, a ray of sunshine nearly blinded her, the sun
was reflecting off a tiny waterfall and the image it created froze

Charlotte in her tracks. She fell to her knees and said, "Forgive me Lord, I've forgotten that which You commanded us to do." The twins heard Charlotte and turned to her, Neon One asked Charlotte, "What is it?" Charlotte answered, "A reminder to me and to you of what the Lord Jesus sacrificed for us." Neon Two asked, "What's that?" Charlotte asked, "What do you see?" Neon One answered, "I see a reflection of a man with his arms spread wide." Neon Two said, "I see a cross behind him and bright light is shining all around." Charlotte said, "That's what I see as well, maybe you two aren't as blind as I thought." The twins laughed and said, "Teach, we see perfectly fine."

Charlotte sat with the twins and told a brief story of Jesus, His life, death, burial and resurrection. Neon One asked, "What's that mean to us?" Neon Two said, "Yeah, I don't see the importance." Charlotte explained sin. Neon One said, "I've never sinned." Charlotte asked if they ever stole, or coveted their neighbor's goods, or loved themselves more than others, she asked if they always honored their father. Neon Two said, "I suppose posing for Porntz wasn't very honoring to father." Neon One said, "So what? We've sinned, everybody sins." Charlotte said, "True, but do you want forgiveness for your sins?" Neon Two said, "Maybe, it depends if I have to work very hard. I don't like working." Neon One said, "Me either." Charlotte said, "It's free, just like receiving a Christmas present." Neon Two got excited, "I love Christmas presents." Charlotte tried keeping the twins on track. She said, "All you have to do to have your sins forgiven is believe on the Lord Jesus Christ. The bible states, "for God so loved the world that He gave his only begotten Son, that whosoever believes in Him, should not perish, but have eternal life." Neon One asked, "That's it, I just have to believe the story of this Jesus dude?" Charlotte said, "Sorta, but it's more than a mental knowledge, it's a heart knowledge, you feel it like when you see a boy you really like." The twins started getting butterflies in their stomach. Neon One Said, "I think I feel Him." Charlotte asked, "Do you want to receive the Lord Jesus Christ as your savior?" Both simultaneously said, "YEAH!" Charlotte said "Great, let's get you adopted into His family." Charlotte prayed with the two asking Jesus to forgive them and come into their hearts. All were crying a river of tears as they looked again at the waterfall reflection, it shined bright and then disappeared as the earth moved away from the sun. All would later swear they saw the image smile and Neon One said, "This reminds me of Kayla Heinze's poem: 'YOU shined light in my eyes that I could never see before. You began to fix my heart that was broken and sore. We went down a road that you didn't see, so what all did you see in me?'" Neon Two giggled interrupting her sister and said, "Silly, she wrote that about a boy." Neon One turned red.

Red continued to slow his pace as he tried giving Jordan and Charlotte less distance to make up. He was worried sick inside but didn't show it. Johnny rode alongside his dad and said, "Don't be concerned dad. You always taught us to have faith that God will take care of us. Show some faith." Johnny left his dad contemplating his words.

Jordan arrived at the outskirts of Libertyless, the city seemed deserted, and Jordan rode slowly and cautiously ahead. He was scared and gave God a quick prayer for protection even though he saw no-one on the streets. He kept riding deeper into the city and at the edge of the business buildings, Jordan saw Rudy and Bobby sitting on the wooden slat sidewalk. He rode his horse to the twins who immediately stood up and approached him, Jordan simply asked, "Where's the teach?" Rudy, figuring this was one who helped cause the chaos in his town, and sensing food in Jordan's bag, was ready to kill Jordan. He didn't answer Jordan but asked, "What's in the saddle bags?" Jordan simply reiterated, "Where's the teach?" Rudy said as he pulled on Jordan's leg trying to dismount him, "She's gone with the others." Jordan's horse, sensing trouble, drew up on its hind legs, when the horse landed, it's left foot landed on Rudy's right foot, breaking all of that foot's bones. Rudy screamed and tried pulling his foot out from under the horse while Jordan jumped off and hit Bobby in his jaw. Bobby backed away. Jordan followed Bobby and then swung his right leg underneath Bobby's left foot as Bobby was resting his weight on that leg backing away from Jordan. Bobby fell and Jordan put his boot to Bobby's throat and asked, "What do you mean she's gone?" Bobby, unable to speak with a boot on his throat, pointed at Jordan's foot. Jordan backed away and Bobby threw sand in Jordan's face. The sand didn't effect Jordan, he simply smiled and said, "I eat dirt for breakfast." He stepped forward and grabbed Bobby's shirt, then continuously hit Bobby in his face making his head bounce opposite what it was accustomed to until he felt Bobby's weight slump to the ground. Jordan cleared his eyes and went back to the whimpering Rudy. Jordan asked Rudy, "What do you mean she left? She came back for the twins." Rudy cried, "The twins are gone too." Jordan immediately realized he screwed up and passed Charlotte somewhere back. He cussed at himself for not watching the ground for tracks as he'd been taught, he mounted his horse and galloped away as Rudy sat trying to nurture his broken foot and Bobby tried gathering some sense.

38 - **The Town Meeting**

A Town meeting was called, most of the townsfolk were too hungry to attend, and those that did attend were hungry, worn, and ragged. When Charles stood up, a voice from the crowd yelled "You liar, you promised to feed, clothe and house us. My family is dying because of your lies." At this, the hungry crowd having their own thoughts voiced, jumped in with their own yelling. Soon Charles heard the chanting, "Liar, Liar, Liar." Charles's first words were "Citizens, I am sorry. I honestly thought I could forever feed, clothe and shelter you." The crowd continued chanting, "Liar, Liar, Liar."

Charles nervously continued. "I did not know the ones paying for your food, clothing and housing would up and leave our beautiful city." When Charles said this, the people quieted, for they too never believed so many would leave their homes. Charles continued. "Citizens, we have the resources to rebuild. We have the manpower to refine our resources. You and me, we can manufacture as we did before and we can prosper once again."

Ben Lazybutt yelled, "You want us to work?" The Wesoo brothers yelled, "Our clients can't work, it'll destroy our lawsuits." Charles answered, "We can sell goods from our factories for gold. With gold we can buy food. With food we can..." A lady in the back yelled, "Someone needs to pay for me and my family to eat. She stormed out and half of town hall emptied as they followed the lady. They were murmuring, "She's right, someone needs to pay for us to eat." Ben and Futureano were the last to leave with the group following the lady. Both truly believed that Charles and Susie should freely clothe and feed them. Futureano said, "Work for food? What crazy person would do that?"

Charles continued speaking to the remainder, "Tomorrow we reopen the wagon factory. Those that want to work in hopes of food can join me there." Charles and Susie left together, a few others laid back grumbling about having to work for food, but they would if they had to. The rest agreed.

As Susie and Charles were heading home, they were mauled by the crowd that first left town hall. They stripped Susie and Charles of their clothing as they ranted "You owe us." When the crowd left, Susie and Charlie lay beaten on the ground nearly naked. A rattle snake slithered between them, paused for a few seconds, and then slithered away. Susie was terrified, she laughed and said, "We should probably learn how to carry and handle guns." Charles hugged his sister and agreed.

Jordan raced back towards his father Red. This time he watched the tracks and made two horses leaving Libertyless, one horse was heavier burdened than the other. Jordan passed Porntz's mansion and the lake, he continued on. By evening he found Charlotte and the twins laughing as though they hadn't a care in the world. Charlotte had a small fire going and they were eating deer and wild berries. Jordan asked Charlotte, "What the heck? You have everyone worried sick about you." Charlotte said, "Oh Jordan, you're so cute when you're angry. We're fine and figure well catch up with Red today or tomorrow. Why are you here?" Jordan dismounted and tied his horse. He sat and started eating with the girls as he said, "Someone had to come rescue you." Neon Two said, "Someone did, His name is Jesus." Neon One said, "Hell yeah, we found Jesus and now we know we'll be alright. He's done kept us fed already." Jordan, excited about the twins kept his mouth shut about the Christian struggle, he helped make camp and enjoyed the joyous talk of the twins and Charlotte.

39 - **The Factories Reopen**

The following day after the city meeting, Charles and Susie
went searching for some guns, none were to be found. They
proceeded to Thomas's old factory and were met by Mr. Porntz,
Murphy and a handful of others. Mr. Porntz said to Susie, "Mighty
fine britches you wearing ma'am, maybe when we get this town up
and running, you could come model for me." Susie had brought a
big pot of potato soup, she heavily sat it down so some splashed
onto Porntz, then she gave her "Don't you dare look at me glare" to
him and he backed to the back of the line. They all readily ate,
searching for any nourishment they could find. When finished,
Charles got up and swung open the huge wooden doors to the
entrance of the factory. They all broke out laughing because not
one had the faintest idea of what it was they were going to do.

A little child dressed in dirty rags and covered in dry dust,
jumped down from the rafters. He asked, "You the onesum who is
comesum to runsum this here factorum?" Susie smiled at him and
said, "We want to, but we do not know how." The boy said, "I
canum showum you, ifum you want." Susie hugged the boy and
said, "Please do." The boy's dirty face showed no sign of the red
underneath.

Susie smiled and asked the boy his name. "People callum me Gopher mam." The boy continued, "All day longum, all I hearum is gopher get me a broom, or gopher get me some water." They all laughed and Gopher started giving a grand tour of the factory. Four hours later Charles said to Susie, "Thisum hereum factory gonna makeum some fine wagonums." The group laughed and Charles asked "Whatum?" The group laughed more.

News of the factory opening drew more townsfolk to the factory doors. After potato soup for lunch, Susie and her clan fixed the vandalized pieces and manned various posts of the factory. Murphy stuck a board in a lathe, the board broke as he tightened the wood into the machine. After the tenth piece of wood broke, Charles moved Murphy to the bearings. Murphy touched a bearing near the bottom of the bin and the cage door of the bearings broke and a thousand bearings scattered everywhere. Charles had Murphy stand outside and be a guard. Mr. Porntz opened the gate allowing water to flow to the water wheel, a few moments later the factory groaned, creaked, and slowly awakened.

Soon dried raw cut wood was guided through saw blades and sanders, refining it to parts and pieces, those were assembled by others and the form of a wagon started taking shape. The people were smiling and humming, then everything slowed to a stop. Susie and Charlie glanced over the crew and everyone glanced back at the two. No one knew why the machines had stopped, anyone could have done anything.

Oshna and Marshna appeared from behind the water gate, Oshna said, "By the power given to me by Susie and Charles, we must stop the work at this factory. Too many safety violations are being broken." They then walked to Charles and handed him a very large stack of safety citations. Charles started reading, ignoring the numerical code. Personal Protective Equipment (PPE) violation. No steel toe boots on any worker. Fine two dollars per worker. PPE Violation, all but two workers not wearing reflective clothing, fine two dollars per worker. PPE violation, no safety glasses, fine two dollars per person. PPE violation, no hard hats worn, fine one dollar per person. PPE violation, no safety uniform, fine five dollars per person. Information Infraction, Minority rights not displayed in locked glass case, fine one dollar per person. Information Infraction, minimum wage not displayed in locked glass case, fine one dollar per person. Information Infraction, State health not displayed in locked glass case, fine one dollar per person. Information Infraction, Equal Opportunity Act not displayed in locked glass case, fine one dollar per person. Information Infraction, Hazardous Material Data Sheets not readily available to employees, fine five dollars per person. Hazard violation, broken glass in break room, fine five dollars per person. Safety violation, trash in walkway 4, fine one dollar per person. Safety violation, trash in walkway 3, fine one dollar per person. Safety violation, dirt pile in walkway 7, tripping hazard, fine one dollar per person, Safety violation, gears 1 - 236 not guarded, fine five dollars per gear. Safety violation, No pre-shift inspection of equipment, fine three hundred dollars. Safety violation, belts 1 - 345 not guarded, fine five dollars per belt. Hazards violation, 1000 roller bearings loose on floor, fine one dollar per bearing. Fatality violation, 12 splintered pieces of wood not disposed of properly, fine 1000 per board. Safety violation, heating oil not stored in flammable proof container, fine fifty dollars. Safety violation, heating oil lamps not inspected, fine five dollars per lamp. Safety violation, ladders not properly stored, fine ten dollars. Safety violation, waste receptacle in lunch room not covered, fine four dollars. Safety violation, Oxen tie down belts frayed...

Charles stopped reading and said, "Oxen, we do not have any oxen." Oshna said, "Laws the law, if you have harnesses, they cannot be frayed." Charles yelled, "What the hell are you doing?" Marshna replied as she wrote another violation for yelling at a government employee, "Just doing our jobs you pay us to do." Charles yelled, "You're fired, now either help or get out." Oshna and Marshna refused to leave or to allow the water to once again flow. Charles had them physically removed and the two continued to yell, "You can't operate this factory, it's unsafe."

Charles commanded the water gate to be raised and soon the lathes were turning and the presses were pressing. At the days end the new factory workers admired their first three wagons, until Big Bill leaned on one and it pummeled to the ground. Gopher laughed. Susie said, "For that laugh my young friend, Gopher get the potatoes."

They were all too tired to go home. After eating potato soup for dinner, they all laid where they sat and slept in the dirt. Tomorrow was another day.

Jordan helped Charlotte hurry the twins along, now they were more giddy and distracted than ever before. The four caught the wagon train heading west. Red was thankful, Johnny said, "I knew he could do it." The twins joined in Charlotte's wagon and with five girls chattering, the others seemed to leave them be, avoiding their wagon. One day the twins rode off on their horse to the front to ride along with Red. Red looked at their cutoff shorts, white shirts with no bras, and cowgirl boots. He said, "You might consider dressing a little more moderately, not good the young boys see you that way." Neon One said, "Quit being such a big boo bear." Neon Two laughed and said, "Oh Red, you love us and you can't deny it." She blew Red a kiss and the two dropped back to Charlotte's wagon. Red had very mixed emotions about the twins, but he did admit to himself he was smiling a rather large smile.

At weeks end Charles and Susie had made twenty quality wagons. Mr. Lenderlee made arrangements to sell the twenty wagons for twenty silver pieces. With the twenty silver pieces, Mr. Lenderlee acquired a shipment of food. The factory team was just finishing unloading the boat, drooling saliva at the thought of their first real meal in weeks when Futureano, Ben, the lady with fifteen kids, and the mob that left town hall believing their sustenance was owed them, rushed and stole the shipment of food from the workers. Futureano said, "You have much, we have little. It's only right you share." Ben said, "You promised us this food." The lady with fifteen kids said, "Someone is responsible for feeding me and my family."

When the mauling was finished, Charles turned to Susie and said, "Maybe we should rethink our thinking."

THE END.

Book 2 – **PUTSCH**

Introduction:

Red was having a hell of a time getting the immigrants from Libertyless to travel. The wagons, built at TFPW, Thomas Factory Produced Wagons, were holding up to the harsh conditions of the travel, the people were not. It seemed to Red that every half hour a stop for some reason or another had to be made. The Neon Twins were a constant rose poking at his side. Gusto and Regina were more interested in site seeing then they were in traveling. Abe continuously moped about having to leave his log cabin. Charlotte continued to teach as best she could while traveling and Kalidascope was bored senseless. The rest seemed to harbor Abe's thoughts, they felt it was wrong to have given up their homes and land.

Sheriff Wright scouted out a perfect place for Red and the wagon train to hold up for a week while food supplies were gathered and restocked. It was beside a lake and large stream where large game trails were seen everywhere. Several large rocks were positioned properly to sustain a secure watch. Red was content, better to give the people rest than try to push them into doing something they no longer wanted to.

Red had seen this behavior before raising his boys Johnny and Jordan. They would beg to go hunting but then complain about the cold and work involved in sustaining camp. After the goal of the kill was achieved, all were once again happy that they had put forth the effort. Red knew that until a new town was established, there would be many complaints. He himself had similar thoughts for having left his wife's mom's ranch. Maybe they had given up too easily, Red thought.

A group had gone fishing and had lost interest as their sight was drawn to a young girl in a canoe paddling towards them. She easily banked the canoe and stood, then spit out a chew of tobacco. Kaleidoscope stood and squared her shoulders to the young girl, both were of equal size and build, 5'6 and very lean. Kaleidoscope took in the 12 gauge strapped across one shoulder, a rifle hanging from the other, and the two six shooters strapped around her waist.

A little blue healer jumped out of the canoe and made its way, wagging its tail, towards Kaleidoscope. The girl in the canoe had brown shoulder length straight hair and a thin face. She wiped her nose, spit, and said "Damn." She looked at Kaleidoscope as if to size her opposition up, then she spit, wiped her nose and said, "Shit." Kaleidoscope started taking a liking to this girl, she walked up to her and introduced herself. The girl spit, wiped her nose, said, "damn,"and then said, "I'm Putsch." Putsch spit, wiped her nose, and said "Damn dog licked her poo then stuck her tongue up my nose." The two girls laughed and started up the hill towards camp, Kaleidoscope introducing Putsch on their way.

ABOUT THE AUTHOR

Trent Smith is from beautiful Colorado. He loves to poke fun at life, he has always said, "A good sense of humor is one of the most importent things in life. It's important to be able to find the humor in problems and difficult times." He truly lives this and has endeavored to pass this gift on to his sons. He has spent years teaching his sons - as well as their friends - that "it's not what happens to you, it's how you handle it."

Trent is happily married because his wife of 24 years says so. ,

www.ingramcontent.com/pod-product-compliance
Lightning Source LLC
LaVergne TN
LVHW041314080426
835513LV00008B/455